THE WIZARD OF

THE WIZARD
OF THE NILE

THE HUNT FOR AFRICA'S
MOST WANTED

MATTHEW GREEN

OLIVE
BRANCH
PRESS

An imprint of Interlink Publishing Group, Inc.
www.interlinkbooks.com

First American edition published in 2009 by

OLIVE BRANCH PRESS
An imprint of Interlink Publishing Group, Inc.
46 Crosby Street, Northampton, Massachusetts 01060
www.interlinkbooks.com

Text copyright © Matthew Green, 2009
Maps by Emily Faccini

Published simultaneously in the United Kingdom by Portobello Books, Ltd

The writing of this book was supported by a Royal Society of Literature/Jerwood Award for Non-Fiction

Library of Congress Cataloging-in-Publication Data
Green, Matthew, 1975–
  The wizard of the Nile : the hunt for Africa's most wanted / by Matthew Green.
1st American ed.
      p. cm.
  Includes bibliographical references.
  ISBN 978-1-56656-736-7 (pbk.)
  1. Kony, Joseph. 2. Lord's Resistance Army. 3. Insurgency—Uganda.
  4. Uganda—History—1979– 5. Uganda—Politics and government—1979–
  6. Acoli (African people)—Religion. 7. Sudan—Politics and government—1985–
  I. Title.
  DT433.287.K66G74 2008
  967.6104'4092--dc22
  [B]
                                              2008028420

Printed and bound in the United States of America

Cover image: Children gather at night in Gulu, Uganda in August 2003. They flee their villages in the late afternoon to avoid abduction and possible death from the Lord's Resistance Army, LRA. Nearly 9,000 children have been abducted in the past twelve months. Up to 25,000 children spend the night outside Gulu in a wet, cold open-air bus station. They rise at 4 a.m. to start the 10 to 20 kilometers walk back to their villages. (© AP Photos: Marcus Bleasdale/VII)

For my parents, John and Susan, and my sister Katie

CONTENTS

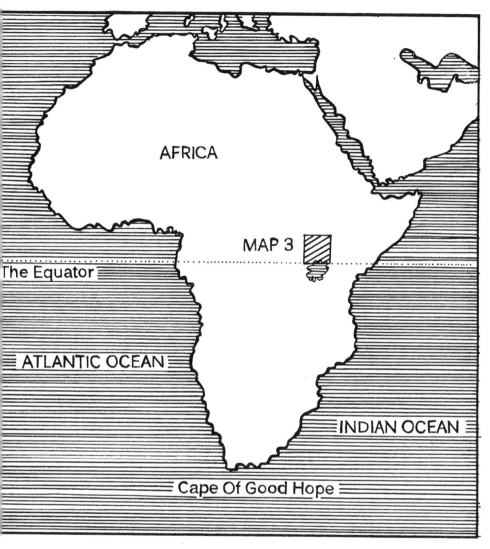

AFRICA

MAP 3

The Equator

ATLANTIC OCEAN

INDIAN OCEAN

Cape Of Good Hope

Map 1: Africa

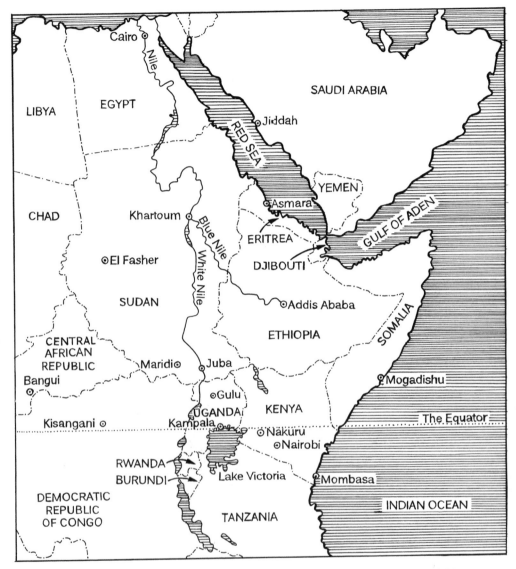

Map 2: East Africa

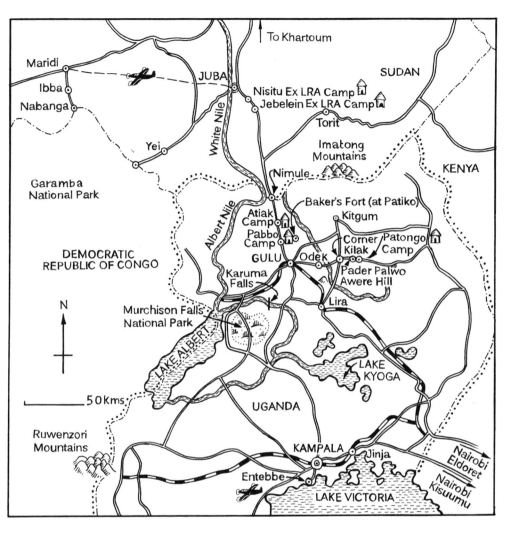

Map 3: The journey

LIST OF ILLUSTRATIONS

"And while the pythons of sickness
Swallow the children
And the buffaloes of poverty
Knock the people down
And ignorance stands there
Like an elephant,
The war leaders
Are tightly locked in bloody feuds,
Eating each other's liver."

—From *Song of Lawino* by Okot p'Bitek

"Better to reign in Hell, than serve in Heav'n."

—From *Paradise Lost* by John Milton

PROLOGUE: A FUNERAL

Alice Lakwena's funeral

I peered into the coffin. A woman's body lay swaddled in a shroud patterned with blue flowers. Her arms hung by her sides, fingers curled into palms. Plugs filled her nostrils, her lips like wax. I took a photo and the flash made the skin glisten.

Her mother sat on the cement floor by the casket, face collapsed in grief. A dozen barefoot friends kept vigil, one holding a baby to her shoulder and gently patting its back. A woman in a red headscarf threw back her head and howled.

Mourners gathered in the garden, waiting by the empty grave. Women wore dazzling dresses, flip-flop sandals, and stoic expressions, the men's shirts were neatly pressed. It was the dry season, and the maize in the field was withered and brown. They sat on chairs, talking quietly. When the sun neared the horizon, pallbearers in black ties, white gloves, and buttoned-up blazers wheeled the casket outside.

The deceased's older sister Betty, now in her fifties, stepped forward and began to read from a spiral-bound notebook. She described how the departed had been a jolly schoolgirl and a formidable javelin thrower. Later she had married, but divorced after failing to bear children. She had supported herself by working as a fishmonger. Then one day a spirit possessed her, and she gained the power to heal.

Betty explained how her sister had prayed for three days, and a mute boy spoke. She prayed for another three days and an impotent man was able to satisfy his wife. Several of the male mourners swallowed chuckles, and then Betty began to describe how her sister became a rebel. Before long a man cut her short.

A sour-faced catechist in a billowing surplice insisted that he be allowed to give his sermon before the sun set. Betty put away her notebook and sat down. Pointing at the casket, the catechist lectured the mourners on the need for their tribe to turn back to God. Selfishness had put up a pillar that deflected their prayers. As he droned on, I realized the most important part of the eulogy would not be told.

When the catechist had finished, the pallbearers began to lower the coffin into the pit. The mother knelt on the mound of reddish earth dug from the grave, head in hands. Her husband leaned on a stick, squinting down through thick-lensed glasses, while mourners jostled for space at the edge of the hole. When the coffin came to rest, somebody tossed in some earth. Others followed, and a shower of pebbles clattered off the lid. I flung in a handful of dust myself. It was over.

Twenty years before her death, Alice Lakwena had raised an army of 10,000 followers, promising to bring a new era of peace to Uganda. Ranks of half-naked soldiers had strolled dutifully to their deaths singing "James Bond, James Bond," their chests and foreheads daubed with crosses of shea-butter oil. Alice told them they would be immune to bullets provided they follow her twenty "Holy Spirit Safety Precautions," which included no smoking, and no taking cover behind anthills. Men must have a regulation two testicles—no more and no less. Stones would explode like grenades.

Her defeat by the Ugandan army in October 1987 should have been the end of the story. In fact, it was the beginning. Somebody else took Alice's place, and he was still very much alive.

Finding him would prove rather more difficult.

1. A PROPHET FROM GOD

Former LRA child soldiers on parade

The bus hurtled north, glittering bush rushing past on either side of the road. "Sexual Healing" by Marvin Gaye blasted from the tinny speakers, alternating with gospel tracks. Passengers dozed or read the back page of the *New Vision* for the football reports. Nobody talked much. Soon the bus would reach the White Nile, and in a few more minutes we would cross into northern Uganda, the home of Joseph Kony.

The newspapers seemed to hold only a handful of pictures of him. One showed a man in his early thirties scowling from beneath a mop of dreadlocks. In another he sported a T-shirt with the slogan "Born to be Wild," a gormless expression stamped on his face. The constant repetition of these same images had a curious effect—it was as if he never aged.

The news reports summed up Kony in crisp paragraphs: "A self-proclaimed prophet who claims to take orders from a Holy Spirit, Kony wants to rule Uganda according to the biblical Ten Commandments. His Lord's Resistance Army rebels have abducted thousands of children for use as soldiers, porters, and sex slaves. They are reviled for cutting off their victims' ears and padlocking their lips."

I knew the paragraphs by heart, having spent the past few years writing them. I had been working as a journalist for Reuters news agency, based across the border in the Kenyan capital Nairobi. We handled stories from volcanic eruptions in Congo to coup attempts in Burundi and starvation in Sudan. Kony's war stood out for the simple reason that it seemed to make no sense at all.

From our crow's nest in Nairobi, the conflict looked like a classic tale of pointless savagery. The rebels had massacred villagers, mutilated hundreds of people and abducted thousands of children—all for the sake of one man's ambition to rule according to his warped reading of the Bible. It was hard to credit, but the rebellion had turned into one of Africa's longest civil wars. After twenty years, the sheer lunacy of the Kony story was so much a part of the wallpaper that I did not think to question it.

Then one day a magazine called the *Referendum* found its way into the newsroom. It was published irregularly by a group of journalists from southern Sudan, a region that lies across the border from northern Uganda. Kony had sheltered there for years. Spelling errors sometimes crept into the layout—in one issue, "messengers" of the truth became "massagers." But the latest edition claimed to have won a remarkable scoop—the first-ever interview with Kony. The anonymous author said the rebel leader wanted to talk to Uganda's president through the spirits, fearing telephones would be used to kill him.

Many people dismissed the article as a hoax, but I couldn't stop thinking about it. If somebody had interviewed Kony, then it might just be possible to repeat the feat. Assuming he was not completely unhinged, he should be able to shed some light on the madness in his homeland. I asked my editors at Reuters for some time off work and made a plan.

I would begin my journey in a town called Gulu. I had the phone number of a Spanish missionary there named Father Carlos Rodríguez, who was one of the few foreigners to have met the rebels. From Gulu I would travel through Kony's stamping grounds in northern Uganda and southern Sudan, loosely following the course of the White Nile. Along the way I would find out as much as possible about Kony and his war. My question was simple: how could one maniac leading an army of abducted children hold half a country hostage for twenty years? \

In the comfort of Nairobi, putting the question to Kony himself had seemed like a fantastic idea. As the coach rushed toward the river, I was not so sure. Things had changed since the *Referendum* published its story. Rumor had it that the rebels had circulated a handwritten note in Gulu in which they threatened to kill any foreigners they found. A British man who had gone to help rafters in trouble on the White Nile had been murdered in the Murchison Falls National Park a couple of months before, and two de-miners had been shot dead in an ambush across the border in southern Sudan.

Some thought Kony wanted revenge. The new International Criminal Court in the Hague had recently issued its first arrest warrants. They named Kony and four of his commanders, accusing them of war crimes from massacring civilians to sexual enslavement. Kony himself faced 33 counts. He might be rumored to dress as a woman, but just then he was one of the world's most-wanted men.

His followers seemed to regard him as something close to a messiah. I had saved a recording of his deputy commander, a man named Vincent Otti, on my iPod. Just before my visit he had called into a radio show in Kampala from a secret location.

"What type of man is Mr. Joseph Kony?" the presenter asked.

Otti's gravely voice sounded as though it was coming from far away.

"Joseph Kony is a prophet."

"Sent by God?" asked the presenter.

"He's really a prophet, I'm telling you. He is and you will even come to agree that he's a prophet."

The recording caught the sound of the studio guests sniggering.

A Canadian journalist on the panel asked if Otti would put Kony himself on the line. For a few tantalizing seconds it seemed as though he might even speak, but then Otti said his boss would talk "next time." The recording ended.

Kampala had been a great place to spend a few weeks preparing for my trip. Nightclubs like Ange Noir and Club Silk stayed open until dawn, and there were plenty of cafés offering wireless internet to hang around in during the day. When the time came for me to leave, I had boarded our coach, misnamed the *Luxury Explorer*, and then waited for an hour while it filled up with passengers.

The bus nudged through chaotic streets in the older part of town, before breaking out into fields of *matooke* trees bearing cascades of spidery fruit. Farms soon gave way to wilderness as we sped further north, the endless green vista strangely sleep-inducing. Kony's fighters had once lined up the bodies of their victims along this road as a warning, but now all I could see were columns of smoke as farmers burned distant fields.

The bus slowed and a smell of roasted meat drifted through the windows. Men and women rushed forward from a line of roadside shacks, thrusting skewers of diced beef at the passengers, dangling flapping chickens by their claws.

A pair of soldiers sat in the shade, manning a roadblock made out of a tree trunk. One of them climbed aboard the bus, shooting glances at the passengers before getting out and hauling the log aside. We rolled toward the bridge.

The land seemed to crack in half, a surge of white water foaming over rocks at the bottom of a gorge. A clean smell filled the coach, and the air was suddenly cool. From the speakers a woman sounding very much like Dolly Parton sang a love song, her voice struggling against the roar of the rapids. We passed another soldier who stared down at the torrent with a rifle slung across his back. A moment later the bus rounded a bend and the river vanished. We had crossed the Karuma Falls, the frontier between the peaceful south of Uganda, and the land of the Lord's Resistance Army. A yellow sign by the roadside said "Safe journey."

The sun was sinking by the time the bus reached Gulu, and I was keen to find a place to stay. A friend in Kampala had recommended the Franklin Guest House. It lay just around the corner from the coach park and only charged the equivalent of a few dollars a night. I set off.

Bicycles whirred through the streets, some with women sitting side-saddle on cushions on the back, heels rushing over the tarmac. A white four-by-four cruised past with the letters UN emblazoned on the side, its radio mast quivering. On the corner, a couple of women clattered out letters on typewriters, marking carriage returns with a satisfying "ping." I found my way to the Franklin and took a small room facing onto a courtyard at the back.

As the light faded and the bicycle traffic thinned, Gulu looked much like any other farming town in East Africa. It had hardly changed since my first visit a few years before. I had stayed less than a week, filing a slew of stories for Reuters, but the images were hard to shake.

I remembered sitting at a table outside the Pearl Afrique Hotel, drinking tea, when a man approached me with a photograph. The snap was a little overexposed, but I could clearly make out a clay pot propped up on stones over a fire. What appeared to be a human leg poked out from the top. Bodies lay strewn on the ground, missing limbs. The man scurried away before I could find out what had happened.

Later I met a boy called Geoffrey. The rebels had chopped off his ears, lips, and fingers, and put a letter in his pocket warning the same would happen to anyone who thought about joining the government army. He was left with just enough purchase to clutch a bottle of Fanta between his stumps. He put it down and shook my hand with his leathery paws. Geoffrey said he had forgiven the people who had done this to him—hate would not bring back his fingers. But it was his last sentence that stuck in my mind. "I need shoes," he told me. He had hurt his toe playing soccer in bare feet.

It was almost obligatory for journalists to visit one of the centers set up to receive children who had escaped after being kidnapped by the rebels. I met a boy called Anthony who had managed to slip away during an attack by the army. Staring straight ahead, he recalled how he had been forced to participate in clubbing five people to death during his eleven days in captivity, a technique used by Kony's men to create a perverse sense of loyalty by bloodying the hands of their new "recruits." He wore a *Star Wars* T-shirt with an image from the film *Phantom Menace*.

Reports issued periodically by human rights organizations provided endless stories of atrocities committed by the Lord's Resistance Army—usually referred to by their initials "LRA." I flicked open a Human Rights Watch report I had found kicking around the newsroom, selecting a random example. On 24 February 2005, a year before my visit, the rebels had abducted a group of women who were on their way to fetch water. According to witnesses, one of the women had a baby who was crying. The five rebels told her they would kill it.

"After some minutes the woman threw the baby down and ran. The rebels grabbed the woman and beat her to death with a gun. When the woman was killed one rebel got a stick and pierced through the child's head. The child was two weeks old."

From reading the reports, and making brief visits to Gulu, it seemed impossible to grasp what was happening. Even after all these years, nobody I spoke to seemed to know why Kony was fighting. They would shrug and say things like "That man is complicated." It was like stepping into a horror film in which everything seemed normal on the surface, but where people were living under the shadow of an unseen monster they preferred not to discuss.

With my visits lasting only a few days, the people I met became little more than caricatures acting out a story I thought I knew was true. Rebels in an obscure corner of Africa were doing awful things to innocent civilians; victims needed more help from well-meaning outsiders; children were suffering the most. This time, I wanted to go deeper.

Before this trip, I had scoured the library at the School of Oriental and African Studies in London for anything I could find on northern Uganda's Acholi—a group of about 1.2 million people. Though communities in the neighboring Lango, Teso, and Adjumani areas also suffered, it was the Acholi who seemed to hold the key. Kony was an Acholi and so were most of his rebels, and indeed most of the people caught up in the war.

I read tales of witches luring snakes into huts with dishes of beer to extract their poison, of rainmakers summoning storms, and warriors stitching the severed heads of their enemies into royal drums. And I stumbled upon a book chronicling an expedition that seemed remarkably close to my own journey.

A British reverend named Albert B. Lloyd, author of a book on Congo called *In Dwarf Land and Cannibal Country*, had penned a later work with a less intriguing title that nevertheless grabbed me immediately. First published in 1906, exactly a century before my visit, the book was called *Uganda to Khartoum—Life and Adventure on the Upper Nile*.

The black-and-white photos were surprisingly sharp, showing a pair of young men in warpaint with the caption "Acholi Swells," and a party of hunters standing knee-deep in a river looking at four hippos that Lloyd had kindly shot for them. The back flap still contained an advertisement informing readers that "Wright's Coal Tar Soap" was to be known as "Soldier's Soap." It included an extract from a letter dated 8 April 1916, from a soldier serving in the trenches in France to a worried parent: "Don't send any vermin powder thanks; I use Wright's coal tar soap, that's as effective and much more pleasant."

Lloyd encountered a chief named Awich who smoked a pipe and wore scraps of soldiers' uniforms, women who leapt off roofs with grief at funerals, and a leader with 50 wives and 60 children, though I doubt he would have recognized the land I visited a century later.

Almost two million people had been forced off their land into squalid "protected camps" as part of the government's counter-insurgency strategy. At Reuters, we faithfully described northern Uganda as one of the world's "worst humanitarian crises," largely forgotten by the outside world. Like Kony, it was just too obscure.

Gulu came to life early. Children in pink shirts walked past clutching exercise books, while a barefoot boy wandered up to the Franklin offering twists of peanuts. Somewhere I could hear a brass band tuning up. I was due to meet Father Carlos at the St.

Monica's tailoring school for young women who had escaped Kony's ranks, but I still had time to buy a newspaper.

The *New Vision* was full of stories about the elections that were due to take place in a couple of weeks. President Museveni had already been in power for twenty years. He had declared at the time of the last elections in 2001 that he would retire after serving a final five-year term, but had apparently changed his mind. Yellow campaign posters plastered shop fronts all over town, showing Museveni wearing a broad-brimmed hat above the slogan "Peace, Unity and Prosperity." The portrait was not quite as out of date as the well-known images of Kony, but he looked considerably more youthful than his 62 years. The banana-colored façade of his "Movement" party's office lay just across the street from the Franklin.

Kony had not made any big headlines in the past few weeks, but there was plenty of speculation that he might have left his base across the border in southern Sudan for a new home in neighboring Democratic Republic of Congo. Already, his deputy Otti had crossed the frontier into the Garamba National Park with hundreds of followers. It was not such a leap of the imagination to believe that his boss might be planning to join him, a move that would perhaps not help my cause.

I walked over to a cluster of men waiting on the corner with their bicycle taxis. One of the riders was quicker than the others and swung his machine round for me to jump on the back. We creaked past the roundabout and along a track that ran the length of a playing field, before reaching the school's gravel drive. A white pickup stood outside the classrooms. A moment later its owner emerged from a doorway.

Father Carlos greeted me with a firm handshake and I followed him inside to a sitting room. With his steel-framed glasses and slightly pensive expression, he reminded me a little of a teacher. I was expecting him to be wearing something like a monk's habit, but he wore jeans and a T-shirt with a design of a child's swing hanging from the knotted barrel of a tank. A young woman washed the cement floor with a rag. She stood up to shake hands, and gave me a curiously lopsided smile.

Carlos had stuck to the missionary's vows he took with the Comboni order twenty years before, his Spanish accent softened by half a lifetime in Uganda. He had arrived in the north before Kony's war had even started, and tried many times since then to persuade the rebel leader to talk peace. For someone looking to meet Kony, Carlos's story was not encouraging.

"I can't forget the first impression that the LRA made on me," he said. "I have met them five times and it's always the same. You can't greet them as you can ordinary people. You go there and you find these two boys, sixteen or seventeen years old, with dreadlocks, without expressions, with their guns just like this." He gestured as if he was pointing a rifle. "You try to greet them, but they don't answer, they just make a sign for you to go ahead.

"You get the feeling that you are not talking to normal people. They may be laughing one moment, but you don't know what mood they will be in the next. You don't feel safe."

I was beginning to realize that Carlos was a master of the understatement. He had been almost killed on one of his trips to the bush, and had stayed on in the north even after the rebels had murdered one of his closest friends. The Italian priest Father Raffaele di Bari was driving to mass one Sunday morning when Kony's followers opened fire from the roadside. They burned his pickup with the body still inside. Carlos buried him at a mission station outside Gulu, wondering why he had been killed. He was 71 years old.

While his friend's death only seemed to reinforce his determination to try to persuade the rebels to negotiate, the closest he came to Kony was speaking to him on the radio.

"For me, the man is a psychopath," he said. "He may be laughing with you and very cordial, saying that he really wants peace, but the next minute he's very angry and shouting and making threats and saying he's going to give orders to kill everybody."

When I thought of all the years he had devoted to contacting the rebels, the sacrifices he had made, it seemed almost impertinent to ask him how to go about reaching Kony, though I had a feeling his story might help. There was also another reason I was intrigued. It was only recently that outsiders had begun to wake up to what was going on in the north, but Carlos had been here for two decades. I was curious to know why he had stayed. After all the risks he had taken, all the reports of atrocities by both the rebels and army he had hammered out on his typewriter, all the columns he had written in the *Weekly Observer* newspaper in Kampala, after all the friends he had lost, the war showed no sign of ending. I wondered what difference he had made.

Carlos was a busy man, juggling projects to pay school fees for former rebels and improve the parish dispensary, as well as his church duties. We arranged to meet again in a few days. As I got up to leave, I asked about the girl who'd been cleaning the floor. Carlos explained that she had been abducted by Kony's fighters. Like thousands of others, she had been given to a commander as a wife. She escaped during a battle with the army, but not before shrapnel had torn her face. Surgeons in Italy had done their best to repair the damage, but she had left half her smile behind in the bush.

Carlos led me back outside. A young Acholi man was waiting next to the priest's white pickup. Tall and lean, with a shaved head, he wore a baggy blazer over a shirt and tie in exactly the same shade of salmon pink. I would have had him down as a university student, perhaps visiting from one of the better colleges in Kampala. The young man beamed at Carlos, who greeted him like an old friend, and we shook hands.

"I am Moses," he said. "Happy to meet you."

Carlos suggested we talk. Moses knew a lot more about Kony than even he did. I took down his number and promised to give him a call.

Tucked behind a row of trees on the edge of town, the Acholi Inn looked like an English country house. Its garden, swimming pool, and nightly buffet acted like a magnet for every foreign visitor to northern Uganda, and I was no exception. It was also a favorite hangout for the top brass of the Ugandan army, and a handful of rebel commanders they had winkled out of the bush. If anyone in Gulu knew how to contact Kony, they were probably sitting right there on the lawn in a plastic chair.

A lone Acholi man sat in the bar watching an African Cup of Nations football match on a television perched on the counter. A sign pinned above the hatch showed photographs of the various kinds of landmines littering northern Uganda, some shaped like pineapples, others like hubcaps. The man clutched a can of Red Bull. I had a feeling I recognized him from somewhere, but could not quite place his face. I headed outside and found a seat in the garden. Pink-and-white strip lights glowed in the trees.

As I watched the congregation gather, I realized I was by no means alone in wanting a chat with Kony. The first to arrive was a Norwegian man with steely-gray hair called Lars, who worked for the United Nations, and had spent some time trying to encourage the rebels to join peace talks. Several attempts to negotiate an end to the war seemed to come close, only to collapse at the last minute. But still the Norwegian persevered. Each evening he nursed his customary Bell beer and often chatted to a former British army colonel called Bob, whose wife worked on a project to help people maimed by the kinds of mines depicted in the bar.

I was hoping to meet their friend, an Acholi woman named Betty Bigombe who retained a touch of the glamour of her younger days as the wife of a Ugandan diplomat in Tokyo. She had tried numerous times to negotiate with the rebels over the past decade, and had even managed to meet Kony. In more recent times she had worked at the World Bank, but still returned from Washington every few months to visit Gulu. Some evenings she would sit in the garden with Lars, sipping a glass of white wine, constantly interrupted by supplicants seeking some favor or other. That night I could see no sign of her.

Investigators from the International Criminal Court tended to cluster around another table in the corner, no doubt wondering when their five suspects would be caught. The Ugandan government had assured them they would soon collar the men, but they had been saying the same thing for twenty years. All the investigators could do was gather more testimony and hope they might one day get to use it.

Accents from Argentina, Italy, and America drifted across the garden, as aid workers pulled a couple of tables together and began stacking up beers. A host of relief organizations were now trying to staunch the hemorrhage of human life from the malaria, tuberculosis, and diarrhea that thrived in some 200 camps created by the government as part of their strategy for fighting the rebels. They had taken their time coming, but there were many more around now than I remembered from a couple of years back. A whole fleet of their uniform white Toyota Land Cruisers was parked out front.

Ugandan officers from Gulu's 4th Division tended to prefer a table near the pool. One in particular hung around more often than most—his name was Colonel Otema, and he was not only head of military intelligence in the north but also the hotel's owner. That night there seemed to be even more uniforms on display than usual. I assumed they had come for celebrations to mark the founding of the army, universally known in Uganda as the UPDF—Uganda People's Defense Forces. Gulu was to host the celebrations in a few days' time, and Museveni himself was due to attend. It was a special moment for him, the 25th anniversary of the day he led 27 armed men in a raid that marked the start of his uprising against former president Milton Obote. A spectacularly successful guerrilla himself—the first in the region to lead an insurgency that succeeded in overthrowing a government—it was no wonder he regarded Kony with such contempt.

I wandered back into the bar. The man with the Red Bull was still watching television. It was only then that I recognized him from pictures in the newspapers. Brigadier Sam Kolo, for years Kony's chief spokesman, looked different without his military fatigues. He had surrendered a year or so before and now lived on a stipend paid by the Ugandan authorities. I tried to catch his attention, but he kept his eyes on the ball zigzagging across the screen.

As I walked back to the Franklin, I wondered if he would talk. He probably had Kony's satellite phone number on his mobile. Then my own phone rang. It was a young British man named Daniel Wallis, the Reuters correspondent in Kampala.

"Hey, there's something you should know," he said.

"What's up?"

"They've killed eight UN peacekeepers."

"What? Say again?"

"Yeah, the LRA have killed eight Guatemalan special forces in Congo. We just got the news out of Kinshasa—I thought you'd like to know."

While I was chatting with Carlos, the Guatemalans had been trekking through the forest hunting Vincent Otti, Kony's deputy. Something had gone badly wrong. Eight of the Guatemalans had been killed and five wounded. Otti was still at large.

It was hard news to absorb. The Guatemalans were supposed to be among the best in the jungle warfare business, the elite forces of the UN peacekeeping mission in Congo. They came from a contingent known as the *Kaibiles,* named after a legendary Mayan prince who fought the Spanish conquistadors. Training involved biting the head off a live chicken. The instructors dropped them in the rainforest with only a knife—if you survived, you passed. They should have made short work of the rebels.

Kony's Lord's Resistance Army was renowned for hacking villagers with machetes or burning people to death in their huts, not for fighting off the likes of the *Kaibiles*. Either the Guatemalans had blundered, or Kony was more organized than he looked.

Moses turned up at the Franklin wearing the same salmon-pink shirt and tie, this time carrying a plastic folder under his arm. We retreated to my room and ordered a couple of plates of rice and chicken. He asked to try my iPod, popping in the white earphones and nodding his head to the hip-hop. I asked him if he wanted a beer, but he said he did not drink much—though he had had a sip of Amarula at Christmas.

He showed me the work in his file, sheaves of paper from a peace studies course complete with diagrams drawn in blue biro. And he showed me a picture that had been taken ten years earlier, a few months before he was abducted.

A sixteen-year-old Moses with a too-long tie beamed at the camera, surrounded by cheering boys on the playing field at his former school, Sir Samuel Baker. He had just been elected health prefect after a campaign that promised to ensure the cooks wore hairnets and the medicine chest was properly stocked. A few months later, Kony's men paid his dormitory a visit. Moses told the story so matter-of-factly it might have happened to someone else.

He was not sure what had woken him—the flashlight shining in his face, or the hand shaking his bunk. The rebels roped 39 boys together and marched them into the night, including Moses and his two half-brothers.

The next morning, the train of captives passed a group of farmers hoeing in a field. They knew better than to look up, and their hoe blades barely missed a beat. Eventually the boys reached a clearing occupied by hundreds of rebels.

"To welcome us there they have their culture," Moses said, "their guerrilla culture."

Young gunmen tore off branches and whipped the new "recruits." Moses knew not to cry out, clenching his teeth through dozens of strokes. Then he watched as an officer singled out one of his brothers, Baptist, for a demonstration. He was given what Kony's men called a "rest." Rebels forced him to lie down and then began to hit his head with a log.

"If you are still new to that community, they pick people at random, so you are afraid to try and escape," he said, his voice suddenly quieter. "Unfortunately, they took one of my brothers, and he was killed."

The commanders told the other boys that they would now become fighters for Kony. They forced Moses to carry a jerry can full of cooking oil, and gave him a stick in preparation for the time he would carry a real gun. Rebels watched the new recruits constantly—escape seemed impossible. It was only when the army sprang an ambush a few months later that Moses saw his chance. Dashing forward, he lunged for a machine gun lying next to a dead soldier.

"I just grabbed it and ran off," Moses said. "I carried it for one week, because I was totally happy."

He chuckled—the gun had reminded him of the film *Missing in Action*, in which Chuck Norris plays a Vietnam veteran searching for American prisoners.

"I watched videos when I was at home, so I used to see this kind of gun, like Chuck Norris! It was beautiful for me. The rebels respected me for capturing it, they told me I was going to be a total soldier. From then on I felt I was no longer going to get mistreated. Before, I was carrying a full jerry can of cooking oil on my back. Then I didn't have to carry it anymore. I became a semi-soldier."

I asked why he did not use the weapon to try and get away.

"Even if you have that gun, you have two minds," he said. "Having this gun gives you some chance to escape, but if you try to escape with their gun they will kill you. But the gun also gives you a chance not to be mistreated, so you feel happier. Sometimes you may feel that it's good even. You think: 'Let's all be in the bush now.' You feel it's good, because all people have to suffer now."

The schoolboy in him had not quite died. When his group of rebels raided St Mary's College in Aboke several months after he was abducted, they escaped with a huge haul—139 young women and a copy of a textbook on tropical biology. Moses stuffed the book into his bag, planning to study in the evenings between marches. He was sure he would be home before long, and he wanted to continue studying for his O levels. His older brother was going to be a doctor, and he wanted to be a vet.

A few weeks later one of the commanders discovered his book and flung it into the bushes.

"They removed it and threw it away," Moses said. "My dream did not become true."

It was getting dark. Moses stood up to leave.

"I have to go and see my mum," he said.

He left listening to my iPod. It was only later I realized that it still contained the voice of one his old superiors, Vincent Otti.

Cymbals crashed, trombones gleamed, and ranks of soldiers goose-stepped in perfect unison across the playing field, boots thudding in time to the beat of the big bass drum. A gust of wind tore off one of the soldier's caps, but he marched on regardless, his shaved head shining. The order came to halt, and a thousand rifles crunched onto shoulders. Watching from the shade of a pavilion, their commander in chief, President Yoweri Kaguta Museveni, must have been pleased.

"They are rather good," said the French military attaché's wife, who occupied the seat next to me under the marquee. "Better than some of the parades you see in France, though it gets so hot here they sometimes faint."

I was beginning to wish I had stayed at the Franklin. Only curiosity had driven me here—I wanted to hear what Museveni had to say about the war. The president sat only a few paces away, surrounded by a gaggle of officers sporting a profusion of swagger sticks, gold braid, and dark glasses. A general gave a speech, repeating the mantra that Kony was defeated. I only pricked up my ears when he said that my quarry might already have crossed into Congo to join Otti. I very much hoped he was misinformed.

Gasps rose from the back of the pavilion, murmurs of surprise drowning the general's words. I craned my neck, struggling to see through the forest of turned heads. A boy of about twelve groped for a seat like a latecomer at the cinema, dreadlocks poking out from beneath his forage cap. A slightly older boy wearing a tattered uniform and torn Wellingtons followed close behind, accompanied by a couple of girls with babies on their hips. They all stared with blank faces, as if they had no idea where they were.

Museveni climbed a set of steps leading to a podium mounted on the back of a pickup, his head shielded by his bush hat. He addressed the parade, his back to the tent. I could not see his face, but I heard his voice booming through the speakers.

"To illustrate how to capture terrorists, I want Colonel Otema to bring out those people recently captured by the army."

The owner of the Acholi Inn ushered out the half-dozen young rebels from the back of the pavilion. They walked like puppets, their personalities drained from their bodies. Photographers began snapping away, as if a showman had just tugged a sheet to reveal an exotic animal trapped in a cage.

"These poor people were captured recently, only two days ago, by soldiers," said the president, gesturing at the children.

The older boy spoke into a microphone, while a man translated his Acholi into English, Uganda's official language, a legacy of its days as a British Protectorate. The rebels had split into small groups, he said, and were wandering around southern Sudan with pregnant women in tow, falling into ambushes laid by the army. Museveni gave him an expectant look.

"I don't know where Kony is," the boy said, eyes downcast.

Looking satisfied, Museveni turned back to his soldiers.

"I will go on the radio one of these evenings and these young people will explain to you so you can hear for yourselves—the army has crushed Kony.

"We told the UN you can't fight Kony, but do you think they listened? They didn't listen, so they got those poor characters from Uruguay. How can somebody from Uruguay come to the African bush and deal with those characters?

"What I want to tell the people of Gulu is that peace is coming and that . . ."

An aide passed a scrap of paper up to the podium. He paused, realizing his mistake. "Apparently, they were not Uruguayans, they were Guatemalans."

Museveni turned to a lean crowd of locals who had gathered on the edge of the parade ground, some sheltering from the sun beneath rainbow-colored umbrellas. He asked them why they were still living in grass huts when the rest of Uganda had been using corrugated iron since the 1940s. Then he told them to be sure to vote for him in the elections, and not listen to any mis-guided Acholi politicians who might suggest otherwise. Speech over, he left in his white Mercedes. I watched the car drive away under a banner slung over the road that said: "Twenty-five years of maintaining our strategic relationship with the people."

2. WE ARE THE ANGELS

Children play at Odek camp

We prayed over the van before we left. I bowed my head and closed my eyes as a pastor led the blessing in her front garden. If somebody had been taking my car to Kony's home village, I might have said much the same thing:

"May the blood of Jesus be on the car! May the blood of Jesus be on the road! Send your angels! Restore what is lost!"

After a few days in Gulu, I had decided to take a trip to Kony's birthplace, a village called Odek about an hour's drive east of town. By all accounts, Kony must have been in his early twenties when he started his uprising, taking on ridiculous odds with zero military experience. I wondered what had been going through his mind—and why on earth anyone would have followed him.

Luckily, I had met somebody at the Acholi Inn who could help, a woman called Joyce Laker who came from the same area. She had worked as an air hostess before Uganda's national carrier folded, and more recently as a local councillor. Now she taught women in the camps to make beads from scraps of magazines and varnish so they could earn some income to support their families. Joyce had managed to borrow her friend's van so she could head home to vote.

I had taken Joyce's advice and obtained permission for my visit from the authorities in Gulu, hoping their letter would help me avoid any awkward questions from soldiers along the way. Joyce told me that Kony's men had beaten to death two of her cousins in the past couple of months, though she thought the road would be safe enough. The most important thing was to travel when the sun was high. The rebels tended to stage ambushes at dawn and dusk.

We drove through Gulu's usual bustle of bicycles, following the tarmac until it dissolved into dirt. Brick houses gave way to thatched huts, then brambles. There was no sign, but this was a frontier as profound as the Nile, the line where the safety of the town yielded to the dangers of the countryside. Speeding into the green, it was impossible not to feel uplifted. I hardly noticed how few people we passed.

Dwarf trees and giant grasses flanked the road, stretching to a horizon broken by knuckle-shaped hills. Though it looked like virgin bush, this was a recent wilderness. Saplings grew through the remains of huts where roofs should have been. A sign for a primary school pointed to silent classrooms. I had to look twice when I noticed a red railway signal sticking out of the undergrowth. A moment later we rumbled over rusting tracks.

"I used to take that line to school," said Joyce. "There haven't been any trains for twenty years."

It would have been extremely cheering to see a locomotive ploughing through the emptiness, but there was only a trio of women wandering along the road with canoe-sized bundles of firewood balanced on their heads. When we reached Kony's home at Odek, I felt a wash of relief. The feeling didn't last.

From the road, the camp looked like a giant brown stain. Mud huts clustered together as tightly as mushrooms, wisps of smoke drifting through thatched roofs from cooking fires smoldering within. Figures wandered through the wattle and daub sprawl, clutching cups or hoes. A leafless tree grew in the center, its branches silhouetted against the sky.

I began walking toward the homes, but a band of barefoot children gathered in front of me. One pint-sized boy brandishing a spear made from a stick and nail giggled at the sight of a stranger. His younger, equally ragged friend hardly noticed me, his face taut as he concentrated on peeling an unripe mango with a razor blade. There must have been two dozen kids, all chirruping a chorus of *"muno, muno, muno"*—Acholi for "white person."

"Mango!" said one of the boys, "Kick the ball!" His companions shrieked in delight as he showed off his classroom English, though I wondered how often they saw the inside of a school.

I pushed through to the edge of the camp and found a group of men sitting under an awning next to a shop made of mud and corrugated iron. Waiting with empty hands, they looked like they had been there for a while. I ordered some Nile Specials from the store and passed them around. The men drank their beers slowly, replacing the caps in between sips to keep out the flies.

"Our land is out there, left alone, with nobody," said an old man in a turquoise T-shirt, revealing rotted teeth. "We're hungry. We can have four or five children, but we are given two mugs of beans for a month. Can it be enough? If you have got a family, is that enough to survive for a month?"

The land of the Acholi was so fertile it could have fed the whole country, but people living in the camps were unable to farm. Anyone venturing back to their fields risked being beaten by the soldiers, or running into rebels. The government had set up the camps as part of a classic "drain-the-lake-to-catch-the-fish" strategy designed to deprive Kony's movement of support by emptying the countryside. But instead of ending the rebellion, they had rendered huge numbers of people dependent on monthly food deliveries from the United Nations. They felt like prisoners, despair strangling hope.

One of the old men reached over and pinched my arm.

"Once I hurt you like this, you'll be afraid," he said. "Even my own child was abducted and never came back. I don't know whether he's dead or alive."

I asked what they thought of Kony. The men gave sheepish grins, as if I had mentioned a relative nobody liked to talk about. One of them suggested I should speak to a man called Lakoch, and the others nodded. A boy led me through the maze of huts toward a tiny door made of flattened tins of vegetable oil sent as a gift by the United States. I pushed it open and stepped into the gloom.

Lakoch p'Oyoo shook my hand and offered me a wooden chair. He had a tired face and kind eyes, a sprinkling of gray stubble dusting his chin. As we sat, his wife prepared black tea while one of his young sons peeped at me from the foot of the bed. I wondered if he could understand the story his father told.

It was hard to imagine two more divergent fates than those of an internationally wanted guerrilla leader and a math teacher, but Lakoch smiled often as he reminisced about his childhood friend. His smile only faded when he remembered the day Kony led him off to war.

"I liked him very much, and he liked me," he said. "He never wanted me to leave him and come back home."

Though their friendship had ended on the battlefield, Lakoch seemed to bear little malice toward his former pal. The way he saw it, Kony's behavior was not his own fault. Lakoch blamed the spirits.

At first, he explained, Kony was just like any other village boy. They had grown up in adjacent farmsteads, not far from where his hut now stood. Kony's father, who served as a catechist, was said to have had seventeen children by three different wives, not an unusual number in Acholiland. By day, the two friends planted maize, sorghum, and sugar cane. At dusk they would lead their fathers' cattle to the stream, strip, and leap shrieking into the water. Older boys would try to provoke the pair into a fight by insulting their mothers, but Kony never took the bait.

"People said he was a coward, that he didn't want to box," Lakoch told me, smiling at the memory. "He just said 'I can't see the use of fighting.'"

When it came to verbal battles, Kony was more than a match for his peers. Lakoch remembered how his friend had mocked his tendency to trip while playing football, and nicknamed another boy *Futa* after a brand of brown soap the same color as his stained teeth.

"Kony was really a jolly man," Lakoch said. "What he liked best was conversation and laughing."

"What did they call Kony?" I asked.

"One of the older brothers who made us fight called him *Ongera.*"

"What does that mean?"

"Black monkey," Lakoch said, and smiled again. Kony's deepset eyes had earned him a nickname of his own.

Kony wore a rosary to school and attended Catholic services, though he never shone in class. Instead, he earned respect with his feet. Parents would gather at Odek primary school for the music festival, where students performed the traditional Acholi dances. There was the *bwola,* the royal dance, the *dingidingi,* the welcome dance, and the *larakaraka,* or courtship dance. Everyone agreed Kony had known how to move.

Kony never completed his schooling. As Lakoch told it, the spirits had other ideas. Some days they stopped him from eating vegetables, or struck him dumb. Other times they would summon him to the granite crown of the nearby Awere Hill where he spent hours in prayer. Kony had been chosen to heal.

"He told me that he never wanted to become a witchdoctor, because he was still young, but he was forced to by the spirits," Lakoch said. "He could even have died if he had refused, so he accepted to become a witchdoctor and healed so many people."

I had reached the limit of my understanding and was about to topple over the edge. Lakoch could no more explain Kony's behavior without mentioning spirits than I could explain the workings of a car without petrol. For him, their invisible presence was an irreducible unit of the universe, as basic as rocks. My problem was trying to grasp what "spirit" even meant.

Turning to the missionary Lloyd's account of his travels, I had found photographs of what he called "Devil huts," straw shrines where Acholi left sacrifices to the ancestors. But the missionary tended to see his hosts as "heathens" in need of Christian salvation rather than try to grasp their beliefs. For a deeper insight, I dipped into a book by one of the greatest African poets, the late Acholi anthropologist, Okot p'Bitek.

In his *Religion of the Central Luo*, published in 1971, p'Bitek launched a counterattack against efforts being made to assert that Africans had proto-Christian beliefs before the arrival of missionaries in the late nineteenth and early twentieth centuries. Describing spirituality in Acholiland, he wanted to show that African religion was more practical in its application than the Protestant and Catholic faiths imported under colonialism. The Acholi system was in a sense more like healthcare, providing ways of seeking therapy in times of distress.

Misfortune or illness was invariably blamed on a spirit, or *jok*. Sounding strange to Western ears, the view made perfect sense. While parents might know malaria had killed their child, blaming an unseen being helped solve the mystery of why it happened to one particular infant and not another. In a world without modern science to tackle disease and famine, explaining reversals in terms of a spirit also offered a way of seeking redress. When there was a problem, all you had to do was call in the experts to drive out the culprit.

Chanting and rattling gourds, a procession of healers would arrive at the patient's house led by a diviner known as an *ajwaka*. Sporting a headdress of hornbill feathers and necklaces of bones, shells, and claws, she would lead her followers in a dance around the sufferer. Perhaps not surprisingly, he would begin to quake. One of the visitors would collapse, a sign that the spirit was near.

"Who are you?" the *ajwaka* would shout.

"I am Whirlwind," the spirit would then reply, speaking through the patient.

P'Bitek says there were an almost infinite number of spirits, with names like "breaker of the home," "mountain splitter," or "the leopard of Nyaga." Each would demand an offering, perhaps a chicken or some honey. The family would oblige, pay the healer's fee, and the patient would return to normal—until the next time.

In more recent years, this belief system helped the Acholi to make sense of their rapidly changing world. When British colonialists arrived, they brought a whole new cast of spirits with them. The *ajwaki* adapted their rituals to suit these times of change, ordering their clients to dress in suits, drink bottled beer from glasses, and eat with knives and forks, preferably while listening to a gramophone, to appease the dreaded "Jok Rumba"— named after the Europeans' curious dancing style.

Sadly, things were not always quite so simple. Sometimes it was not a normal *jok* that had possessed the person, but a *cen*, a spirit of ghostly vengeance. If somebody was murdered, a *cen* would haunt the killer, but might end up plaguing almost anyone. Relatives would cluster outside a hut while a healer engaged in a fierce argument with the spiteful being, finally emerging with it corked in a jar.

Not all intermediaries with the spirit world were as benign as the healers, however. A boy who behaved strangely was sometimes said to have inherited the evil arts of witchcraft. Fathers blew the curse into their sons through the anus.

P'Bitek's witches made Lakoch's account of Kony's teenage eccentricities seem rather mild. Usually male, they would run around naked, smeared with white ash and hissing like a python. Plucking out the eyes of lizards, they would turn the skins into fetishes and place them in front of doors. Anybody who stepped on one would sicken and die. The witch would then exhume his victim.

"He took the corpse into the wilderness and, together with other witches, held a cannibalistic feast," writes p'Bitek. "They used the bones of the legs and arms for stirring their dishes, and the skull as a water cup."

There were ways to fight back. Fearful homesteaders would rub special herbs onto a stool and leave it outside at dusk. When the witch sat down, he would be stuck fast until morning—wide-eyed and stark naked. Villagers would dispose of him by hammering a nail into his head.

Fortunately for Kony, whatever forces had possessed him seemed to have other plans. Lakoch remembered his worried parents summoning a procession of *ajwaki*, but no matter how many goats they sacrificed it made no difference. It seemed the spirit, or whatever influence was working on Kony's mind, was adamant that he would heal. It was not long before his skills eclipsed those of his older brother, an established medium who worked in the family compound. Kony became the consultant, lifting curses and curing barren women. Some said he would sit in his hut with a hand placed on a Bible, or peer into a cracked shard of mirror to foretell the future.

"He was a very strong witchdoctor," Lakoch said. "He would take a calabash and start shaking it, and you would hear a voice. It told you the problem."

Kony was doing well in his field, but when his friend passed his primary school exams he looked destined for bigger things than anything Odek had to offer. Lakoch sat his O levels at Sir Samuel Baker while Kony was still shaking his rattles, before heading down to Kampala to make something of himself. Lakoch soon landed a job at a factory that made nylon nets to catch Uganda's tilapia, lungfish, and Nile perch. The manual labor that had defined life on the farm seemed to belong in the past, but his newfound prosperity was not to last.

When Museveni's guerrilla army captured Kampala on 26 January 1986, and installed their leader as president, large numbers of defeated Acholi soldiers from the government army ran home, fearing reprisals. Civilians fled with them, Lakoch included. Museveni's troops soon followed their former foes, crossing the White Nile at Karuma Falls and reaching Gulu. Soldiers began to beat and kill suspected rebels. Families fled into the bush, angry and afraid.

One day Kony summoned his neighbors to the family homestead.

"He gathered people to tell them that he had received a new spirit, the Holy Spirit, which had come to him so that he could go and fight to overthrow the government," Lakoch said. "The voice was coming from his mouth, but it was not his normal voice."

Lakoch became one of Kony's most loyal followers, recording the orders of the various spirits that possessed him in an exercise book and learning their names. There was "Juma Oris," named after a minister under the late dictator Idi Amin, a Sudanese woman called "Silli Silindi," an American called "King Bruce," and, most mysterious—and unpredictable—of all, "Who are You?"

"He told people that when he's speaking, when the spirits are in him, he doesn't understand. So he chose me to be his secretary. People really trusted in him—how could I miss that chance? I was happy to get that post."

Kony's mother Nora Oting was against her son's talk of rebellion, but he ignored her, instructing his followers to bring him white objects—a dove, plates, a Muslim robe—as well as seeds from the red-hot poker tree. Acolytes wearing bamboo rosaries gathered at his homestead, awaiting orders.

"Very many people went to join Kony," Lakoch said. "I believed that he would do as he stated, that he would overthrow the government and that I would get a good position."

Then their leader vanished. For three days his devotees searched, until one of his brothers found him praying on Awere Hill. Clouds were marching through the sky but Kony told his brother not to be afraid, vowing to hold back the storm. He made good on his promise. His communion with the spirits now complete, Kony was ready.

The young rebel left Odek with eleven followers on 1 April 1987, taking the road toward Gulu. Lakoch had noted the date in his exercise book. One of the girls carried the white dove perched on her head, but they had not a single gun between them. After a few days they met up with a group of Acholi soldiers known as the "Black Battalion," part of the army defeated by Museveni. Kony told them their new president was bent on slaughtering all the Acholi, but that his powers could help. He daubed them with sacred water from Awere Hill to deflect bullets, and sprinkled it on wire models of the enemy's weapons.

"He said, 'Water, you have power!'" Lakoch explained. "'Any hot thing can be cooled by you, so make the guns cool when they attack us!'"

When his followers raided Gulu, Museveni's soldiers fled, just as Kony had predicted. Soon, however, the little band of rebels began to take casualties. Kony explained it was inevitable, quoting an Acholi saying: "When you go to the bush to hunt, you want to catch game, but grasses might cut you on the way." Lakoch was not convinced. Realizing he might die if he stayed much longer, he returned home.

He kept cows, farmed a little, and began to teach math at Odek primary school, which he had attended with Kony. Some years later the rebels abducted one of his brothers—he was never seen again. Kony's men had since attacked the camp, killing more than 40 people, including Lakoch's other brother. He was left to look after their orphans. Good times in Kampala belonged to a different life. Like everyone else, he was trapped in the war.

Lakoch led me out of the hut and through a cassava field to the tumbledown remains of Kony's homestead, now just a scattering of mud bricks. Broken glass and pots lay strewn in the grass. There was nothing left.

I joined Joyce in the camp that evening. She was sitting outside the family hut on a tiny chair. A cluster of women arranged themselves on the ground around her, eager for tips on the bead business. A little farther away, men gathered under the leafless tree to listen to a radio. The BBC reported that police had again fired tear gas to disperse opposition supporters in Kampala, just a few days before the election.

Museveni's biggest rival had not had an easy ride since returning from exile in South Africa a few months earlier. Kizza Besigye had served as the president's doctor during the bush war that brought him to power, but was now his strongest challenger. Fans had set up roadside shrines with bananas or bottles of soda perched in front of his grinning portrait, as if offering a sacrifice. For some people, Besigye seemed like their only hope of stopping Museveni from ruling Uganda for the rest of his life. But now he was facing charges of treason, terrorism, and raping his housegirl.

Farcical proceedings only reinforced the impression that the courts were being used to keep "the doctor" off the campaign trail. When a judge ordered fourteen of his co-accused in the treason case to be released, paramilitaries from the hitherto unknown "Black Mamba Urban Hit Squad," wearing bandanas and brandishing submachine guns, turned up at the High Court to rearrest them. They wisely opted to stay in jail. A furious general told a talk show on KFM radio that the courts were helping "terrorists," insisting: "It is the generals who liberated this country when the judges were hiding under their beds." A replacement judge in the trial quit two days later. "I still love my dear life," he said, "I do not want to die a martyr." It was becoming increasingly clear who held the real power in Uganda.

Joyce showed me into a hut where her relatives served dinner. A girl appeared with a tray carrying plastic bowls of millet paste, sesame sauce, and tiny fish stewed with aubergines and okra. She knelt down and poured water over my hands from a jug, catching it in a bowl she held in her other hand. Like the other families, they relied on beans and maize delivered by the United Nations, but they had somehow conjured up a spread for their visitors.

Joyce used a plate to carve a steaming chunk from the lump of millet, known as *kwon-kal*. Looking a little like chocolate cake, tasting like dough, it forms the traditional staple in the north. The Acholi would claim it made their bones stronger than *matooke*, the more mushy plantains served by the Baganda in the south. I struggled to copy Joyce's knack of rolling the *kwon* into a ball, making a thumb-tip depression and scooping up the relishes, but the technique defeated me.

I asked about Awere Hill, where Lakoch said Kony had prayed before he began his rebellion. Part of me felt drawn to climb it, though I was not sure quite what I expected to find. Some said Kony had to come back to the outcrop every three years to make sacrifices to the ancestral spirits, though I had a feeling the chances of bumping into him on the summit were slim. Joyce suggested I ask the soldiers at the next camp to escort me; it would not be a good idea to go wandering around alone.

When night fell, the camp descended into almost total blackness. Women emerged from doorways with flaming sticks to light the way, then vanished back inside. I was startled when a shape detached itself from the wall of a nearby hut, but it was only a furtive boy. Faint light spilled from under ill-fitting doors as families crowded around cooking fires or crammed onto papyrus mats, trying to sleep. Darkness transformed the camp into a labyrinth of curved walls, identical whichever way I turned. I would never have found the way back to my hut from the latrine, had I not noticed the silhouette of the leafless tree.

I heard a strange swishing outside my door the next morning, and it took me a few moments to realize it was the sound of wives flicking dust from their thresholds with fistfuls of straw. A dirge of mewling children filled the air—the camp was so crowded it felt like a giant nursery. Somewhere a radio was playing Madonna's "Like a Prayer," while another broadcast a sermon.

"There is a high level of immorality in the camps, there is a high level of fornication in the camps," said the preacher—I could almost hear the spittle hitting the mic—"You need to repent, you need to come back to the Lord."

I strolled past a row of men who sat on a bench passing around reeking beakers of a spirit known as *lujutu*. Women brewed it from cassava to earn a little money, though it often rendered their menfolk insensible, and sometimes violent. Many Acholi said alcoholism worsened a kind of general breakdown in morality they blamed on the misery of life in the camps. But for farmers driven from their land, it was easy to see why drinking was appealing.

Left to their own devices, children sought entertainment in the lanes between the huts. Girls in torn frocks played hopscotch in the mud, while boys left clay pellets baking in the sun—homemade ammunition for their catapults. A group of them sat playing cards with a pack so tattered it might not have lasted another game. They looked like mini convicts, whiling away their stretches.

I took a bicycle taxi to the next camp, passing a strip of fields where people could still farm. A girl stood with a tiny dish of seeds perched on her head, passing them one by one to a boy of about eight who slammed a hoe into the soil then popped them into the holes he'd made. We crossed the bridge over the stream where Kony and Lakoch had once bathed, and a group of kids was wading in the brownish water. The road passed the primary school the two men had attended thirty years before. I could hear cheering. A huge crowd of children in bright-pink shirts had gathered on the field between the tin-roofed classrooms, shouting wildly. Young runners hared bare-chested around a makeshift track. I had turned up just in time for sports day.

I found the headmaster in his office, where the roll of pupils was recorded in marker pen on a piece of pink paper stuck to the wall. The school had several hundred children, 241 of whom had lost one or both parents. We wandered back out to the field, where boys were warming up by clapping hands under their kicking legs.

Teachers were supervising a weigh-in conducted with a set of bathroom scales and a wooden height measurer that still bore the sticker of the charity Action Against Hunger. I supposed they had donated it to help record malnutrition in the camp. Now it was being used to sort the competitors into categories according to a certain height–weight ratio. Age alone was an unreliable guide to strength, since so many children lacked a balanced diet. Boy scouts in khaki shirts, oversized caps, and blue-and-white neckerchiefs kept young spectators in order with sticks.

I watched the races for a while, and noticed that there were a number of soldiers deployed around the grounds, just in case Kony's men decided to grab a few more recruits. Their officer sat at one of the desks placed in the shade and exchanged the occasional sardonic remark with the teacher sitting next to him.

'A child died from this exercise," he muttered.

"That's bad," said the teacher.

"From javelin," the officer said. "Heard it on the radio this morning."

I got back on the bicycle and resumed my trip toward the next camp. Thick shrubs grew by the roadside, but I managed to catch a glimpse of Awere Hill as we rode past. The summit was shaped like a giant stone loaf. Some time later the rider dropped me at a row of ramshackle shops. The massed huts looked identical to those at Odek, but here a river snaked around their edge, flowing toward the Nile.

I followed a path up a small mound toward a circle of huts occupied by the soldiers that guarded the camp. The lieutenant in charge sat beneath a tree, peeling a clove of garlic to spice his lunchtime plate of beans. A spear leaned against the trunk, and a walkie-talkie radio hung from the branches. I recognized one word from the flow of transistorized voices—*adui,* Kiswahili for "enemy."

The lieutenant, an energetic man who wore his green beret at a jaunty angle, scrutinized my letter from Gulu. Then he beamed, promising to take me to the hill the next morning and ordering one of his men to clear a hut for me. I watched him amble up a nearby anthill where he peered at his mobile phone to see if he could get reception. By the look on his face, I guessed he was used to being disappointed.

Later that evening, the lieutenant invited me into a large, round hut that served as a kind of dining room for officers. Wide windows afforded a view across the plain rolling out below. We sat in silence, listening to the sound of drumming that drifted across the river from the camp. Somewhere nearby, I could hear the *thunk thunk* of a woman chopping firewood.

I regretted not bringing a gift from Gulu, perhaps a few bottles of V&A Imperial Cream—a popular tipple among soldiers. Its label declared it was made with molasses and "sherry flavors." All I had to offer was a rather whiskery copy of the *New Vision* and a bumper pack of sachets of Empire Vodka I had picked up at the shop. But I soon learned my host was a teetotaller.

"Shoes!" called the lieutenant, and a young soldier appeared, placed them at his feet, then vanished back into the cook hut. He called out orders throughout the evening—"Chili Sauce!" "Radio!" "Tea!"—and the young man waited on him like a doting wife.

The lieutenant explained that he was not an Acholi, but came from western Uganda, the area inhabited by Museveni's Banyankole tribe. He had joined the president-to-be's guerrilla army at fourteen, while he was still marching toward Kampala, and had stayed on ever since. In the past, Museveni had often extolled the virtues of the hundreds of child soldiers recruited by his National Resistance Army (NRA) during his struggle. They were known as "Kadogos"—"little ones" in Kiswahili—and they often acted as bodyguards for senior officers. But the president was less inclined to mention them these days. The recruitment of children was one of the charges the International Criminal Court had thrown at Kony.

Soon the lieutenant was no more than a silhouette in the chair in front of me, the orange tip of his cigarette glowing in the darkness. The only other light came from the red diode on his hissing radio. Though I did not normally smoke, I suddenly felt a powerful desire for a cigarette. He offered me his packet and I tore inexpertly at the foil until he tapped the base so I could pull one out.

"Is it really harmful, this smoking?" he said. "I had heard that a doctor said the smoke kills 99 percent of bacteria entering the nose and mouth, so it could be good?"

By now it was completely dark outside, pinpricks of light winking in the camp below. I felt as though I was on a ship, watching lanterns on distant vessels. After hearing from Lakoch how the spirits had influenced Kony, I wanted to ask the lieutenant why he thought his opponent was fighting, but he broached the subject first.

"This is a senseless war," he said, blowing out smoke. "Now what are they fighting for? God has given these people a punishment."

I asked him what he meant, and he referred to the *New Vision* I had given him.

"This man is trying to say war is caused by Satan," he said, casting his flashlight beam over an article written by an American evangelist. He traced the lines with his fingers, reading aloud.

"'Rebellion began in Heaven when Satan decided he was better than God. He was the number-one angel and he rebelled against God. Satan is the source of the start of war and destruction.'"

He looked up and laughed.

"This man is telling us the truth," he said, leaning back and swinging his arms. "It's Satan, not politics. Kony is Satan and Museveni is God! And we are the angels!"

Flying ants dove through the flashlight beam and the radio played a reggae song: "*Ain't no doubt, Bible must be right.*" I could not see the lieutenant's face in the darkness, but I imagined him grinning broadly, the mystery of the war solved. It was simple: Kony was driven by some nameless evil, perhaps the Devil himself.

Boots thudded past outside the hut, magazines clicked into rifles. I struggled out of my sleeping bag and opened the little door. Dazzling sunshine silhouetted a group of soldiers forming up nearby. Awere Hill lay less than an hour's walk away, but the lieutenant had organized a guard of twenty troops. I fell into the single file behind an Acholi sergeant carrying a spear, his gun slung across his back.

The path twisted through the undergrowth, leaves sparkling with dew. I imagined Moses, my newfound friend in Gulu, trekking through similar bush after his abduction, long grass forming prison walls. Luckily we had a landmark to guide us— the hill's rocky dome.

We passed an old woman, barefoot and bare-breasted, hacking a hoe into a patch of soil, then reached an almost sheer cliff. I removed my shoes to gain a better grip, the granite warm under my feet. It only took a few minutes to clamber to the flattened peak, but I could see why Kony had come here to pray.

Space and light flooded my head after the claustrophobia of the bush, sunlight glinting on veins of quartz embedded in the rock. Smaller mounds rippled on the horizon. Awere was considered the first wife to a cluster of boulders called "Moro," the husband. Another hump was named "Ayamo," the second wife. Beyond the trio of hills, I felt as if I were looking at infinity; I was the highest living being in the world. Only a hawk cruising on the thermals came close.

In the old days, Acholi rainmakers would climb such outcrops to call down the storm. Even as recently as the 1980s they risked a beating from farmers during droughts. I imagined Kony kneeling here praying, his brother urging him to come down as the clouds boiled, the young man oblivious to the danger.

The lieutenant called for shoes—mine this time—while he walked around in his green socks, listening to his walkie-talkie. I caught snatches of radio traffic: "Zero Four Zero . . . under disciplinary action . . . Fiver Hotel Zulu." In between bursts of static, he explained that Kony had climbed up here to collect water for his rituals.

"I just heard that he prays," he said, "then after praying, the water comes."

I walked to the edge of the summit with the sergeant, while another soldier scratched his name into the rock alongside signatures carved by previous climbers—Okellos, Omonas, and Okots. Acholi names formed a language of their own. I knew Okot means "born in the rainy season," but others have more intriguing histories—Komakech is "unlucky," Ocan means "born in poverty," while Otto is "death." Oringa means "run away"—sometimes used to refer to a man who has deserted a pregnant woman. Ojok alludes to some kind of physical defect—a reference to the *jok* presumed to be the cause. Kony is a particularly unusual name, meaning "helper." I had a look around, but there was no sign of a "JK" chiseled in the stone.

The sergeant pointed his spear toward the horizon, explaining how there had once been homesteads scattered all over the land. Now everyone was crowded into camps.

"They've all run away," he said. "Kony won't surrender, he will die in the bush."

We lingered on the summit for a while, before the soldiers began to trek back down the path. A crocodile of kids walked past in the other direction, on their way to school. A pair of girls dropped to their knees to greet me then stepped up again in one fluid motion, barely breaking their stride. The gesture took me by surprise, but I remembered reading that it was a traditional sign of respect given by Acholi women.

"Maybe they think you're Jesus!" said the lieutenant, and laughed.

We sat down outside a shop near the river by the camp. The lieutenant joined in a game with one of the locals, clattering beads into holes scooped in a block of wood. I had no idea of the rules, but the lieutenant seemed to be winning. An old man joined us and I bought him a beer, a Coke for the lieutenant, and another beer for one of his soldiers. I wanted to ask another question: why, after all this time, had the army's infantry, tanks, and helicopters failed to defeat Kony's band of rebels?

"They are like groundnuts," said the lieutenant. "When you harvest groundnuts there are always a few left which can grow again. Now we are uprooting even those ones."

He groped for another analogy, settling this time upon the *anyeri,* the giant rats speared by Acholi hunters and brought home for the pot.

"You know *anyeri?*" he said. "They can be hunted one by one, but they are still surviving out there." He pursed his lips and nodded. "Rebels are like *anyeri*."

"But you have not won the war," said the old man. "The war is not ended."

The lieutenant shook his head, like a teacher who hears a foolish question for the umpteenth time.

"This is not a war," he said. "A war would be with a thousand of them. There are now only groups of five."

"Yes," said the old man, setting down his beer and raising his palms. "But why can you not crush them, defeat them completely?"

"So how can you crush two individuals?" asked the lieutenant. "It is very difficult."

He squinted at the old man.

"And they have support," he said. "Even you, you could be going out on your bicycle after buying them soap and medicines, and then come back saying they have robbed you. You tell us your story to deceive us."

The old man spluttered and the lieutenant smiled.

"It is only an example," he said. "But there are collaborators every-where. Why do the civilians not go and get those last remnants?"

"We cannot go and do that fighting," said the man. "*You* have to crush them and destroy them."

The lieutenant looked thoughtful.

"Now the problem is this," he said, raising his forefinger. "Acholi only know three things in this world: fighting, hunting, and dancing. How can we change their ways? The Acholi are the easiest people to deceive."

The younger soldier, also from western Uganda, struggled to suppress a grin: "How could anyone believe that a stone can burst like a grenade?"

The two men chuckled, shaking their heads. The old man nar-rowed his eyes.

The strange thing was, however many times the rebels had been uprooted in the past twenty years, they had always grown back. For all the talk of spirits and Satan, I was beginning to sense that the secret of Kony"s longevity might be more down to earth. Perhaps inadvertently, the lieutenant had given me a clue.

3. DAUGHTER OF THE MOON

Supporters celebrate President Museveni's election

hants of "No change! No change!" mingled with the sounds of an Arsenal vs. Blackburn football match blaring from the television in the Franklin bar. I stepped onto the veranda and looked down the street. A small crowd had gathered outside the yellow façade of Museveni's party office. Blowing whistles and swapping high fives, the president's men were celebrating even before the final results had been declared.

Clouds massing above Gulu threatened to unleash one of the town's magnificent downpours, but Museveni's supporters looked as though they would dance regardless. A grinning young man wearing a bandana held one of the president's posters aloft as if it were the portrait of a saint.

"He's our president," said one of the young women, "the life president of Uganda!"

Lost in their gloating, Museveni's cadre of fans seemed oblivious to the hard stares of people watching from across the street. For a few months, the election campaign had kindled hope in the north that a change of leader might break the stalemate with the rebels and end the conflict. Now that hope had vanished. Although the great mass of Acholi had rejected him, Museveni had won a slim majority countrywide.

Cheering soldiers rolled past in a truck, flashing the thumbs-up sign for the president's Movement party. Often they were reluctant to have their photos taken, but this time the troops reveled in the attention, waving branches and whistling. The message was clear: their commander in chief was still in charge.

Kony was doubtless as disappointed as the rest of Gulu. I had often written in my Reuters stories that the Lord's Resistance Army had no discernible political agenda, but visits to some of the camps had taught me its leader was not above using the ballot box in his fight against Museveni. I had heard stories of women venturing out to collect firewood carrying cards bearing Besigye's picture, to prove to any rebels they met that they were voting for the opposition. Kony had even declared a ceasefire during the 1996 elections to allow villagers to vote against his foe. The fear was that he would take out his displeasure at these latest results on his own people.

"This man will punish us," muttered a woman standing near the Franklin, as the army truck rolled by. One of the minority of Movement supporters, she was decked entirely in the party colors, wearing a yellow dress, yellow plastic shoes, yellow earrings, a yellow handbag, a yellow hair band, and a yellow whistle on a gold chain around her neck. The effect was seriously yellow.

"The rebels will say the few people who voted for the president should be beaten," she said. "They will cut off their lips, they'll be looking for us."

Wind whipped up sheets of dust that flew down the street like brown ghosts, and I retreated to the shelter of the Franklin bar. Everyone looked glum, especially the Arsenal fans, who had to bear a Museveni victory as well as watch their team's bid for a Champions League place the following season slip further away with a 1–0 defeat at Ewood Park. I called Moses on his mobile phone and together we wandered down to the Acholi Inn. He shared the sense of resentment at the government, though he was coy about how he had cast his vote.

"We are tired of war, we are tired of being in camps with no proper protection," he said. "Even when I was abducted, it was because of poor security by the government. Why should a big school be attacked when soldiers are nearby?"

We followed the road through a patch of swampy ground where long-horned cows browsed in the grass. A trail of splatted frogs run over by cars the previous night led almost all the way to the Acholi Inn; their sun-dried skins were the color of peppermint. By the time we reached the gates, Moses sounded angry.

"The government says these rebels are only terrorists, that we are thieves—those are their kinds of prejudices," he said. "But Kony has objectives: he wants to overthrow the government, not just loot; he wants to restore Acholi culture, to rule Uganda according to the Ten Commandments."

Moses shook his head.

"People were forcibly taken to camps—they did not want to go," he said. "But the soldiers burned all their houses, all their crops were slashed down, they beat people. We northerners, we are not given any respect, we are just like slaves."

We made it to the inn as the first drops of rain began to fall. The sign warning of the landmines in the north was still pinned above the bar.

"The civilians and the government don't trust each other now," Moses said. "The rebels come and tell the civilians: 'You are supporting the government.' And the government tells them: 'You are supporting the rebels—they are your children.' So we end up being caught in the middle. We are neutral, who is on our side?"

As the rain fell harder, Moses's mood lightened just a little.

"In Acholi, if it rains, it means it's good," he said. "It's not a curse, it's a blessing."

That evening was the first time I had seen the Acholi Inn deserted. The usual buffet odor of cabbage, stew, and chapatis wafted from the dining room, the same pink-and-white strip lights glowed in the trees, but the garden was empty. Maybe it was the music. An ode to the "Yellow Man" washed over abandoned tables, the singer urging her listeners to quote Museveni's words of wisdom.

"He's a preacher, a lecturer, a teacher—yellow people, yellow president, yellow country!"

The part about "yellow country" was very much wishful thinking. The *New Vision* had splashed a map on its front page showing the voting pattern. While the south of Uganda outside Kampala was almost entirely yellow for Museveni, the country north of the Nile was blue for Besigye. The river cut the country in two not just geographically, but politically as well.

Looking at the map, I thought again about what the lieutenant had said after we climbed Kony's hill. He had compared the rebels to groundnuts that kept growing back. To take his metaphor a step further, I wondered what kind of soil had nurtured these "groundnuts" for so long. Looking at the north–south divide revealed by the map, I wondered if I had found part of my answer.

After only a few weeks in Gulu, I was beginning to recognize that the seeds of war had been sown in northern Uganda long before Kony's time. Echoes of what I considered ancient history kept cropping up in conversations about the conflict, as if the antics of a wayward village healer were a footnote to a much larger story.

I was most struck by this when I was sitting in the garden one afternoon, chatting to two Acholi men who had spent most of the war fighting each other. One was a colonel in the Ugandan army, the other an ex-rebel brigadier named Kenneth Banya. Now gray-haired and almost pathetically friendly, he had been granted amnesty by the government, though many people wondered why the prosecutors from the International Criminal Court did not issue an arrest warrant for him for what he had done in the bush. Like his old crony Sam Kolo, the rebels' former spokesman, Banya always asked for Red Bull. Kony banned alcohol among his followers and the enforced temperance seemed to have stuck.

Banya described Kony as a man who hated educated people, sometimes asking his commanders "Did Jesus go to school?", but his discussion with the colonel was more revealing. They plunged back through time—to the civil war Museveni fought in the 1980s, through the years under the late dictator Idi Amin in the 1970s, right back to the days before independence when Uganda was still part of the British Empire. Banya even remembered a royal visit in 1954, when schoolchildren were treated to projector shows of ballroom dancing. He was probably the only former member of the Lord's Resistance Army who could claim to have met Queen Elizabeth II.

The link with Britain went deeper still. Both Banya and the colonel remembered their fathers being shipped off to Burma to fight the Japanese during World War II. Survivors returned with tales of their white officers blacking up with boot polish to blend in with their African soldiers and confuse snipers. Banya even claimed his grandfather had taken up his spear in a rebellion against the British almost a century ago.

Gradually, a picture began to emerge from the fragments. It was as if, over the past 150 years, the people of northern Uganda had been thrust into a confrontation with a series of outsiders. Each wave had played a role in shaping their destiny, whether

Arab slavers, British colonialists, or even governments that exerted their authority from distant Kampala, where the inhabitants spoke a different language and followed different customs. Ultimately, the Acholi were the losers, confined to camps, preyed on by rebels, fearful of soldiers, and politically powerless. The man who claimed to be fighting on their behalf had turned them into his chief victims. To grasp the story of Kony, I would have to try to understand the story of his people.

Elders begin the saga with a legend. Turning on the murder of a young girl for the sake of a glass bead, the tale is far from cheerful. But when it comes to the history of the Acholi—and their most notorious son—it is as good a place as any to begin.

Hundreds of years ago, as the story goes, migrants began to drift southward across the savannah of southern Sudan and into what is now northern Uganda, searching for fresh pastures. They spoke Lwo, one of the Nilotic languages originating along the Nile. One of their clans was led by an old man and his two sons. The eldest was called Labongo, his younger brother Gipir.

One misty morning, Labongo's wife was looking for firewood when she heard a crashing sound. Seeing an elephant approaching, she screamed. Gipir ran into his elder brother's hut, grabbed the nearest spear and threw it into the beast's side. When the fog cleared, both elephant and spear were gone.

Had Gipir flung any old lance, the story might have been different. Unfortunately, he had lost the ancestral spear, entrusted to Labongo by their dying father to be handed down for eternity. Labongo was furious. "You must get it back!" he ordered his brother. "You must go right now!"

Muttering curses, Gipir wandered for many months in the forest before eventually meeting an old woman. "My son," she asked, "what has brought you here?" Gipir was exhausted, but he managed to explain. The crone nursed him until he felt a little better, then whispered that she knew of a place where the elephants brought spears. Together, they managed to retrieve the heirloom. She also gave Gipir some sparkling beads, the most beautiful he had ever seen.

When Gipir arrived home several months later, he marched up to his brother and plunged the spear into the ground. Joyful villagers mobbed him, oblivious to his anger. In the tumult, the beads fell from his pouch. One of Labongo's youngest daughters picked one up and popped it into her mouth.

Gipir grabbed the girl and turned to Labongo: "My brother, she has swallowed one of my beads, I want it back now!"

Now it was Labongo's turn to plead. Eventually, he lost his temper, slit open the girl's stomach, and thrust the bloody bead into Gipir's hand. The girl died.

The brothers performed a ritual to destroy their relationship, turning their backs and cursing the woman who had breastfed them, before going in opposite directions. Gipir reached the Nile, parted the water with an axe and crossed to the western bank. He founded a tribe known as the Alur. Labongo remained on the east side of the river and became the forefather of the Acholi. To this day, the tribes are neighbors.

The legend says more about the Acholi's sense of themselves as a distinct community than about what actually happened, and variants of the story are repeated by Lwo communities in Kenya and Sudan. But what does seem clear is that what it meant to be an Acholi took on new interpretations as a succession of visitors arrived in their land. Long before Kony's day, whether you were considered to be an Acholi became a matter of life and death.

Given the Acholi's eventual fate, it was perhaps no wonder that the older generation felt a certain nostalgia for a lost age before slave hunters, imperial agents, and missionaries turned up. Tales of children sitting around the fire learning the names of stars from elders sat uneasily with the scenes I witnessed of kids wandering the camps in gangs as their parents got blitzed on homebrew. Reading about the life Labongo's descendants might have led, even I found myself slipping toward a rather rose-tinted view of the past.

Fought with arrows and spears, the wars of old sounded like rather genteel affairs compared to the wholesale slaughter familiar from the region's modern-day conflicts. Young men would set out to seize cattle from neighboring tribes to pay the bride price needed to marry, earning honor on the battlefield into the bargain. A plan would be hatched, the spirits consulted, blades blessed by an old woman at the village shrine. Warriors had to be pure—they were not allowed to sleep with a woman on the eve of battle. They attacked at dawn.

Killing was in fact relatively rare before the arrival of large numbers of guns in the late nineteenth century, and custom dictated that a returning warrior must ritually cleanse the spilling of human blood. A fighter would sacrifice a black-and-white billy goat by running it through with a spear to appease the spirit of his slain opponent. He might even cut off his victim's head and take it to the ancestral shrine to show what he had done so the violence could be "neutralized." Cuts would be made on his arm—three for killing a man, four for killing a woman, and he would be given a special name. Every morning and evening the killer would wander out of the village and shout an invitation to the dead person's spirit to visit. Nobody wanted to be haunted by their victim's ghost, the vengeful *cen*.

Festivals designed to ask the ancestors for help in bringing good health, abundant rain, and plenty of children helped unite the clans that made up each of Acholiland's many chiefdoms. According to the poet p'Bitek, a priest would periodically emerge from the chief's enclosure shouting, *"Diki teero jok,"* shorthand for "tomorrow is the day for taking food for the spirit." The cry would spread through the village, and women would scurry to prepare beer and flowers. P'Bitek recalls a curse once laid on wayward girls: "Explode the eyeballs of any woman who marries outside the chiefdom!"

Followers lowered the priest into a cave infested with snakes and hornets, rendered harmless on the day of the spirit so he could scoop up sacred sand for use in medicine. Priests were sometimes said to take the shape of an animal themselves—one morphed into a huge serpent with a human head and eyes that shone like fireflies.

Even when Lloyd visited at the turn of the twentieth century, old ways were still intact. He described how, each night, dust would be sprinkled beneath the ladder leading up to the young men's huts to capture footprints of any amorous teenagers who ventured in or out. It was a different world from the cramped mudscapes of today's camps, where adults, children, and the elderly were forced to live on top of each other.

Many societies have looked backward to a mythical "golden age" in times of crisis, but in my view the Acholi could be forgiven for feeling they really had suffered a fall. Long before the camps were created, life in northern Uganda took a definite turn for the worse. In the middle of the nineteenth century, the slavers arrived.

Rampaging down the White Nile in ships full of Nubian soldiers, the hunters came to feed Egypt's ravenous appetite for captives to work its sugar plantations and irrigation schemes, and to fight in its armies. Thriving slave markets in Khartoum, where the White and Blue Niles converge, lured adventurers and cutthroats seeking quick riches. Counting everyone from Arabs, Kurds, Turks, and Copts in their ranks, as well as companies from Britain, France, and Austria, the traders laid waste to southern Sudan before reaching the fringes of what is now northern Uganda. Penetrating the area that would eventually be called Acholiland, they found plenty of fresh villages to plunder and plenty of elephants to shoot. The slavers did a lucrative business in ivory, which were used in Europe to make piano keys.

Compliant chiefs would help raid villages and hand over the captives in exchange for muskets. Conflicts took on a new and deadly hue as local leaders suddenly saw new opportunities to expand their influence and accumulate prized copper and beads with their new guns. The word Acholi was not yet commonly used, but the slavers soon began referring to their new "hosts" as "Shuuli," perhaps based on their linguistic similarity with a group farther north called Shilluk.

There is some debate as to precisely when the loose grouping of chiefdoms began to be identified by others—and themselves—as a distinct Acholi tribe, but it seems to have had a lot to do with the British. Early administrators deemed that the various communities living in the region around Gulu formed a single unit, and stuck the label "Acholi" on top. The poet p'Bitek argued that the British actually "invented" the Acholi "tribe" as it is now known in the 1920s, although others argue that the collective identity of Acholiland has much deeper roots.

Whichever version holds more truth, most people agree that under colonial rule, this emerging "Acholi" identity took on a whole new significance. To be an Acholi was to be a warrior, an arbitrary designation that would induce a whole saga of bloodshed, in which Kony was only the most recent chapter. And, like many fateful encounters, it began almost by chance.

The site of Sir Samuel White Baker's old fort lies less than an hour's drive from Gulu at a place called Patiko. The ever intrepid Lloyd had visited, and the redoubt had been home at one time to Arab slavers. So many ghosts from northern Uganda's past seemed to congregate among the ruins, I could not resist a visit. A guide called Constantin led me toward the crag.

As I scrambled up the heap of boulders, I could easily see why Baker had chosen this place for his castle—it was the perfect lookout. With a little imagination, you could just about make out the blueish smudge of the Ethiopian highlands. Apart from a glinting tin roof on the Nile floodplain below, I imagined the view had barely changed since he had first arrived more than a century before.

A bear of a man with a barrel chest and black beard, Baker was the archetypal Victorian adventurer. He was the eldest son of a family of West Indian sugar planters and had tried his hand as a tea farmer in Ceylon, then helped to build a railway down the Danube. Somewhere along the way he liberated a beautiful Hungarian woman from an Ottoman slave bazaar. Fifteen years his junior, Florence made a robust companion. The Acholi called him "Pasha," or even "lion's mane," while his partner's long blonde hair earned her the name *Anyadwe*—"daughter of the moon."

For a man of Baker's passions, Africa presented one irresistible challenge—to discover the source of the White Nile. More than just a scientific puzzle for Victorian explorers, "settling the Nile" was an obsession. Herodotus had written that the river flowed from "fountains" at the heart of the continent, but there was not much else to go on. By the time Baker arrived, the most reliable geography of East Africa had been written by the Greek mathematician and astronomer Ptolemy in about 150 AD. Not to be deterred, Baker set out to win his place in history.

Heading up the Nile from Cairo with Florence in April 1861, Baker was blissfully unaware of the news that awaited him upstream. The couple reached Khartoum, then made it to a river station at a place called Gondokoro, near present-day Juba in south Sudan. It was here that Baker met the rival explorers John Hanning Speke and James Augustus Grant on 15 February 1863. The pair told him they had found the source on the shores of Lake Victoria a few months earlier.

Baker refused to be discouraged and set off to find another lake the two men had mentioned. He "discovered" it on what is now the border of Uganda and Congo, dubbed it Lake Albert and won a knighthood for his trouble. Reading his account of the journey, the award sounds well deserved: food supplies fail and the couple are forced to eat grass; hippopotamuses overturn their boats and raiders shoot at them with poisoned arrows. Remembering a more relaxed moment, Baker describes passing through Patiko, where the locals prepared a sheep for his lunch. The explorer wrote that he "took a great fancy to these poor people." But for all the couple's scrapes, Baker's accounts of the ravages of the slave trade are what resonate most strongly today. Full of descriptions of burned huts and seized captives, his reports could have been describing the predations of Kony's rebels.

"For many miles circuit from Shooa, the blackened ruins of villages and deserted fields bore witness to the devastation committed; the cattle that were formerly in thousands had been driven off, and the beautiful district that had once been most fertile reduced to wilderness."

The Scottish missionary David Livingstone had done much to alert the British public to the evils of the slave trade in East Africa; Baker's reports only added to the clamor for the government to take sterner action. The obvious target for diplomatic pressure was Egypt, with its huge slave population and dominion over the hunting grounds in Sudan. Hoping to win favor in the eyes of his London creditors, the Khedive in Cairo hired Baker to rein in the slavers. He was appointed "Governor-General of the Equatorial Nile Basin," and given a salary of £10,000 a year. Sir Samuel Baker and Lady Florence returned to Patiko on 1 August 1872.

While stamping out slavery was nigh-on impossible, Baker loved the life at the fort, describing it as his "little paradise." When not riding around on horses blasting elephants with his gun—which was said to break the shoulder of a lesser man—he indulged in vigorous constitutionals. Our guide pointed to a gap between two huge boulders.

"That was 'Baker's Leap,' he used to jump across it for exercise," he said. "I don't know why he did it."

The chasm looked a little too big to try, but in between bayonet charges with enemy caravans and encounters with African wildlife, it was probably the least of Baker's worries. The slavers were bad enough, but the Nubian troops he left stationed in his garrisons were often even more predatory, many of them ex–slave hunters themselves. Baker himself would not shrink from razing a few villages or stringing up locals from trees when he saw fit, though he was fondly remembered in Acholiland even several decades after the couple began the long voyage home in 1873.

Lloyd encountered a man named "Sululu" who would climb an anthill and blow a piercing blast on Baker's old bugle to summon his men, while one of Baker's former retainers told the missionary the "Pasha" had shared his people's joys and sorrows.

The respect was not always mutual. Despite the risks he took to defend them, Baker frequently asserted his pet monkey was more civilized than the Africans.

"The treachery of the Negro is beyond belief," he wrote. "He has not a moral human instinct, and is below the brute. How is it possible to improve such abject animals? They are not worth the trouble, and they are only fit for slaves, to which position their race seems to have been condemned."

Our guide led us to another boulder, motioning for me to climb up and take a look. Somebody had spent many hours scratching a cross about the diameter of a teacup into the granite. Constantin insisted the mark was made by none other than Lady Florence herself, though he explained the slavers had found less artistic uses for the rocks.

"You would be beheaded here," he said, pointing to a slope leading down into the undergrowth. "Your body would roll down there, and the hyenas would take advantage of it. I grew up here but we never went down there. We expected to find skulls."

Not for the first time I wondered if Constantin was indulging in a little poetic license. It was clear, though, that the accounts penned by Baker spawned the first British interest in Acholiland. Soon emissaries of the Empire returned in force, initiating an encounter that would have far bigger consequences for the subjects than for their masters.

When Britain established a Protectorate over Uganda at the close of the nineteenth century, Baker's old stamping grounds were not even included. British interest focused on Buganda in the south, where the kingly Kabaka and his courtiers bore a much closer resemblance to European monarchies than the scattered clans and chiefdoms of the north. Even Baker, who kept up a voluminous correspondence from his country house in Devon, began to argue that administering his former haunts would not justify the expense.

But these were the days of the "scramble for Africa." As Britain vied for influence alongside France, Germany, and Belgium, the imperial authorities began to look at Uganda in a new light, noticing that the Acholi occupied an important square on the chessboard of great power rivalry. Again, the Nile brought visitors.

The river had gained new importance with the opening of the Suez Canal in 1869, linking Britain to India, her most important possession. To control the Nile was to control Egypt, and the artery of Empire. Farfetched as it sounds, there was a real fear that a hostile power might block the river completely. Legend had it that an ancient king of Abyssinia had diverted the waters of the Blue Nile until the sultan of Egypt sent presents, while Baker cited biblical references that seemed to confirm the danger.

Protestant and Catholic missionaries were also eager to win converts, some enticing worshippers with gifts of salt or pins. "Shuli country is ready for putting to the sickle," wrote one English bishop, while another missionary wondered why a station founded by Austrian Catholics had not made more progress; "they had three years' innings but they do not seem to have got hold of any of the people." The competition between churches added another fracture into society, and a new layer to existing spiritual beliefs—often rather confusingly. An early missionary from the Verona Fathers translated the name of the Christian God as *jok rubanga*, the same spirit the Acholi blamed for causing spinal tuberculosis. Despite Lloyd's attempts to attract followers to the Anglican Church with magic lantern shows, and what was probably Acholiland's first football match, the majority flocked to the Catholic faith. Congregations began to wear the rosaries that Kony would cherish as a schoolboy, and follow rituals he would later adapt to cement his grip on his own followers.

When the British authorities began to set themselves up in Gulu in the early years of the twentieth century, they were unimpressed. The Acholi's reluctance to abandon their crops in order to grow cotton to feed Manchester's hungry mills was seen as clear evidence of their laziness. Although many farmers did eventually embrace the imperialists' favored crop, Acholiland also served as a labor pool for the tea, coffee, and sugar plantations established in the "productive zone" in the south. Certainly they were not deemed fit for the limited opportunities offered to the Baganda for advancement into the civil service, though there was one career option they were welcome to try. In the words of one colonial administrator, the Acholi took to soldiering "like ducks to water."

The British preference for recruiting Acholi into the military was based partly on racist stereotyping that decreed certain tribes were good for certain things. Officials wrote of the Acholi's "superior physique" and "habits of discipline," theorizing that the tribe bore the martial imprint of earlier Asiatic invaders. Beyond the pseudo-science, there was a more pragmatic reason for putting northerners into the army: the classic British strategy of divide and rule. There was no telling what might happen if they armed the Baganda, who were organized enough to rise up against their imperial masters. The Acholi were too divided to pose a threat themselves, though they could be mobilized to deal with other communities who showed signs of rebellion.

When the British found themselves facing World War II, they called on the Acholi to fight, entrenching their military identity even further. I met one of the veterans in a camp outside Gulu. Leaning on a polished wooden stick, Adelino Lagara did not look a day younger than his 92 years. He had been sent thousands of miles to fight for a foreign king, and had risked his life on both sea and land, but looking back, he was grateful.

The old man's voice quavered, but there was nothing wrong with his memory. I asked his rank and he snapped to attention, barking: "Driver, 5788!" For him, World War II counted as recent history. He began his story by reeling off a list of ancestors stretching back ten generations to the spear-obsessed Labongo himself.

It turned out that Lagara had been an accidental participant in the war. Signing up to be a government driver in Gulu just before Germany invaded Poland, he soon found himself learning to drive a Chevrolet truck at a British army base in Kenya. The smell of the brand-new upholstery was still fresh in his nostrils. After serving in Ethiopia, he boarded a ship at Mombasa, sailed through the Suez Canal and passed the mouth of the Nile at Alexandria. He could remember the alarms warning of German submarines as he crossed the Mediterranean. "If you sank, the fish would eat you," he said. "But I was not scared, I just had to do my duty."

The Allies had already defeated the Nazis in North Africa by the time Lagara arrived, but many other Acholi soldiers were less fortunate. Sent off to Burma, they joined the British 14th Army's pursuit of the retreating Japanese through the jungles of the Kabaw Valley—the "Valley of Death." Starving Japanese troops made death pacts to shoot one another, or blew themselves up with hand grenades, their bloated bodies swelling in the rain. British Tommies found postcards of cherry blossom and snow-capped Mount Fujiyama on corpses. Veteran John Nunneley described the fighting in his book *Tales from the King's African Rifles*: "In the huge loneliness of the jungle violent death comes at the hands of half-naked, demented soldiers turned into hunting packs killing the weak and robbing the dead for the last handful of mouldy rice." Horrified at the idea of surrender, the Japanese elite "White Tigers" division nevertheless staged a fierce rearguard action, in which many Acholi were killed.

Britain felt the debt had been repaid when the government built a sports ground at Pece on the edge of Gulu, and Sir Samuel Baker School, from which Moses would be abducted half a century later. The Ugandan soldiers may be largely forgotten, but older Acholi look back on that pivotal experience with a curious mixture of nostalgia and bitterness.

Many veterans thrived. Lagara's salary paid for the cows he needed to marry another wife, and founded a herd that supported his family for a generation. Having discovered a much wider world than his ancestors could have imagined, he chaired a committee to promote development in his locale. Others wondered why Britain had forgotten their relatives' sacrifices. "If my uncle died in the King's African Rifles," said one woman, "how many Britons have died in the cause of helping northern Uganda?"

When the war ended, Britain faced a growing clamor for independence in its colonies. The country Winston Churchill called the "Pearl of Africa" was no exception; Uganda's turn came in 1962. Soon the pearl was stained with blood. The Empire had been about maintaining control, not fostering democracy. The constitution adopted at independence failed to resolve the competing demands of Uganda's various communities, and politics took an increasingly ethnic hue. The first prime minister, Milton Obote, was a northerner from the Lango area, adjacent to Acholiland. He began by forging an alliance with the Baganda in the south, but it proved short-lived. Within a few years, Obote had dissolved the constitution, imposed a one-party state and assumed the post of president. Shells blasting the Kabaka's palace made the point in no uncertain terms—the army was now the arbiter of power.

A veteran of the King's African Rifles named Idi Amin grasped the point better than most and overthrew Obote in 1971. One of the general's first acts was to summon Acholi and Langi troops back to the barracks, where his men massacred them. Amin was anxious to ensure there was nobody left in the military to stage a counter coup. Survivors fled into Sudan, saying they were going to "skin the elephant," a euphemism for joining the forces gathering in exile to fight Amin's dictatorship. He wiped out a generation of officers, intellectuals, and churchmen, simply because they might pose a threat. Some Acholi trace the source of the present-day conflict to the murder of a prominent Acholi brigadier named Okoya in 1970, saying it brought down a curse that resulted in Kony's war. Legend had it that his coffin was buried vertically to ensure his *cen* would take revenge.

Amin sealed his own fate by sending his troops across the southern border into Tanzania. The Tanzanian army retaliated by invading Uganda in 1979, supported by factions of Amin's exiled opponents. Acholi formed a substantial part of the Ugandan contingent, as did Museveni and his followers. Perhaps 500,000 people were killed during Amin's rule, but his defeat only marked the start of a new phase of bloodshed.

When Obote emerged as winner of elections in December 1980, Museveni accused him of rigging the result. He attacked a barracks the following month with 27 armed men, and this was the moment commemorated at the parade I had seen in Gulu. Again, Uganda was plunged into a cycle of conflict played out largely along ethnic lines. Led mainly by Bantu-speaking fighters from south and west Uganda, Museveni's rebel National

Resistance Army found itself battling government forces dominated by Lwo-speaking northerners, including many Acholi.

The fighting focused on an area north of Kampala called the Luwero Triangle, and it turned increasingly ugly. Obote's army massacred tens of thousands of civilians suspected of supporting Museveni during the notorious "Operation Bonanza," with troops looting, murdering, and raping on a grand scale. The history of exactly who did what in Luwero remains contested, but Acholi soldiers, and Acholi more generally, were increasingly demonized.

As the war ground on, tensions between Acholi and Langi officers from Obote's tribe divided the army. Two Acholi commanders—General Tito Okello and Brigadier Bazilio Olara-Okello—overthrew Obote in July 1985, triggering a breathtaking round of looting in Kampala by their soldiers. (I had at first assumed their common surname meant the two were somehow related, but later learned that "Okello" means a child born after twins.) The generals signed a peace deal with Museveni in Nairobi, but he seized Kampala a few weeks later. Feeling betrayed, the Acholi called the peace talks "peace jokes."

Fearing Museveni wanted revenge for the "skulls of Luwero," the Acholi soldiers fled north, crossing the Nile at Karuma Falls and heading as far as south Sudan. When the new president urged them in a broadcast on Radio Uganda to return to barracks, they remembered how Amin's men had used a similar call to slaughter them. Some returned home, many handed in their guns, but others waited.

In the following months Museveni sent his soldiers to establish control in the north, but their heavy-handed tactics only seemed to confirm the Acholi's fears. Troops burned granaries, executed civilians, raped women and looted goods, telling villagers they were settling scores from Luwero. "We want our mothers' clothes back," they said, "we want these bicycles." Warriors from the neighboring Karamojong tribe plundered huge numbers of cattle with the collusion of Museveni's officers, dealing an economic blow from which the region never recovered. It was perhaps no wonder that many Acholi decided to fight back. The civil war that raged in southern Uganda during the early 1980s between Acholi soldiers in Obote's army and Museveni's guerrillas had crossed the Nile and resumed in the north. The difference was that now Museveni's men were the army, and the Acholi were the rebels.

By the time Kony appeared, he was a minor player dwarfed by much more powerful Acholi leaders. By far the most famous was the fishmonger called Alice Auma, better known as Alice Lakwena after the Acholi word for "messenger." Her career lasted only a fraction of Kony's twenty-plus years, but it was far more spectacular. If anyone was a prototype for him, it was Alice. Her sister's brief eulogy at the funeral I'd attended only hinted at the story. I hoped her father, Severino Lukoya, might fill in the rest.

Zigzagging through a slum on the edge of Gulu, the lane eventually opened out into a patch of swampy ground housing a blue building with a tin roof. A white cross with a heart-shape at its center had been chiseled above the door, a star perched on one arm, a moon on the other—the sign of the New World Meltar Jerusalem temple.

I stepped inside to find a man in blue robes contemplating a large wooden crucifix that leaned against the far wall. He turned and smiled, pointing to the corner. I looked around and saw an old man lying on a bed. Naked apart from his white shorts, and with his gray-bearded chin resting on his chest, Severino Lukoya looked like a prophet from the Bible he was reading. Fixing me with bright eyes, he motioned to a chair.

Working as a mason in between preaching, Severino had managed to fall off a ladder while doing some plastering. Recovering in his temple, he was more than happy to tell the story of his daughter's ill-fated uprising, salted with tales of meteors, speaking crocodiles, and a memorable trip to heaven where he met Abraham, Moses, David, and God himself, sitting on a three-legged stool. Asking his priest to bring him a Coke to "warm his blood," he finally veered back to the subject of Alice.

She had been selling fish in a village called Opit, not far from Kony's birthplace, when the spirits summoned her. Father and daughter took the train, still functioning at the time, and then trekked through the forest to the Murchison Falls. Splashing cowries and coins into the Nile, they heard the "authorities of the water" instruct Alice to heal.

Severino raised himself in his cot, remembering how the Acholi soldiers ran wild after Museveni seized Kampala. Six of them chased a train driver into his daughter's temple, who cowered behind Alice for protection. The men had wanted to kill him for working for the government, but when they cocked their guns to fire, they all jammed. Awed by Alice's powers, the soldiers begged for her help.

"The commander of the group said, 'If it's because of sin that we were overthrown, then I am ready to die in the name of Jesus Christ,'" Severino told me. "When they returned to Alice, the spirit bathed them in water, he purified them. After washing them he anointed them with shea-butter oil, just like Jesus was anointed. Almighty God sent a message to Alice that she should cleanse everyone in Acholiland."

And cleanse she did. Alice became the most popular Acholi in living memory. Ex-soldiers, villagers, schoolchildren, even a former education minister named Isaac Newton Ojok joined her

Holy Spirit Mobile Forces. She was not just offering protection from Museveni's soldiers—she also promised redemption.

When Kampala fell, the Acholi soldiers fled home with trucks full of loot and blood on their hands. Vanquished, terrified, and out of control, they feared not only the retribution of Museveni, but the *cen* of their victims in Luwero. Acholi had never seen a crisis quite like it. It would take a new type of leader to restore the balance.

Blending Christian symbolism with older Acholi beliefs, Alice created a genuine sense of rebirth among her followers, washing her tribe clean of collective guilt. They began by killing witches and sorcerers, and rooting out other presumed sources of evil. Not only would her army redeem the Acholi, but it would cleanse the whole country of violence.

Alice sought to create a sense of invincibility in her rapidly swelling ranks of foot soldiers, promising that they would be immune to bullets if they followed strictures like not eating before battle and respecting water. Although these might sound bizarre, her Holy Spirit Safety Precautions reflected a tradition among Acholi elders of laying down rules in times of disaster to appease unseen powers. Enlisting the forces of nature, she promised her fighters that squadrons of bees would sting their enemies, snakes bite them, rivers wash them away, while an army of 140,000 spirits would rally to their side.

Alice's horde enjoyed some remarkable successes, despite her unconventional tactics. Eschewing conventional military wisdom, she would send letters stating the time and place of planned attacks. Locals would wait for the gunfire to start at the appointed hour, wryly calling it the "disco." Sometimes the tactics worked. Confronted with thousands of rapturous warriors glistening with oil, soldiers often fled. At other times, they mowed down her followers in their hundreds. Recruiting more volunteers to plug the gaps, Alice promised to part the Nile and seize Kampala. She was within only a few days' march of the capital when things went badly wrong.

Museveni's soldiers routed her peasant army near Jinja, not far from the spot identified as the source of the Nile by Victorian explorers. Alice escaped to Kenya on a bicycle, where she lived out her days in a refugee camp, preaching, knitting, and concocting "remedies" for AIDS. She rebuffed various attempts by the Ugandan government to convince her to return, demanding compensation for cattle lost during Museveni's takeover. She died during a bout of sickness in January 2007, aged 50. Nobody knows how many people were killed in the course of her uprising, but the figure is probably in the region of 10,000.

As Severino spoke, a boy of about fourteen walked into the temple and knelt before the cross. The priest balanced a calabash on the boy's head like a bowl, then mumbled some words before it clattered to the floor with its mouth up. The priest repeated the ritual until the calabash landed mouth to the ground. He tapped a stone on the top three times, then smeared an oily cross on the boy's forehead, ensuring he was free of any malignant spirits before his exams at Sir Samuel Baker School.

"Now the spirit has been trapped," whispered Severino. I noticed a mouse scurry along the wall behind the altar.

Given Alice's stunning, albeit short-lived success, Kony's initial appeal becomes easier to understand. He drew on the same pool of Christian and Acholi beliefs at a time when people desperately needed a redeemer, and he was by no means alone. Severino himself had enjoyed an inglorious career as a rebel at about the same time as his daughter, though he was from the Madi tribe, rather than an Acholi. He was jailed for a while, before eventually finding his way back to Gulu. Suspecting he was up to his old tricks, the authorities arrested him once more, this time for collecting shea butter in old Fanta bottles.

Many people say Kony and Alice were cousins, though Alice's relatives tend to deny any connection. Family trees I assembled during my visit to Odek suggest they were distantly related, but the connection was hard to pin down. Severino had once referred to a "Trinity," with him representing the Father, Kony the Son, and Alice the Holy Spirit. Now Alice is dead and Severino retired, only Kony survives.

Severino had few good words to say about "the Son," whose followers had broken his crook and burned his Bible many years before, making him cry.

"Kony believes that he is a messenger of God, and everyone on Earth must follow whatever he has been sent to do," Severino went on. "Kony says he wants to carry the cross, to give people suffering, to give people pain."

I took his photo before I left, his face twitched, his eyes twinkled. For a few seconds he was possessed once more, by whom or what he did not say.

Several weeks later I told an Italian priest living outside Gulu about my encounter with Severino, but he did not give his reams of testimony much credence.

"Ah, Severino," he said. "He's mad."

After six hours talking to Severino I needed a drink, so I headed for the Acholi Inn. As usual, I got to chatting to the former British colonel named Bob. There was talk that the rebels were thinking about joining peace talks across the border in Juba, the new capital of southern Sudan. If those negotiations began, there might be a way for me to contact Kony.

I wondered whether I should head to Juba straightaway. The town lay a couple of days' journey further down the White Nile, and so I would have to set off soon. But before I left, there was a man I wanted to meet. He would only be in northern Uganda for a few hours, but he had an interesting goal—to galvanize the world into stopping Kony.

4. FEEDING THE PRISONERS

A healer prepares to summon spirits

With headlights blazing and UN flags snapping from radio masts, the convoy pulled up in tight formation in the middle of Patongo camp. Car doors swung open and figures clad in blue flak jackets and helmets emerged from the air-conditioned interiors. Ripping Velcro seals on their vests, they dumped the cladding on the back seats. Their leader had no need for armor—his whole car was bulletproof. Sporting a safari jacket and spectacles, Jan Egeland stepped back into Kony country.

Egeland, a plain-speaking Norwegian, was head of disaster relief at the United Nations. He spent his days dealing with wars, famines, and earthquakes. His remit was the planet. Soon after assuming his post as emergency relief coordinator in August 2003, Egeland had dubbed the crisis in northern Uganda "the biggest forgotten and neglected humanitarian emergency in the world." Having campaigned to raise awareness for several years, he now felt there was a chance of a solution.

I wondered if anybody had known he was coming. A pair of boys kicked a ball between some huts near the parked cars, while a girl wandered past with a saucepan balanced on her head. Patongo camp lay some hours from Gulu in the Pader District, which was renowned for being violent, dangerous, and depressing, even by northern Ugandan standards. That was partly why Egeland had chosen to visit.

Journalists sometimes felt a little jaundiced by the various permutations of the word "neglected" that aid officials used to describe whichever African crisis they happened to be visiting, whether it be in Sudan, Congo, Chad, Somalia, Uganda, or an even obscurer location. But whichever phrasing you used, Patongo could fairly claim to be more neglected than most. Fighting had continued there even when the area around Gulu had fallen quiet. Soldiers had skirmished with rebels in the surrounding bush on the day of our visit.

Egeland found his welcome in a hall in the center of the camp, where a group of residents waited patiently on wooden chairs. He said a few words about how their plight was beginning to attract greater attention abroad, then opened the meeting to the floor. A man shot up his hand and asked Egeland if he could do something about the latrines. Apparently, the holes they dug for long-drops kept collapsing. Others asked for more food or more teachers, but none raised the possibility of ending the conflict. It was as if war was so normal that the idea of peace had slipped everyone's mind—or perhaps experience had blunted expectations of outsiders. Egeland nodded as his officials made notes, then stepped into a closed meeting with a group of mothers.

A posse of journalists from the Ugandan media, as well as the BBC, Reuters, and Associated Press, had turned up from Kampala, but they were dwarfed by the gaggle of threadbare children who trailed Egeland's brief tour of the camp. For all his efforts to attract attention, northern Uganda still dwelt in the "news in brief" columns; no big television networks or international newspapers were covering his visit. The lack of interest played in my favor—it was easy to grab a place in the back of his car.

A couple of other journalists squeezed in, pointing tape recorders in Egeland's face as he craned his neck around to speak. A former television reporter himself, he chose his words carefully as we rolled out of the camp.

"For me, northern Uganda has become a little bit of a quest ever since I came here," he said. "I asked which was the most neglected place on earth, and then my staff said, 'Basically, if you want to hear it, it's northern Uganda.'

"I'm a hardened relief worker now, but I was really moved to my bones by the stories of these mothers. I asked them 'Is there anyone here who has had a kidnapped child?' and they all raised their hands, I would say 95 percent of them. One had lost four children and hadn't heard anything yet, a couple of others had gotten back their children totally traumatized.

"It's just a terror like no other place in the world. It's not the West which is the epicenter of terror—this is complete terror, 90 percent of the population being displaced. For me it's mindboggling."

"So why did it take the world so long to notice?" I asked.

"Uganda has done well on many other fronts, and that should not be forgotten," Egeland said. "Somehow the international community in Kampala didn't look over its shoulder and see what was in the north."

I thought of Father Carlos tapping out his reports on carbon paper by the light of a kerosene lamp, and posting them off to organizations that filed them in the wastepaper basket. For years the diplomats and UN officials in Kampala had hardly ventured north of the Nile. In some ways it was not surprising. In the shorthand of our Reuters stories, Museveni had become a "darling" of the West. Contributions from donor countries like Britain and other members of the European Union funded half his government's annual budget. Everyone wanted to believe the miracle.

It was easy to see why Museveni had been so appealing. After the chaos under Amin and Obote, the new president had pulled off a stunning turnaround. The economy recovered quickly, particularly in the south. He spoke about AIDS when the disease was still a taboo subject in Africa, and he lambasted leaders who stayed in power too long. Even better, Museveni not only adopted the kinds of free-market reforms advocated by the World Bank and the International Monetary Fund, but seemed to make them work at a time when activists were increasingly questioning their wisdom. He even invited back the thousands of Asians expelled by Amin, asking them to help rebuild. For a time, Museveni was arguably the most influential head of state in sub-Saharan Africa after Nelson Mandela.

In the early 1990s, the contrast with Uganda's neighbors could hardly have been more stark: civil war festered in Sudan, Congo—then known as Zaire—was traveling at full speed in reverse gear under President Mobutu Sese Seko, while in Kenya President Daniel arap Moi was presiding over the wholesale looting of the economy by his cronies. Rwanda's old rulers were busy drawing up plans for a genocide. Desperately short of credible allies on the continent, few in London or Washington wanted to look too closely at Museveni's failings in the north. It was only later that things began to change.

Revelations that his army had plundered neighboring Congo during a war in which millions of people died did little to enhance Museveni's international standing, although his growing authoritarianism at home probably had an even greater impact on his image. Intimidation and violence tarnished his victory at elections in 2001, held under his "no party" Movement system in which candidates in theory campaigned on individual merit. When parliament voted to change the constitution to lift a two-term limit so he could run again in 2006, many Ugandans wondered whether Museveni was turning into the kind of classic African "Big Man" dictator he had always pledged to fight. On top of all this, the crisis in the north was worsening.

Egeland had done his best to shine a spotlight on the conflict since his first visit in November 2003, when he dubbed it the world's biggest neglected humanitarian crisis. The phrase became a cliché that was recycled in virtually every Reuters story, but it had an impact. Suddenly, there was a humanitarian scramble for northern Uganda. Foreign workers set up projects, from teaching jam-making to landmine victims to providing quinine drips for malarial children. The problem was they were only treating the symptoms. Nobody was tackling the war's underlying causes.

"We keep people alive now increasingly well," Egeland said, "And I see courageous young girls from NGOs who stay overnight in places where peacekeepers would not necessarily want to stay, but it's very clear that it's not this work that will put an end to the conflict."

Aid workers faced another, more serious dilemma, one I only began to appreciate after I'd spent a few weeks in Gulu. By agreeing to feed the people in the camps, the United Nations had become a vital component of the government's strategy. The problem was that the camps had shown no signs of stopping the war. On the contrary, studies showed hundreds of people were dying each week from preventable illnesses that thrived in the crowded, unsanitary conditions. More people were burning up with fever or watching their life bleed out through their bowels than were being killed by the rebels. At one point, the number of IDPs—jargon for "internally displaced persons"—in northern Uganda reached around two million. Only a few countries, such as Sudan and Colombia, had more. The camps were the crisis.

I thought back to my days sitting in the Reuters office in Nairobi, obediently typing up appeals from the United Nations World Food Program (WFP) for more funds to feed the inmates. It had always struck me as an unambiguously good cause, and certainly worth spending a few minutes on to turn into a brief story. (What is more, WFP's Nairobi office had a very attractive spokeswoman.) I had always assumed people had fled to the camps purely by choice, and hadn't realized the picture was more complex. While it was true that in many cases farmers had spontaneously rushed to towns for protection, I had never realized that the government had adopted a policy of systematically forcing hundreds of thousands of people from their homes. The army had broadcast radio ultimatums telling families they would be considered rebels if they refused to leave. In some cases soldiers shelled recalcitrant villagers who preferred to take their chances with Kony's men rather than endure the slum conditions in the camps. The UN appeared to have been sucked into underwriting a system that had caused terrible suffering.

It had been a hard trap to avoid. The World Food Program had started feeding people shortly after the government began creating the camps in late 1996—according the to government a temporary measure while they crushed the "bandits." At the time, the policy may have seemed like a viable short-term measure. Ten years later, food trucks were still rumbling out of the WFP depot in Gulu. The strategy did little to end the war, but it did create giant incubators of disease, alienation, and despair. The problem was that once the UN had started to feed people, it was impossible to walk away and let them starve. A Norwegian aid worker summed up the dilemma over a beer in Gulu:

"The people are prisoners, the soldiers are the jailers, and we're feeding the prisoners."

"So why feed the prisoners?" I asked.

An American relief worker answered, "Because we're worried about what would happen if we didn't."

Many people thought aid agencies should have sent out stronger calls for action long before Egeland rang the alarm bells. A senior member of the UN's internal displacement division told me during a separate visit to Uganda that the UN and other organizations should have put much more pressure on the government to alleviate conditions in the camps, rather than simply agreeing to spend hundreds of millions of dollars feeding their residents indefinitely in the absence of a credible plan for ending the war.

"The key donors should have got their act together ten years ago, or five years ago, and said 'Look, we're not going to just do a prolonged humanitarian aid program, there has got to be a solution,'" he told me. "Solutions aren't easy when you've got this mad group across the border, and you don't have a very good army, but they should have had a strategy. Sure, you have to feed the people, but it's very easy to get locked into it."

Kony's reputation as the leader of a "mad group" had in many ways distorted perceptions of the conflict, distracting attention from conditions in the camps. The plight of children abducted by his fighters made better copy than the quiet suffering of a generation growing up in squalor. The young "night commuters" who traipsed into towns each night to avoid being abducted by rebels became poster children for the war, though they represented only a tiny proportion of the people affected by the conflict. I visited a center set up for them in Kitgum town. As night fell, about 200 children turned up and began to make an almighty racket with xylophones and drums dished out by War Child Holland. I wanted to record them, but one young boy asked for money.

Concentrating on children also tended to perpetuate the idea that Kony was leading an army of infants. Although it was often reported that at least 80 percent of the Lord's Resistance Army combatants were children, researchers pointed to data that suggested the assertion was closer to myth than reality. An independent study called "A Hard Homecoming," on the plight of returnees, showed that of almost 29,000 people registered as abducted between 1990 and 2001—some for only a day—less than a third were below the age of eighteen at the time they were taken. Though large numbers of children undoubtedly did serve in the rebel front line, it was difficult to prove that they were in the majority. Ugandan soldiers mostly found themselves fighting adults.

Given Kony's image as the arch villain of the piece, a kind of Pied Piper with an army of children at his heels, it was logical for the International Criminal Court to focus its investigations on him and his commanders. But forcing civilians from their homes without adequate provision can in certain circumstances also be considered a crime against humanity. As far back as 1999, Amnesty International had written a report arguing that the Ugandan government had in this respect failed in its obligations under international law. But for years the architects of the policy of creating camps had come under remarkably little scrutiny.

Some argued that donor countries like Britain and the United States—who provided much of WFP's funding—had in effect become partners in the plan by allowing their strategic aim of supporting Museveni to eclipse the suffering caused by his counter-insurgency policy. Foreign governments, the UN, and relief organizations all became part of the system. "In many instances, these can be regarded as complicit bystanders," wrote Chris Dolan, a British academic who had spent years conducting fieldwork in northern Uganda. "Like doctors in a torture situation, they appear to be there to ease the suffering of victims, but in reality they enable the process to be prolonged by keeping the victim alive for further abuses."

It would have been an interesting question to explore when I was filing for Reuters, only it never occurred to me at the time. I was too caught up in the idea of evil rebels kidnapping children and infallible outsiders doing their best to help. As our armored car cruised toward Pader town, I asked Egeland whether he thought aid agencies should have considered their approach more carefully.

"It's only an ethical dilemma for, like, ten seconds, and then you will understand—we have no other job than to save lives," he said. "The World Food Program was very much alone in actually caring for and averting a much greater loss of life. We could have seen mass death on a much larger scale, but I feel very strongly in places like this that we, as a humanitarian community, should not be the alibi for lack of security and political action."

The kind of action Egeland had in mind involved a whole range of schemes, most of which hinged on persuading donors, including the United States, Britain, and other European Union countries, to bring the conflict higher up their list of priorities. He wanted the United Nations to encourage Congo and Sudan to cooperate with Uganda to tackle the Lord's Resistance Army, and appoint a special envoy to galvanize increased international engagement.

Twenty years after the conflict started, there were signs that Museveni's powerful allies were beginning to take more of an interest. Egeland briefed the Security Council in New York on the humanitarian situation in the north in April 2004. When many of Kony's fighters crossed into Congo the following year, the rebel leader began to look less like an irritant for Uganda's northern fringe, and more like a threat to regional stability. In January 2006, the Security Council finally passed a resolution expressing "deep concern" about the "brutal insurgency." A few months later, the top US diplomat for Africa, Assistant Secretary of State for African Affairs Jendayi Frazer, said it would be a priority for President George W. Bush's administration to "get rid" of the Lord's Resistance Army by the end of the year. Such sentiments were perhaps cold comfort for people languishing in camps, or whiling away their lives serving Kony, but the conflict was no longer quite so easy to ignore.

Our convoy parked in a compound on the edge of Pader town. Huge tents housed sacks of UN food aid, while air-conditioned offices sheltered the administrators and their computers. Staff served pastries and juice to the journalists, while Egeland went to meet several dozen aid workers. He began by acknowledging how many more relief organizations had appeared in the north since his first visit, which rather invited the question of where they had been for the past decade. I would have liked to listen, but it was a private session and an irritated press officer bustled me out. It didn't help that I had taken his seat.

Egeland was due in Sudan next, first in Juba in the south, then the Darfur region in the west, where massacres committed by government-sponsored militias had generated more headlines in the past few years than northern Uganda had ever managed. Then it would be another country, and another crisis.

Heading into Pader town later that day, I ran into two of the "young girls" Egeland had perhaps had in mind when he mentioned aid workers who ventured into places where peacekeepers would fear to tread. One of the women was British, the other Dutch, and both worked with an organization called Medair with a strong Christian ethic which provided boreholes and mobile clinics to serve the camps.

The British woman opened her laptop and showed me a picture taken by one of her colleagues of some kind of creature. A crowd of villagers peered down at the remains of something with the body of a hippo, giant paws, and a pig's head. Its fingers looked disturbingly human. By the time the next shot was taken the locals had chopped the carcass into dripping red chunks. It must have fed them for weeks.

"They call it a *muok*," she said, sharing my bemusement.

There was nothing like it in any animal encyclopedia I had seen. Lloyd made no mention of the like in his book, though I was willing to bet that Samuel Baker had bagged one with his elephant gun. For a second I was tempted to abandon the search for Kony and devote myself to catching a *muok* instead.

But there was a more serious decision to make. I could try to hitch a lift with Egeland to Juba, where I would be able to follow up on rumors that the rebels would join peace talks. In the end, though, I decided to return to Patongo camp for a few more days before starting my journey to Sudan. Now that the humanitarian circus had been and gone, I was keen to test my theory about the soil that had nourished Kony. If I was right, then his fighters had much closer links to their community than I had imagined. Patongo seemed like the ideal place to ask a few questions.

When the Medair women dropped me off the next day, the only accommodation I could find was a half-built hotel at the end of a row of drinking dens. Naked concrete pillars sprouted from the second story where construction had ground to a halt; a sign saying "KURNGET BAR LODGE" hung at a crooked angle. A surly-looking man with heavy-lidded eyes, who wore a purple polo shirt with the logo "ID please, it's the law," led me down an alleyway to my cell-like room. Surrounded by bare walls, I felt a pang of nostalgia for the much cheerier Franklin. Apart from a lone soldier and a young man with dreadlocks wearing a red tabard who hung around at the bar, I was the only guest.

The owner lounged in a tracksuit at one of the plastic tables in front of his hotel, which overlooked the road Egeland's convoy had taken the day before. An Acholi major in the army, he had watched the visitors swoosh past with a cynical eye.

"You know, when these white people come with ten vehicles, people are asking why don't they stop the war? Are they just enjoying watching Africans suffer?" He spoke without looking at me, answering his own question. "They don't stop the war because if there's no war, there's no jobs."

The aid industry was an obvious cause for resentment—it was one of the few businesses thriving north of the Nile. Growing fleets of white four-by-fours were conspicuous emblems of the wealth and power controlled by outsiders. I often encountered a kind of schizophrenia among the Acholi, who would call for more help on the one hand, while bemoaning their loss of dignity on the other. It was hard to shake the feeling that the agencies sometimes, perhaps inadvertently, reinforced the sense of dependency. T-shirts given out by UNICEF bore the slogan "Love your Children"—as if parental neglect were the problem rather than the pressures of life in the camps. I saw another man wearing a T-shirt with a World Vision logo and the slogan: "With your support I can lead a better life"—the emphasis again on raising money to save poor Africans from themselves. But for all the aid, the war went on.

"People wonder why whites are here, walking around, when they just do nothing?" the major said. "Is it because they enjoy coming here to Africa, or what? Are they making money from this war?"

I found myself nodding along to the tirade, until he asked me for a donation to go toward finishing his hotel. Changing the subject, I asked him about the name on the sign—Kurnget. His explanation turned out to be more complex than I had anticipated. I never completely grasped it, but the word meant something between a philosophical concept of the imminence of death, and the hoe used for digging graves.

Leaving the major to his musings, I wandered down the track past the makeshift bars. Men and women huddled around plastic barrels of cappuccino-colored beer. Some grinned and raised their mugs in a silent toast, others stretched out their palms for coins. More sober women bustled through the shade of the market, selling secondhand dresses from coat hangers, or waving away the flies that crawled through the mouths of dried fish. Raised voices emanated from a tin shack.

"Don't screw up! Going against me is like going against God!"

"We respect our God. We don't respect you!"

I peered into the video hall, where a crowd of teenagers and a couple of soldiers sat on benches watching a badly dubbed kung fu movie. Frayed video sleeves pinned up by the entrance advertised the next feature—*Missing in Action* with Chuck Norris, one of Moses's favorites. Wandering back down the road by the Kurnget, I passed a deserted pool hall, then caught sight of a red-and-white flag hanging from a pole. There was no wind, but I could just make out the logo in the folds: *Médecins Sans Frontières*—"Doctors without borders." I sensed a chance to dig a little deeper.

I had run into medical staff working for *Médecins Sans Frontières* all over Africa when I was reporting for Reuters, invariably relying on them to explain their take on whatever crisis they happened to be tackling. Working with local doctors and nurses, they often developed a pretty good grasp of what was going on beneath the surface. Stepping through the gate into their compound, I sensed I was in luck.

An American doctor named Cameron invited me into a seating area and told me to help myself to an instant coffee. He had arrived in Patongo a few months before to run a small hospital on behalf of the organization's French section. Diarrhea, malaria, and tuberculosis thriving in the cramped conditions were among the main killers, as well as the odd bullet wound. In fact, he had dealt with one a few weeks earlier—a teenage boy hit in the stomach.

"I didn't know at the time that it was an LRA soldier," he said. "He had an abdominal gunshot wound and his guts were spilling out."

Nurses had laid him on the floor of the hospital tent, sluiced the gash with saline solution, repackaged his intestines, and wound a crepe bandage around his stomach. Pumping him with painkillers, they loaded him into car to take him to a bigger hospital run by Italian missionaries a few hours down the track.

The boy's mother rode with him. The rebels had taken him five years earlier when he was coming home from school. She was not going to let him go again. Writhing in pain, he was strong enough to claw a tube from his nose.

"He was really a tough kid," Cameron said. "But the odds are he probably did die, he was already very, very close when he left here."

I too wondered whether he had survived. Seized from his mother by Kony's men as a schoolboy, he had returned to her arms as a fighter. It seemed too much to ask for a happy ending. But although it made me curious, the boy's story also seemed to point to something about the relationship between Kony and his people. For all the cruelties inflicted by the rebels, Cameron said the locals had thanked his staff for treating one.

"They said: 'We are grateful, these are our children.'"

Finding the wounded boy's mother among the camp's 33,000 residents did not sound like the easiest of tasks. Fortunately, a team of health visitors recruited by *Médecins Sans Frontières* would be doing their rounds the following morning, led by a formidable Acholi woman called Margaret. If anyone could find the mother, it would be her. I went back to the Kurnget where the dreadlocked boy was sitting in the bar, still the only customer.

Striding into the maze of huts on her latest sortie in her war on disease and dirt, especially dirt, Margaret left her younger colleagues straggling. Within moments she had noticed a toddler wandering around covered in mud, which prompted a gentle dressing-down for the mother and some hygiene tips.

No violation was too insignificant to escape her attention, whether it be discarded mango stones acting as a magnet for flies, or basins filled with rainwater that bred mosquitoes. She waved at one woman to discourage her from poking a stick into her child's ear to scrape out the wax, then told another to place the soap on a plastic bag as she washed her child, to avoid picking up specks of grime.

I asked what sustained her neverending battle, but she just shrugged. Unlike most of Patongo's inhabitants she had been educated by no-nonsense Italian nuns who ran a school for leprosy patients. The drugs had cured her while she was still a teenager, and she wanted to pass on the medical knowledge she had gained since then to her people.

"Most of them don't know the basics of health care, that 'This is bad' and 'This is good,'" she said. "We are the ones to make them understand."

There was only one snag. The doctors and nurses offering free care at the clinic where Cameron worked did not enjoy a monopoly on treatment. Many patients had more faith in the longer-standing pedigree of existing healers. One appeared to have done the rounds shortly before us. Margaret pointed out the signs—little pouches of herbs tied around babies' necks. We rounded a hut to meet a young girl whose arms were covered in tiny nicks made by a razor blade—a recipient of Acholi acupuncture. Then Margaret asked the question I had wanted to hear: "Would you like to visit the witchdoctor?"

The hut looked like any other, but Margaret pointed out the telltale sprig of fresh herbs tucked into the thatch above the doorway. We stooped to enter. As my eyes adjusted, I had the distinct impression we were interrupting something.

A woman knelt on a mat, clutching a wand covered in blue beads and wearing a headband encrusted with shells. Three sick children were sprawled on the ground in front of her, their mothers waiting in silence for the healer to begin her work. She nodded as we entered, but there was a flash of annoyance behind her smile.

Shutting her eyes, the medium began rattling a calabash—the spirit did not take long to hear the call. Sucking in her cheeks, she whirled her finger around her temple, moving her lips in muttered discussion with something we could not see. Casting a handful of coins, she peered intently at the pattern as if reading runes. The women were transfixed, leaning forward as she gave her instructions, though Margaret could not hide her smirk.

"She is telling the mothers they have to winnow rice over their sick child," she whispered. "That will drive away the spirit."

We had entered the house of an *ajwaka*, much like the kind described by Okot p'Bitek in his accounts of Acholi beliefs.

When the prescriptions had been dispensed, it was my turn to ask a question. There was only one thing I wanted to know, but I felt too embarrassed to raise it. I decided to go for something more neutral.

"When will I get married?"

Turning her back to us, the diviner crouched in the corner as if deep in prayer. A few seconds later, we heard a subterranean voice.

"You are already married."

Perhaps the spirit had thought it was a trick question, but it was wrong in any case. I handed over a few notes, suddenly regretting that I had not asked what I most wanted to know: whether I would meet Kony. As we left, Margaret could hardly hide her frustration, blaming the mothers as much as the healer.

"We tell them to go to the clinic because this magic cannot help them, they might even lose the child," she said. "The money they are spending to pay the witchdoctor is supposed to buy food to give a balanced diet to a child, rather than just wasting it for nothing. That woman is just sitting there, cheating the community. Some people understand, but many don't."

Walking back between the huts, I remembered the way the mothers had looked at the *ajwaka*, desperate for her to make their sick children well. Women like this had been offering solace for centuries; it was no wonder they were more popular than the doctors who had turned up only a few months earlier. Even Moses, who was far more educated than most people in Patongo, had spoken of Kony's "invisible magic." Watching the woman at work, I felt I had seen something of his power.

As Margaret led me back toward the clinic, a man emerged from a hut playing a finger piano, a block of wood with metal keys. Drifting through the warren of mud and smoke, the sound was as haunting as a harp. The musician followed us for a moment, absorbed in his tune, then disappeared back into the sprawl. Margaret left me at the hotel, saying she was sure we would find the boy's mother the next day.

When it got dark, the only electric light in the street spilled from a bar a few doors down from the Kurnget, packed with camp dwellers and soldiers who could afford the bottles of Bell and Nile Special sold through a cage protecting the counter. Music blared from a television mounted on the wall showing pop videos made in Kampala.

A soldier threw his arms around my neck. It took me a second to recognize him as one of my fellow guests at the hotel. His name was Josphat and he wore an army T-shirt with the slogan "*Hakuna Lala*"—Kiswahili for "We don't sleep." Slurring his words only slightly, he persuaded me to buy him a bottle of V&A Imperial Cream, the priciest drink in the bar. I wondered which of his comrades had shot the boy.

Disentangling myself, I found a seat next to some older men who were watching the screen. Images of Ugandan girls splashing in a pool flickered before their eyes, the camera lingering over the honey-colored midriff of a young woman dancing in one of the capital's nightclubs.

"I like that face," said one of the drinkers, mesmerized by the show.

His features were long and worn. I guessed he was in his forties, but he seemed older. At first he rehearsed jokes based on the names of drinks—Fanta became "Foolish Africans Never

Take Alcohol," and Bell, "Better Education, Less Labor"—but he became serious when I said I was writing about the war. I asked him if he had met Kony. He put a finger to his lips and promised to come and find me at the Kurnget.

The following morning Margaret found the boy's mother sitting on the ground outside her hut flanked by two teenage daughters. She mustered a gap-toothed smile. With a tenderness I could never have managed, Margaret coaxed out the story of her youngest son. Even his name, Otoo, was laden with sadness—it meant he was born after her two previous children had died at birth.

Otoo had been something of an artist. The teacher had even called her in to see his drawings of cows, dogs, and motorcycles scribbled in biro in his exercise book. Kony's men grabbed him as he walked home from school in his blue shorts and pink shirt. He was twelve. When he returned five years later, he was wearing the uniform of a rebel.

His mother was waiting for him. Another boy had escaped from the rebels a few months before and told her he had seen Otoo in the bush. After years without news, the hope that he was still alive was almost worse. Lying awake one night, she heard shooting on the edge of the camp. She had no idea what had happened until the next morning when a neighbor summoned her to the clinic.

"I'm dying," her son cried, "I'm dying without seeing my dad." Otoo tried to lift himself, begging her to summon his father. The nurses advised her not to tell him the truth. While Otoo had been fighting, his father had sickened and died. His mother joined her son for the journey to a bigger hospital in Kalongo. Squirming and thrashing, he looked strong until the last.

Later she hired a wheelbarrow to take his body to a relative's house, covering him with a sack. Mother spent the night lying alongside dead son, as was the custom. A small party of mourners went into the wilderness and dug a shallow hole, then lowered Otoo's body. They did not use earth to fill the grave, only covering him with rocks and branches to ensure his spirit could rise up and avenge his killer. His mother returned to the clinic in Patongo, where the nurses gave her all they could—two bars of soap.

When she had finished her story, Margaret whispered a few words to her in Acholi.

"I'm telling her not to think of anything," she said as we got up to leave. "This is how life is."

We visited another hut where there was a girl who had recently escaped from the rebels. She looked about twelve. Whispering answers to Margaret's gentle questions, she barely raised her eyes as she explained how she had been forced to carry a baby belonging to one of the commanders' wives on her back. When an army helicopter attacked their group, she put the newborn down in the grass and ran. Now she lived with her aunt, who peered out of the hut with glazed eyes, her breath heavy with drink.

"If I think deeply, I will become sick," said Margaret, as we walked away. "I just say that everything is in the hands of God."

It was only then that I learned she had watched Kony's men abduct two of her own sons. The rebels had ambushed a pickup they were riding, executing two women passengers and a man before dragging away her boys and three other "recruits." Her sons had come back alive, but the experience marked them.

"I may feel sorry, but what can I do?" she said. "I will not manage to do something for the others. If they see me crying, what will these children think? I just say that this is life. You are given a brain to think, and it is written in the Bible that you should work. You have hands to help you."

There was one part of Otoo's story that I learned only later. He had been among a small group of rebels coming to collect food that somebody had left for them in an abandoned hut. Watching the war from Nairobi, it had seemed inconceivable that anybody would donate even a grain of rice to Kony, but the more time I spent in places like Patongo, the more I heard stories of people willingly helping his men.

Some did it for cash. Known as "collaborators," they would buy everything from Wellington boots and batteries to tubs of Blue Band margarine and credit for mobile phones on the rebels' behalf. Some would even develop their films, often bearing images you would hesitate to take to your average chemist. Charging big markups, the collaborators made good money. People would point out houses they built for themselves in the camps, referring to Kony's spies as CID—"Criminal Investigation Department." Others donated food simply because they wanted to help abducted relatives survive life in the bush. As Cameron had said, people were grateful his staff had treated Otoo, telling him the rebels were "our children."

But there was yet another part to the story that also only emerged later. When the boy was found curled up in the hut the morning after he had been shot, clutching a shirt to his ripped intestines, a crowd began to pick up rocks. They would have stoned him, but for the intervention of an army officer.

Always there seemed to be a tension in people's feelings toward the Lord's Resistance Army. Over the years, Father Carlos had witnessed locals welcoming surrendering rebels with crates of soda, speeches, and prayers, waving branches of the *olwedo* tree—

a sign of blessing. "A lot of people see them as perpetrators," he had told me. "But on the other hand, they see them as victims. They want to let their children come back home, let them surrender rather than be killed." Yet I had also heard reports of captured rebels being lynched by their neighbors, their bodies torched.

The clash in attitudes toward the rebels seemed to be part of an ambiguity that ran through every aspect of the war. It was a conflict in which the people who chopped off people's noses were also victims, having been abducted and forced to kill in Kony's name. It was a conflict in which people would give food to the very rebels who could wipe out their whole village, hoping it would help their lost sons and daughters survive. And it was a conflict in which people felt betrayed by both the rebels who terrorized them and a government who left them to rot in camps.

An old Italian missionary told me once how he had seen a woman looking up at a mural on a church wall of Mary and Joseph fleeing Bethlehem to save Jesus from the slaughter of infant sons. She turned to the priest and said: "We are caught between two Herods—Museveni and Kony."

Attitudes toward Kony were also divided. While people were appalled by the massacres and abductions he ordered, there were those who would admit to sympathizing with his number-one aim—the overthrow of Museveni. Scratch a little under the surface, and you would find people in Patongo who agreed with Kony's ambitions, if not his methods.

The man I had met watching videos at the bar turned up at my room at the Kurnget the next night. He swigged bottle after bottle of Bell as the sun went down, until my room was almost dark. I was relieved I could not see his face. At least he would be spared the indignity of showing his tears.

"A soldier can sleep with my daughter in exchange for a bowl of beans like this," he said, gesturing to the small plastic basket he'd used to carry his beer. "How can we spend another year in the camp?" Shaking his head, he said, "Sorry, sorry."

As he spoke, I realized that he was suffering from more than just frustration at life in the camp—he felt impotent. He was supporting more than ten boys and girls himself, caring like so many others for the children of dead brothers, yet he was unable to provide the kind of food, education, or even hope expected of a father. With their men powerless and penniless, it was perhaps no wonder some of the women turned to soldiers to support them. To him, the camps looked more like a means of punishment than protection.

"Is it because of revenge? For what my father did? But that is not me!"

By now he did not need to spell it out. It was the unspoken conviction I had encountered everywhere I went in the north—the idea that Museveni was persecuting the Acholi in revenge for the atrocities their soldiers had committed during the civil war. I had seen images of the "skulls of Luwero" lined up in rows, like monuments to massacres in Rwanda or Cambodia. One even figured in Museveni's campaign video—a way of saying "I will protect you from this if you vote for me again." My friend spoke in metaphors, but it was obvious that, deep down, he wanted to resist.

"What happens when you have a bicycle tire—you keep patching and patching it, until one day . . ." he trailed off.

"It bursts?"

"Aha!" he nodded. "If the people were treated well, if they could have businesses, if they could go to school, why would they help the rebels? We have no guns or money—that is our problem in Acholi."

He thought for a second, then quoted the tagline from *Missing in Action*.

"'The war's not over till the last man comes home," he said. "I don't want to be buried. I want to rot in the fields."

I thought of Otoo, his body lying under the branches. This man seemed to want to die the same way—fighting. Footsteps broke the silence between us. The barman with the "ID please" shirt wandered down the alley outside my room.

"That one was a very big rebel," my friend said, "a very senior commander."

By now, I was not even surprised.

After a few nights in the Kurnget, I couldn't bear the idea of spending another evening in my cell with only a candle for company. Josphat and some other soldiers had taken women into the adjacent room, and the sounds carried through the walls. I was beginning to see a new meaning to the slogan "We don't sleep" on his T-shirt. Escape routes were limited. The thought of more videos in the bar was too much. Then I remembered the pool hall I had discovered when I first arrived in the camp.

Deserted during the day, the room came alive at night. Young men turned up in ones and twos, lining up around the walls until the place was packed. Some smoked, others sucked clear liquid from sachets, probably Empire Vodka, but most lacked the money needed to buy a soda, let alone play a game. If I had wanted to start a rebellion, this would have been the place to find recruits. Flying ants spun round the bulb hanging above the table. A man reached out and pinched one.

"You want this?" he smiled. "We eat them."

Players put coins on the table's edge, the winner staying on after each game. Spectators slapped their hands on the side to applaud a notable shot, but generally appreciated the clack of balls spinning over the baize in silence. There must have been about 50 young men watching when my turn came, and I felt the pressure.

For a start I managed to brush the talc sprinkled on a small table for the players' use onto my wrong hand, the one that grips the cue. I sensed my faux pas did not go unnoticed by my opponent, an enormous guy in a string vest. Despair swallowed my already meagre store of confidence as he blasted in his reds with unblinking precision. Spectators whispered encouragement—"Play wide! Don't worry!" and, more obscurely, "Go east! Go east!"—which only made me more nervous. I managed to sink only a single yellow before my rival cleared the reds and smashed the black home. I slunk back to the Kurnget, hoping the soldiers would keep the noise down.

I was anxious to head to Sudan, but before leaving Patongo I managed to strike up a conversation with the young man I had seen in the Kurnget bar. He seemed to wear the same crimson tabard and matching tracksuit trousers every day, but it was the dreadlocks that really marked him out. Considering the only person famous for his tangled mop in these parts was Kony, it took some chutzpah to copy his hairstyle.

He explained he was a singer called Rasta Lawstone Key—stage name "Wrong Government"—who had come to Patongo a few weeks earlier to run the sound system for one of the election candidates. He shrugged when I asked him how he managed to get away with dreadlocks, the unofficial emblem of the Lord's Resistance Army.

"I dress like a musician," he said. "You have to be smart full-time. I'm a true Rasta. I've seen a lot of bad things in the north here, so I don't fear anything."

Rasta was one of a crop of young northern musicians who blended traditional rhythms from finger pianos, Acholi harps, and rattling calabashes with the American rap and R&B they heard on the radio, adopting names like "Black Fish," "Doctor Jelly D" and "Fire Man." Although they idolized American gangsta rap stars, the northerners tended to choose more wholesome topics than guns, sex, and drugs, often crafting musical appeals for the rebels to return home. I had heard a few of them drifting from the speakers in the trees at the Acholi Inn. Rasta's repertoire of more than 400 songs included his hit "Women of the Market," praising mothers who sat all day at their stalls to feed their families, and a duet entitled "Woman, Open Your Eyes."

Rasta explained the lyrics: "I tell my wife 'Let's come and join hands, we'll build our home; if we don't, nobody will build it for us.' The woman is saying 'You used to get drunk, and love many women.' I try to cool her down."

Before I left, Rasta scribbled down a list of things he thought I might be able to obtain for his show, including speakers, bass bins, mid-ranger and tweeters, professional mixing equipment and a 2,000-watt amplifier, disco lights and smoke machines, "good material for stage uniform," a "very good generator," a video camera, four pairs of wireless microphones, and a piano.

The next morning, I heard Josphat arguing with his friend.

"I will kill her! I can even kill a person now!"

"You tell her that she will get a profit! Why can't you tell her?"

I heard a dropped coin spinning on the floor and the shuffling of feet. Rather reluctantly, I left my room to make my way to the brick enclosure with a resident bucket that served as a shower. I bumped into Josphat in the alley.

"Matthew, you are my best friend," he grinned. "I love you."

He broke into a drunken rendition of one of Uganda's latest pop songs.

Josphat was still lingering in the alleyway when I returned from washing. He pointed out a spot of shaving foam caught on my ear, and asked me to buy him another beer. I shook my head and went back into my room.

"What is wrong with this woman?" he said, his voice again muffled by the wall.

"Don't take us to be a fool!"

"Muthafucker!"

It was definitely time to go to Sudan. I found a place in the cab of a pickup heading back to Gulu through more deserted roads. Just outside Patongo, we passed a row of abandoned shops, the place where the rebels had cooked several people a couple of years back. I had heard the story a few times now. Rumor had it that a commander had been taking revenge on the family of an abducted boy who had run away with his gun while he was bathing in a river. It must have been the incident shown in the photo I had seen on my first visit to Gulu.

I spent a night on the way back at a place called Pajule, visiting the grave of Carlos's friend, Father Raffaele di Bari. Wearing a flat cap and neatly trimmed white beard, he stared out from an oval-framed photo set on a cairn behind the mission house. Hymns drifted from an evening choir practice in the church, mingling with the mournful cry of guinea fowl preening on the lawn. An inscription on the black marble gravestone said: "May he continue to pray for his people, whom he loved so much."

The next day I found another truck heading toward town. We passed a white cross that marked the spot where di Bari had been killed. Until recently, this had been the most dangerous road in

Uganda. I was glad to get back to Gulu, but I was more eager to hit the trail leading north.

I was about to find out that Kony was a lot closer than I thought.

5. A THUG WITH A CROSS

Father Carlos Rodríguez

Barcelona, the summer of 2002. Father Carlos was taking one of his rare holidays, visiting his sister and friends on the Spanish coast. He had spent the day at the beach, then eaten seafood. The evening had been a pleasant one, and he'd ended it nursing a whiskey in an Irish pub. But his vacation was about to be cut short.

It was after 2 a.m. when Carlos got the message, and he returned the call. An Italian priest explained that he planned to venture into the bush with another missionary in a few days' time to try to convince a group of rebels to come home. Carlos only went back to Spain once a year and he knew his parents would be disappointed, but he agreed to go with his friends. He had been following the news from the north on the internet, and it was far from good.

The Ugandan army had just launched an offensive they called "Operation Iron Fist," advertising it as Kony's nemesis. Generals had been vowing to crush the "dreadful dreadlocked one" for years, but they insisted this would be different. For the first time the Sudanese government in Khartoum had given the Ugandans permission to cross the border and overrun Kony's bases in southern Sudan. The theory was that the Lord's Resistance Army and its leader would have nowhere left to hide.

Sending thousands of troops across the frontier was like shoving a stick into a hornet's nest. Instead of scattering, the rebels launched a counteroffensive. Hundreds of Kony's fighters streamed back into Uganda to abduct, kill, and burn. The number of people huddled in camps soared after Iron Fist was launched in March 2002, eventually peaking at around two million. The closest the army came to capturing Kony was seizing one of his suits.

Carlos arrived back a few days after receiving the call. Within 24 hours of reaching Gulu he was with the rebels. The meeting went well. Despite the carnage, persuading Kony to return home suddenly began to seem possible. One of his commanders assured Acholi churchmen that the rebels wanted to negotiate. Museveni made a radio announcement saying he was also willing to give talks a chance. Carlos and Father Tarcisio, a 40-year veteran of northern Uganda, and the other Italian, Father Julio, obtained permission from the local authorities to visit another group of fighters in August. Carlos had no idea he was walking into a trap.

I remembered hearing about his misadventure while I was still with Reuters in Nairobi. I had been at the Congolese nightclub Deep West when an editor called from London. The Ugandan army had detained three priests—two Italian, one Spanish—on suspicion of collaborating with the rebels. Stumbling back into the Reuters office, I filed a few lines, quoting the army spokesman: "For all intents and purposes," he had said, "they do not look like they were on a peace mission." Four years later, Carlos told me what actually happened.

"I must tell you, our mood that day was as if we were going for a picnic," he said, telling the story at the Acholi Inn. "I mean, we had already been with the rebels a number of times. For us it was becoming a routine. We were very enthusiastic."

With the benefit of hindsight, he should have been more suspicious. They were carrying an official letter, but soldiers manning a roadblock bombarded them with hostile questions and confiscated syphilis drugs they had promised to take to the rebels. Shaken, the trio of priests, accompanied by a couple of Acholi catechists, continued toward the rendezvous.

When they finally located the rebels, Carlos tried to explain to them that Museveni wanted to negotiate. But the commander, a man named Lapaico, had no faith in the president. "If Museveni doesn't want peace, then everybody's going to die," Lapaico said. "Even small children are going to die. We're going to kill everybody." Carlos tried to reason with him, but was interrupted.

"I see this Lapaico just opening his eyes like this," Carlos said, giving a wild stare. "Then they disappeared in less than a second. They even left one of their walkie-talkies there. Then we started hearing gunshots—*tatatata*—close by."

Grenades exploded in clouds of dust, shots whined through the branches. Tiny fragments of shrapnel tore into his arm. It was only later that he realized how badly his skin had been burned. Soldiers appeared, one of them cocked his rifles and Carlos was sure he was about to be shot. "They said, 'Just look at the ground and don't move.' That's when I started thinking that this was not a mistake."

The three men spent the night locked in a metal hut at an army base with no food or water. When Carlos asked what the charge was, an officer said: "Talking to the wrong people at the wrong time." He managed to beg a small bottle of mineral water from one of the guards, but they had to relieve themselves in their prison.

The next day the priests were made to sign a paper admitting responsibility for the whole incident. Carlos was loath to comply, but he was worried about being expelled from Uganda on the false pretext of helping the rebels. That evening he drank the most delicious beer of his life, but the ordeal was only beginning.

"I started hearing rumors, nasty stories: 'Finally we have got him, Father Carlos is an anti-government collaborator.' I was already well known by many people in the government and intelligence services, and I was beginning to sense that they were looking for a way to kick me out of the country."

The *New Vision* ran a story claiming the priests had been taking an "amazingly huge" amount of drugs to the rebels. In fact they had been carrying one packet of syphilis medicine about the size of a matchbox. Coining a phrase that Carlos would never forget, one politician branded him a "thug with a cross" on national radio.

"He said that he had reliable information that I was a sergeant in the Spanish army, and that I had deserted my post," Carlos said. "He claimed that I'd taken a ship and come to Mombasa as a soldier of fortune, that I'd linked up with the LRA and started selling them weapons."

Another station made an equally absurd claim, saying he was a colonel from the Basque terrorist group ETA. "I think it's one of the principles of military propaganda," Carlos said. "If you tell a lie a thousand times, some people will believe it is true."

Fearing something worse might happen, friends told Carlos he should return to Spain, but he decided to carry on as normal. The following Sunday he prayed for the soldiers during the homily, telling them he had seen how stressful their work was. His arm was still in a sling from the burns.

The more Carlos told me about his life in the north, the more I wondered why he didn't just call it quits. I could understand his eagerness to try to persuade the rebels to return home, however dangerous and frustrating it was. After all, they were supposed to be the bad guys. But the job looked distinctly less appealing when powerful men in the military seemed bent on foiling his efforts to help end the war.

Stories of senior army officers making money from the conflict were so common in Gulu it was simply taken for granted. Sitting in the garden of the Acholi Inn, I had to look no further than its owner for a prime example: Colonel Otema did a roaring trade catering for the aid workers, mediators, investigators, and journalists drawn to a war he was supposed to be fighting. Some might have seen the competing demands of catering and combat as a conflict of interests, but it was positively commendable compared to the way many commanders made their fortunes.

Shortly before I arrived in Gulu, the International Court of Justice had ordered Uganda to pay reparations to the Democratic Republic of Congo for looting and human rights abuses committed after Museveni sent his army into the east of the country in 1998. Congo's government was demanding a cool six to ten billion dollars. The tribunal found Ugandan forces had committed a list of violations strikingly similar to the charges leveled by prosecutors at the International Criminal Court, an entirely separate institution, against Kony. These included razing villages, acts of killing and torture, and training child soldiers.

The fact that Museveni had sent so many troops to Congo to fight a separate group of Ugandan rebels while Kony was still at large entrenched the feeling of neglect among the Acholi, but it was easy to see why his generals were keen. United Nations investigators documented their massive plunder of Congolese resources, from gold and diamonds to timber and coltan—a mineral used in mobile phones. Acting like warlords in uniform, Museveni's men armed rival groups of ethnically based militias to protect their commercial interests, fueling more slaughter, rape, and robbery. Congo's multi-sided war became the deadliest conflict since World War II—four million people were estimated to have died, mainly from war-induced hunger and disease. Museveni's most loyal officers fanned the fires simply to make money. Given their behavior in Congo, it was no surprise to hear tales of soldiers importing truckloads of teak felled in Sudan during Operation Iron Fist while they were supposed to be hunting Kony.

When they were not pillaging neighboring countries, army commanders simply stole from their own troops. An internal inquiry into the scandal of the "ghost soldiers" in 2003 found that superiors were pocketing huge amounts of pay for dead or missing soldiers, or even entirely fictional battalions. "Financial implications of this ghosts saga are mindboggling," the report's authors wrote, estimating that officers might be stealing as much as two-thirds of the army's annual wage bill. The investigators warned that perhaps half of the military's official tally of 56,000 personnel might not exist.

One sergeant told the "ghost soldiers" inquiry that her comrades fighting a group of Kony's soldiers led by Vincent Otti lacked even Wellington boots. "Sometimes the rebels look better than us. They eat well because they operate among their people who give them food," she said. "For me, I think there is an enemy within. He does not want the war to end, for that is how he makes his money."

The fears of an "enemy within" committed to the continuation of the conflict went beyond cases of individuals lining their pockets. Many northerners believed Museveni created the camps to neutralize them as a source of potential political opposition, often citing a remark he was supposed to have made about the fate of "grasshoppers eating each other up in a bottle." Others said he used Kony to keep alive memories of the atrocities committed by Acholi soldiers in Luwero, a constant reminder of his role as protector for voters in the rest of the country. Some took this idea further still, accusing Museveni of deliberately prolonging the war to justify the high levels of spending on the army, the most important pillar of his power base.

Among the most eloquent supporters of the theory was Andrew Mwenda, the political editor of the *Daily Monitor* newspaper who had interrogated Otti on his talk show on KFM. I visited him one day in his office in the industrial zone in Kampala, finding him tapping out his latest column with his feet up on the desk. Swinging around in his chair, Mwenda seized my notebook and in big, extrovert handwriting wrote down figures that showed the defense budget swelling in the past few years. Then he jotted down the names of the various commanders, showing how Banyankole from Museveni's home area in the west of Uganda dominated the security forces. Westerners also held the most powerful cabinet posts.

"The war serves a vital purpose," Mwenda said. "It is a reward for officers who are given access to plunder. The brutalities cast Uganda as the victim of a demented cult and international sympathy brings aid. The war is financed by Sudan, which is Islamist—so to fight Islamic influences, the US gave its support to Uganda in the 1990s. The war places Museveni at heart of geopolitical interests. What does he lose? Kony is an inconvenience in a remote part of the country—not a threat to his power—and he kills a population who are not a core constituency."

A container train clanked past outside, giving a woeful honk.

"So the war, if you look at it, benefits Museveni right, left, and center. Why would he end it? Me, I am an economist. If you do a cost-benefit analysis of the war, the benefits far outweigh the threats. Kony could not take Kampala in a hundred years, but the only way you can keep the army in control, and oppress political rights, is by having a rebellion."

Popular as the argument was, I met a succession of people involved with the peace process who believed Museveni had given talks a genuine try on various occasions, pointing out that the rebels were far from easy negotiating partners. Museveni's degree of commitment to ending the conflict had clearly varied; his approach had been erratic and contradictory, often larded with threats, insults and hubris, but he had never entirely closed the door.

As Father Carlos put it: "If peace talks failed, 10 percent of the blame would go to the government, 90 percent to the LRA. There were times when the president was ready to give negotiations with the LRA a serious try, but the LRA never kept any ceasefire, they never presented any agenda for discussion. You can criticize Museveni, he was very impatient, but in the final analysis, you could always find a way out with him."

I was left with the impression that figures in the army itself were perhaps among the biggest obstacles to attempts to seek a peaceful solution. Carlos had the burns and shrapnel wounds to prove it.

"On one hand they were saying 'we're going to use the military solution,' on the other hand they were not taking the military solution seriously," he said. "What's the result? People were left unprotected.

"Something I've seen from the beginning is that in the army there are people who are in favor of peace talks and people who are completely against peace talks," he continued. "There may be different reasons why some people just want complete or absolute defeat of the enemy. For me it's a question of pride."

A few months after he'd been attacked in the clearing, Carlos ran into the soldier who had given him water when he was locked up with his two companions. It was sunset, and the man was glugging down a beer.

"He said, 'I have been in the front line for five years; I haven't seen my family in all this time. Every evening, at this time, I get scared to death. If I don't drink I can't sleep. This is an unbearable life.'

"You don't feel hatred for people like that," Carlos said, "you just feel pity. You also learn with experience that things you think are the end of everything can be the start of something new."

Kony's father died a few months after Carlos was wounded. I knew little about Luizi Obol, having heard only that he'd served in the King's African Rifles before raising cattle in Odek. A Requiem Mass was held at the Holy Rosary church in Gulu. The archbishop sent a letter of condolence to Kony via one of the rebel's contacts, saying a death in the family was traditionally a time for reconciliation in Acholiland. A letter came back saying the rebels were still willing to talk. Carlos prepared for another trip into the forest, this time to speak to Kony himself.

The violence had become so extreme he felt he had no choice. Not even the mission was safe. One evening in early 2003, Carlos was about to have supper. A deaf cook who worked at the house was explaining how he had prepared some lovely pork when Carlos heard gunshots. Oblivious to the sound, the cook took a moment to read the shock on the priest's face. The rebels began to hammer on the door, threatening to blast it down with a rocket-propelled grenade. Carlos could only look on helplessly as they dragged away a twelve-year-old altar boy named Joseph who had hidden under a bed. "Don't worry," the boy told Carlos, "let me go with them. God will help me." The raiders took the cook too, though they let him go the next day.

"You asked me why I stay," Carlos once told me. "It's not boring, that's one of the reasons."

His chance to speak to Kony came on 1 March that year, when he joined a delegation of elders for another trip into the bush. Teenage gunmen with expressionless faces led them to a makeshift camp. Carlos took in the details: emaciated women with downcast eyes; boy soldiers as young as ten or eleven; powerful weapons like mortars and recoilless rifles positioned in the trees. One of the rebel lieutenants arranged the chairs so the meeting could begin. He was tall, lean, and intelligent-looking, trusted enough to help raise the "Chairman" on the radio. Carlos asked if it was one of the sets they had looted from the mission last time they dropped by. The commander just smiled.

Finally, Kony's voice crackled over the airwaves.

"Who are these people," he asked. "What do they want? Have they been sent by the government?"

Carlos muttered a few more words to try and lighten the atmosphere, but the commanders gathered around the radio maintained a solemn silence, indicating Kony was consulting the spirits. Minutes passed, static hissing from the receiver.

"Are those people still there?" came Kony's voice.

"Yes, they are still here," said one of the officers.

"Tell them to come closer."

As they took turns to greet him, Kony started laughing.

"I'm very happy that you are there," he said. "You are welcome."

Kony's tone veered from flippant, to angry, then apparently happy again, but he seemed to listen carefully as the delegation pleaded with him to declare a ceasefire. To Carlos's delight, he agreed. Then Kony made a request.

"Father Carlos, are you there?" he said. "I would like you to pray five rosaries for peace."

"If it is for peace," Carlos replied, "I can pray ten."

As they prepared to leave, the young lieutenant who had helped arrange the chairs managed to catch Carlos's eye.

"My name is Moses," he murmured. "Take my name, you tell my mother that I'm here."

Carlos nodded, and the delegation began to head back to Gulu. He was anxious to broadcast the tape of Kony's truce declaration so both the army and the people could hear it. If the ceasefire held, there might be a chance for serious negotiations. Years of painstaking effort finally seemed to have paid off.

It was only later that Carlos heard Kony's fighters had beheaded four soldiers near their meeting place on the very day he had spoken to him on the radio. The rebels said they had in fact only executed one army officer who had been sent to spy on them, accusing the military of planning a surprise attack on their leadership under the cover of the next peace meeting. Kony's attacks against soldiers and civilians continued.

"I got some information from the army," Carlos said. "They told me that I should be very careful because Kony had given orders to kill me."

Escaped rebels confirmed it was true. Kony was angry that Carlos had been trying to persuade his rebels to come home. The army had killed many of his senior officers during Operation Iron Fist, and he didn't want to lose more.

"We were so downcast, so traumatized, so exhausted those days," said Carlos. "I remember that was the time I couldn't sleep for months and months. I was always worried, I was always afraid."

In May 2003, Carlos received a text message in the middle of the night from a friend on the edge of Gulu: "SEMINARY BEING ATTACKED," it said, "SEMINARIANS BEING TAKEN." He called the terrified man, who explained the rebels were still outside, having just abducted 43 trainee priests.

I wondered again what Carlos felt he had achieved. It was only later that I discovered that for Moses, his trip to the clearing to talk to Kony had made a very big difference indeed. It might even have saved his life.

6. "GOD IS A KILLER"

LRA fighters in a clearing near Nabanga

At first I was worried about asking Moses to show me the place where he had been abducted, but he seemed happy enough to return. We left the Franklin on a pair of motorbike taxis, finding his old school on a bluff on the edge of Gulu. He had not been back since the night the rebels came knocking a decade earlier.

Sir Samuel Baker himself guarded the gravel driveway. Thrusting out a bearded chin, the cement statue gazed across the plain as if he were still on the lookout for slave traders. I imagined he would have approved of the painted sign. There was an almost Victorian earnestness in its exhortation to students to work for "better understanding and friendship."

Moses led me across the football pitch, the scene of his landslide election win as health prefect. He had designed his campaign posters himself, inscribing the slogan "Peace, Unity and Good Health" in pencil around his picture, then running off 50 photocopies with some money from his father. I remembered the snap taken on his day of triumph, his face plastered with a huge grin as cheering friends slapped him on the back, a too-long tie dangling past his belt. The field was silent now, deserted apart from a woman walking past netless goalposts with three small children in tow and a basket on her head.

Mauve jacaranda blossoms and the crimson flowers of red-hot poker trees blazed in the boughs above iron-roofed classrooms, but the buildings looked as though they had seen better days. Cement steps were chipped, cream paint peeled from walls. Signs still showed the names of the dormitories—Stanley, Grant, Livingstone, Burton, and p'Bitek. Moses led me toward Speke.

A metal door blocked the entrance, corrugated iron covered the windows. I tried the handle, but it was locked.

Moses stood in the shade of a mango tree, hands on his hips. A few minutes passed before he spoke. He simply said, "I cannot forget."

Moses had told me what had happened that night during one of our talks at the Franklin. The story began before dusk. Moses had gone to a kiosk outside the school gates to buy tomatoes, planning to fry them alongside the beans served up by the cooks before settling down to study. He saw a procession of men, women, and children heading into town. Some carried bundles on their heads, others creaked along on bicycles. An old woman turned to him and muttered a warning.

"They have reached Akonyi Bedo," she said, then continued on her way.

Clutching his bag of tomatoes, Moses walked back across the playing field. Akonyi Bedo was not far from Sir Samuel Baker, not far at all. The woman's words worried him, but he wanted to study for his geography exam the next day. In any case, cycling home to his parents' house in Gulu was not an option. A girlfriend of his had become pregnant just a few months before. His parents had offered to look after the teenager before she gave birth, keeping the affair as quiet as possible. Moses was afraid that if he was seen with the girl his friends would start whispering. And he had heard rumors of rebels before.

Back at the classrooms, Moses's friend Geoffrey told him to cycle home. Moses lent him the bike instead, assuming he would see him the next morning. Poring over notes on forestry in British Columbia, flood control in the Tennessee Valley Authority, and the formation of the Ruwenzori Mountains, Moses pushed the woman's words out of his mind. But he slept in his clothes, just in case.

The images from that night were jumbled—flashlight beams dancing in the darkness; Wellington boots squeaking on the cement floor; a face floating by his pillow. But Moses could remember clambering down from his bunk, joining the other boys spreadeagled on the ground, his two half-brothers among them. The intruders dragged his trunk from under his bed, flung open the lid and rifled through his things, tearing his exercise books to shreds. Then the rebels ordered the boys to their feet and pushed them through the doorway.

Moses showed me the mango tree where they had made the boys squat, before roping them together—just like a train of slaves. One of the fighters had produced a knife, dug a small hole, and planted an anti-personnel mine in case anybody tried to follow. Moses pointed to the path they had taken, leading away from the school and into the bush, terminating many months later in Kony's kingdom.

We lingered for a few minutes then walked away, passing a row of eucalyptus trees that grew by the gates. Moses brightened a little, explaining that he had helped plant them when still a schoolboy. They were much taller than he remembered, leaves shimmering in the dying sun. We headed back to Gulu.

Turning up each afternoon at the Franklin Guest House, Moses would wander into my room and, bit by bit, tell the story of his career as a rebel. Ranging back and forth across years, and from place to place, I sometimes grasped little more than fragments. As the weeks passed, the pictures became clearer.

He recalled the *wuh wuh* sound of the branches as the rebels flayed him and the other boys on their first day in captivity. He described stripping the uniform from a dead soldier, the stream swirling red as he rinsed out the blood, putting it on wet. He reminisced about playing Snake on a mobile phone between ambushes, then told a rather tall story about Sudanese guerrillas tying a goat to the trigger of a machine gun so it could join in the fighting. Once he used the sewing skills he had picked up as a boy to stitch up a wound in his commander's scrotum. And he described the first time he saw Kony.

In the months following his abduction, Moses's column had wended its way across northern Uganda before finally reaching one of the Lord's Resistance Army bases in southern Sudan. The commanders summoned the recruits into a clearing. Moses glanced around at the circle of young men and women sitting on the grass. Hands clapping, faces shining, they lifted the sweetest chorus they could muster:

"Heaven, heaven, Jesus save us! We need a straight path to take us to heaven!"

They were about to meet the "Chairman."

A group of officers stepped into the glade and the singing faded. One of the commanders struck Moses as particularly imposing, a rangy figure who shunned military fatigues for a short-sleeved shirt. He began to speak.

"You, the stupid Acholi, you think that Kony is bad? Kony is not bad! Kony is fighting for the Ten Commandments, Kony is fighting to restore Acholi culture, Kony is fighting to overthrow the dictatorship of Museveni!"

Raising his hands in divine supplication, the man raked the audience with his stare.

"Kony is a messenger from God. We follow the commands of the Holy Spirit. Kony told you that you have to come and join hands to fight Museveni, but you didn't want to, so Kony had to abduct you. Because if Kony went to the village and asked the elders: 'We want twenty youths to be our soldiers,' they would not agree.

"So we are not abducting people, we are just taking members of our tribe so they can join us to fight the government. The stupid Acholi who are at home, they think education is good. But will that education take us anywhere? Our people are suffering while Museveni's tribe is enjoying life. But by next year, Kony is going to overthrow the government. Kony is going to be president."

The speaker paused—Moses stared.

"Now, are you thinking of going home? There is no point in going home, because Museveni has killed all your parents. All your parents have been killed now, and you still want to go back home? Why? If anyone tries to escape, I will know his plan and will kill him straightaway. We have to fight until we succeed."

On the way back to the camp, Moses asked one of the older rebels who the man was.

"That one?" The man smiled at his stupidity. "That one is Kony."

"The real Kony?" asked Moses.

"Yes, it was the real Kony."

Kony's priests purified Moses a few weeks later. Men in white robes paced up and down flicking the circle of bare-chested recruits with water. Moses felt the drops tingle on his skin. He stood still as one of the men smeared white clay from Awere Hill into crosses on his chest, palms, and forehead, before moving onto the next young man in the line.

Moses was clean now. Bullets could not touch him. All he had to do was follow the rules: respect water, no shouting when crossing rivers, and no eating of mutton, pork, or pigeon. Nobody was to touch an abducted girl before she was given to them as a wife by Kony. No smoking, no drinking. Obey, and you would be invincible; disobey and you would be killed. Moses wanted to live, so he would do as Kony commanded.

Kony commanded him to fight.

As a schoolboy, Moses had only been dimly aware of the war. He had seen trucks full of soldiers trundling through Gulu, heard the crump of distant artillery as chalk squeaked on the blackboard, but life had gone on as normal. He and his brothers would take girls to watch the football at Pece Stadium, maybe buy a few Cokes at the Diana Gardens disco. Moses seemed to have had quite a few girlfriends, including the one he got pregnant just before he was abducted, but it was a young lady called Peace whom he mentioned the most. Kony barely crossed his mind. Moses imagined the rebels lived lifestyles akin to the gorillas in the Impenetrable Forest national park he had heard about in western Uganda. As for Kony, he wondered if he was even human. Nothing could have prepared him for what he had found when he reached his dominions in Sudan. He had stepped through a looking-glass into a twisted version of the life he had left behind.

Kony adopted the role of teacher, holding endless sermons to instruct recruits in their new religion. Sitting in the shade, groups of abductees would scribble down his edicts in exercise books, as if they were back at school. Kony told them to concentrate on the Rosary, the Holy Spirit, and Holy Mary when they prayed, promising to perform miracles to defeat their enemies. Repeating the homilies years later, Moses bulged his eyes and chopped the air with his forefinger as if drilling home his old master's dictates. It was as if Kony himself had materialized in the Franklin.

"Go to the Bible, this verse: God killed the people of Sodom and Gomorrah, so God is a killer," said Moses, mimicking Kony's harsh voice. "God was a soldier; he gave orders to the angels to go and kill all these first-born children in Egypt, so God is also a killer!"

Moses pointed at me, furrowing his brows.

"If someone has done something bad to you, you have to kill them, as they have done something bad! Go and read in Matthew, chapter what and what, it is stated that if your right hand causes trouble, cut if off! If one of your legs causes trouble, cut the leg off! If one of your eyes causes trouble, remove it! It is there in the Bible! Cut the hand of people!

"You see," he continued, "we are not abducting young girls, we are following what is in the Bible. You compare to Abraham—Sarah was fifteen years old. It is also in the Bible that you have to be with as many wives as you can, because King Solomon, in the Bible, was having 74 women, and King David was having 47, so it is in the Bible. You have to have as many wives as you can hold."

Nodding along, the young recruits took the lessons to heart. They were the "New Acholi," the lucky ones. The rest of their tribe, those who refused to support Kony, were doomed to be killed by Museveni or the disease called AIDS. Kony was the redeemer who would topple the government and revive Acholi culture, recover their stolen cattle, and foil the government's plot to steal their land. Calls for greater democracy, an end to the policy of putting people in camps and the healing of Uganda's ethnic divisions may not have corresponded to Western ideas of a "political agenda," especially when imposing the Ten Command-ments was thrown into the mix, but they spoke to Kony's followers.

Older commanders would reinforce his tales, telling how mountains had split in two to allow the rebels to escape, how speaking trees had given directions when they were lost. I heard a rumor that Kony could turn himself into an old woman to give Museveni's soldiers the slip. I thought of tales p'Bitek recounted of branches reaching down to lift warriors to safety, of birds warbling to confuse their enemies. Feast days, not so different from the "day for taking food to the spirit" the poet described in old Acholi, reinforced the sense of a parallel world. Commanders slaughtered bulls to celebrate 7 April, Juma Oris day, commemorating the moment the Holy Spirit appeared to Kony.

Exploiting old Acholi beliefs, respected Catholic rituals and the Acholi's deep-rooted fear of Museveni, it was no wonder that for many people Kony's lectures began to make sense. Transported into a different dimension where rebel commanders replaced teachers, military training replaced lessons, and where disobedience was punished with death, even Moses began to hear his message.

"This is all what he preached, just to disorganize your brain," Moses said. "Kony has a kind of invisible magic. Somehow you believe."

The first task for the New Acholi was to learn to fight. Kony's officers taught abductees standard infantry drills, hand signals, ambushes, and shooting. Section commanders learned how to use range cards and gun stakes to direct arcs of fire, while recruits were taught to pick up their dead comrades' rifles, or at least pull out their firing pins so the army could not use them. Instructors showed them how to march backward in their Wellingtons to confuse their pursuers, to communicate using Motorola radios, and to conceal the solar panels used to power them. Older rebels taught how to start a fire by breaking open a bullet and pouring out the powder.

Moses learned the basics like everyone else, but his education guaranteed he would be marked out for promotion. Moses took on the role of battalion administrator, compiling charts of the "parade state," "nominal roll," and "particulars of soldiers," along with detailed records of the parents, ages, and birthplaces of abductees so escapees could be traced. He used British military abbreviations like AWOL for "Absent Without Official Leave" and KIA for "Killed In Action," hand-me-down terms from the days when imperial officers commanded the King's African Rifles. As meticulous with his new duties as he was with homework, Moses was eventually put in charge of keeping records for a whole brigade of several thousand troops. He even learned radio call signs for his commanders—Kony would go by "three-five."

Moses's artistic streak did not go to waste either. I showed him a digital photo I had obtained of an insignia from one of the rebels' shoulder flashes and he grinned in recognition, saying "I sewed that one."

It was the first time I had seen the Lord's Resistance Army coat of arms. Twin palm fronds embraced a blue heart shape with an open book in its center, the crested crane symbol of Uganda capping the emblem. I wondered if the palm leaves reflected Kony's dreams of entering a new Jerusalem, and the book the Ten Commandments. The national bird was even more intriguing, chiming with Kony's claims that they were fighting dictatorship not just for the Acholi, but the whole country. Moses had used a pedal-powered Singer sewing machine his father had bought him to make shirts and dresses to earn some pocket money when he was back home in Gulu. In the bush he had to improvise, employing a 200-shilling coin to get the curve of the palms exactly right. His stitching won him even more respect from the officers, who proudly displayed his badges. Gradually, he moved closer to the center of power.

Moses took my notebook and began marking triangles to represent huts arranged in concentric circles. Junior rebels lived on the outer rim, with more senior officers behind them, until the lines gave way to a blank space for Kony's compound in the middle, and the rectangular "yard" where he communed with the spirits. It seemed like an exact replica of the descriptions I had read of the Acholi villages of old, arranged in circles with the chief, or *rwot,* protected in their center. Like the leaders of the past, Kony was not only the director of war, but the intermediary with the realm of the ancestors. And he too had plenty of wives.

The Reverend Albert B. Lloyd had once come across a chief called Ogwok with 50 wives and 60 children, reducing them to fits of laughter by recording their voices on his phonograph one night. Kony's harem was even bigger. The district chairman of Gulu gave me the most up-to-date estimate in early 2007, putting the number of Kony's women at 88.

Our Reuters reports tended to call the women "sex slaves." In a sense this term was correct, but it obscured the strict rules governing the treatment of women and girls, who were given out to commanders as rewards. Anyone who approached a woman belonging to another rebel, or a girl who had yet to be assigned, could be flogged or shot. Kony once demoted all the officers of Sinia Brigade to the rank of private for having sex with women in the villages—they would have to be cleansed again.

The rebels often seized prepubescent girls, assuming they would be less likely to have AIDS, a disease Kony seemed understandably concerned about. The fighters called these girls *ting ting*, at first using them as servants. They were told to consider their commander as their "father" until they matured enough to be distributed as wives in their new "families." Moses was given his teenage bride just a couple of years after he'd been abducted. He missed Peace, the girl he'd left behind in Gulu, but he seemed to get on well enough with his new companion. She eventually became pregnant.

Kony's clan began to grow as more recruits were seized, and more children were born in captivity. At one point in the late 1990s, they counted more than 10,000 men, women, and children in their ranks. Some put the figure closer to 20,000—all armed, fed, and hosted by the government of Sudan. The majority were abductees.

Life in Kony's domain followed the rhythm of the seasons, just as it had back home. In the drier times from November to April, the rebels remained in their camps. When the Sudanese army delivered enough food, they could eat relatively well. When they did not, raiding parties went out to steal supplies from villages occupied by southern Sudanese, whom Moses referred to as "wild tribes." Or they dug up wild cassava, roots, and leaves to fight the hunger pangs. Some recruits were put to work cutting trees for charcoal to be sold in Juba. Moses himself supervised the deliveries, riding in the truck that took them to market.

In better times, Kony's abducted subjects performed the *larakaraka* courtship dances he had enjoyed as a boy. Kony would sometimes join in, perhaps thrumming a few notes on a finger piano, laughing alongside his commanders. Football matches helped pass the time—battalion vs. battalion, brigade vs. brigade. Like Acholi in centuries past, the soldiers would form hunting parties and wade into the savannah in search of antelopes, wild pigs, and the edible rats known as *anyeri*, using guns instead of spears.

Moses again grabbed my notebook and began to draw. A dog-like creature took shape on the page, quickly developing spines. He did not know the English word, but I could see it was a porcupine. Moses had shot one then carved off its hind leg and given it to his commander at the time, a man named Raska Lukwiya, later slapped on the International Criminal Court's wanted list. He had paid his tribute, just as the clansmen had done to their *rwodi*.

When the rains came, recruits were forced to labor in fields around the bases to grow millet, sorghum, peas, and beans. Slackers were given a beating. Even Kony took up a hoe, perhaps remembering his days tilling the soil as a boy.

Wet season was also killing season. The land of the Acholi turned from gold to green, the grass sprouting from the stubble of scorched fields providing perfect cover. Leaves unfurled on branches, sheltering the rebels from the army's helicopter gunships. Soldiers often laid ambushes around boreholes, but when the rains came, natural springs flowed freely, making it easier for Moses and his comrades to find water.

He was about to describe something of his life as a fighter before he noticed it was almost dark. Uttering the words that ended each of our conversations, Moses got up to leave:

"I have to go and see my mum."

It was when Moses talked about fighting that I found him hardest to understand. Plucked from his school, he had been forced into the front line in countless skirmishes in southern Sudan and northern Uganda, and bore the scars to prove it. Perhaps time had taken the edge off the terror he must have felt. Years later, there was never a trace of self-pity, but there was an occasional flash of defiance.

It was Moses's birthday and we were sitting on the veranda of the Franklin, drinking Fantas. I could hear a Liverpool vs. Manchester United match on the television in the bar. These days almost every Ugandan male I met was obsessed with the Premiership, invariably supporting Manchester United, Chelsea, or Arsenal. Many Ugandan soldiers supported Arsenal—the

"Gunners"—because they assumed they must have something to do with the military, though Kony's former spokesman Sam Kolo was a die-hard Chelsea man. Moses never seemed that interested in sports. As usual he was "empty," meaning broke. I mumbled something sympathetic, but he smiled, remembering his bush days.

"Me, I'm multi-purpose," he said. "I can survive any conditions."

I tended to agree. Some days earlier, Moses had lifted up his shirt and pointed out his scars like a grizzled trooper. There was a wound in his shoulder where a bullet had torn it, another in his side where a piece of shrapnel had ripped into his abdomen and stayed there. He bore wounds on his legs and one on his foot from the time he had fired a mortar on marshy ground—the blast had hammered the tube into the soil and the handle had speared his foot. A bullet had grazed his scalp, causing so much blood to pour out he was sure it was the end. "I thought I was a moving dead man," he said, "but I could feel the blood was hot. It was the only reason I thought I was still alive." It was a wonder we were celebrating his birthday at all.

Moses had brought a couple of girls along to share in the occasion. Christine was six years younger than Moses and laughed as if the world were an endless procession of hilarities. She giggled when the other girl, Lucy, rejected one of the soda bottles. The manufacturers were promoting a new design with a bulbous end and studded surface.

"It is like Lifeguard," said Lucy.

"Lifeguard!" said Christine, and slapped her knees.

"Lifeguard?" I said.

"Yes, Lifeguard," said Christine. "You know Lifeguard?"

Then I remembered it was a brand of condoms. As the waitress exchanged it, I tested out some of the Acholi Moses had been teaching me.

"Amito camo dek! Kec tye ka-neka!" I said—"I want to eat food, I am hungry!"

Christine scrunched up her eyes and threw back her head.

"You are stealing our language!" she said. "You are a thief!"

It would have been hard to guess, but both of these girls had once been *ting ting*, abducted and given to commanders, and bearing their children in the bush. I tried to ask Christine what had happened, and the laughter ceased.

"You want to know my story?" Christine said. "Why should I tell you?"

I would also have found it impossible to tell Moses had been a rebel. Even after everything he had told me, I still couldn't imagine him carrying a gun. He had a certain thoughtfulness, an earnestness and a sensitivity that simply didn't fit with my notion of a hardened guerrilla.

"Do you have groundnuts at your home? No groundnuts?" he asked one day. "What about soya beans? No? You're missing some nice food. When you go back, I'm going to make groundnut paste, and put it in a tin. Take it to your family for them to see what is in Uganda."

But the memories could surface at any time.

Some days after his birthday, we were once again sitting on the veranda at the Franklin, munching biscuits. One of the government's armored cars rumbled down the street. Known as *mambas*—Kiswahili for "crocodile"—and bristling with machine guns, they sometimes filled up at the Caltex garage just down the road. Moses shook his head as he remembered being chased by a trio of the vehicles:

"That day I was about to give up, there were three of them," he said, shaking his head again. "Then I went into the tall grass, I escaped!"

Talking to Moses at times like this felt like talking to any veteran about his war. Somewhere along the line, he had begun to feel more like a soldier than a schoolboy. I had read numerous reports of abductees being forced to beat would-be escapees to death, their commanders believing they would find subsequent killings easier once the first one was out the way. But from the way Moses spoke, I sensed there was another bond that held Kony's rebels together. The natural reflex of camaraderie under fire glued commanders like Moses to their comrades, making the organization more disciplined than I could have believed. As he put it one time: "There's no joking with rebels."

When I wrote about the war in the Nairobi newsroom, there was one word that always sprang to mind when describing the Lord's Resistance Army—"ragtag." It came almost unbidden, perhaps reflecting an underlying assumption that the rebels were essentially savages who killed for the sake of killing. The occasional photos of captured fighters in torn fatigues, toes poking out of Wellington boots, only reinforced this impression. But the more Moses talked about his life in the bush, the more it sounded as though he was describing a well-drilled fighting machine rather than a rabble. He would defend their military prowess to the hilt, tut-tutting at the government army's incompetence.

"A guerrilla is a guerrilla!" he would say, when recounting one particularly fiendish trick played on the soldiers. "They died and died! They couldn't touch us! They must have been very weak and stupid! We couldn't feel afraid of them!"

Divided into brigades—Stockree, Gilva, Sinia, Trinkle, and Control Altar—the rebels used the same kinds of ranks and formations as a regular army. This was perhaps not surprising, given that Kony had initially linked up with defeated Acholi officers who had served for years in the government forces under ex-president Obote. Kony adopted the highest rank as "general," while his deputy Otti was one step below as "lieutenant-general." Moses reached the much lowlier, though not insignificant position of lieutenant, rewarded for his hard work on the battalion records. It was also his responsibility to ensure proper hygiene in the ranks and to monitor the sick, almost as if he were resuming his duties as school health prefect.

While the rebels were best known for bludgeoning villagers to death, Moses described an armory of sophisticated weapons— from the Soviet-designed SPG-9 recoilless gun to the B-10 anti-tank rifle, assorted landmines and rocket-propelled grenades. There was of course no shortage of small arms, from the trusty AK-47s common throughout Africa to rarer Heckler & Kochs, right down to Browning 9mm handguns. Some said the rebels even had SAM-7 anti-aircraft missiles—a more sophisticated item than many African armies could field—all courtesy of Khartoum. I looked up the assorted arms at one of the internet cafés in Gulu. Moses examined the diagrams with interest, recognizing them all.

I was most struck by this sense of martial pride when he described an attack where the rebels accomplished the unusual feat of setting a tank on fire. As I listened to him recounting the details, it dawned on me that I had filed a story on this raid from Nairobi in August 2002. I had been writing about Moses's exploits long before I met him.

According to the Reuters version, the rebels had stormed into a camp called Achol-Pii for Sudanese refugees who had sought shelter in northern Uganda from their own civil war. The attackers killed more than sixty people and took six aid workers hostage, all of whom were free within a week. The 24,000 refugees living in the camp fled. I had even written a line, courtesy of the

Ugandan army spokesman, about rebels firing "indiscriminately into terrified crowds."

For Moses, it had been a victory.

He told the story in the Franklin, leaning back in his chair with his hands folded behind his head. Kony had given the order over the radio: all units were to destroy a tank. The commander of Moses's Stockree Brigade gathered his officers in a clearing for a briefing, telling them they would attack just before first light. Whooping and cheering, the rebels burst into a chorus of their war song *"weka moto, weka moto Achol-Pii"*—*"burn, burn Achol-Pii."* At the refugee camp, soldiers waited in their trenches.

Moses joined the rebels padding between the thatched huts in single file, clutching his AK-47 with six extra magazines in his pouches—about 200 rounds in all. He also carried four hand grenades and a Motorola walkie-talkie. "You have to go into battle fully loaded," he told me those few years later, and he grinned.

As the rebels brushed between the huts, they found Sudanese sleeping outside in the cool evening air. One man stirred and asked "Who's that?" It took only a second for him to realize his mistake. He dropped his head again and feigned sleep, knowing what the visitors would do if he raised the alarm.

The lead rebel spread his arms, a signal for the rest to adopt extended line formation, a regulation five paces apart. Footsteps tapped in the darkness as another sleeper awoke and scuttled across the road to alert the soldiers. Moses pushed his way into a patch of maize and listened to the voices:

"There are strange soldiers out there and they don't want to say who they are."

"Commander, this civilian says there are soldiers."

"You go and find out what is happening."

"I'm not going out there to die."

The rebel on Moses's right opened fire with a machine gun. Shooting from the hip, Moses let loose single shots—the rebels were trained not to fire on automatic, to save ammunition. Red tracers flicked through the night. He grabbed one of his grenades, pulled out the pin and hurled it across the road.

Headlamps shone through the darkness, and a whirring sound made Moses start. He realized he was standing right in front of the tank, traversing its barrel in search of a target. He joined the flight of rebels scampering back into the shelter of the huts and heard three explosions as the gunner began to fire. The rebel commander waved a pistol at his retreating men, swearing he would shoot them if they did not go back and fight. Moses and the others ran back toward the tank, gunning down the two crew members firing machine guns from the turret. The remaining crewman wriggled out of a hatch and fled. By now, the sun was rising. Rebels swarmed on top of the tank, chanting *"Allah Akhbar! Allah Akhbar!"* to praise God, just as they had learned in Sudan. One of them snapped a picture before they scrambled off and set it ablaze.

Moses did not have a copy of the photo, but I could see the image in my mind's eye. I pictured him surrounded by cheering comrades, beaming in triumph, just as he had when he was elected health prefect six years before.

Moses took a look at the dead soldiers in the trenches to see if there was anything worth taking. Peering inside one of the huts, he found a body sprawled on the floor, a wound gashed in its neck. Moses began removing the uniform. The dead man had a lanyard around his arm, a strip of blue and green cord worn as a mark of soldierly authority. Moses picked it up and tucked it into his jacket pocket. His transformation from schoolboy to rebel was complete.

The story finished and Moses rose with his nightly mantra: "I have to go and see my mum."

I thought again about the line I had written about rebels firing "indiscriminately into terrified crowds." Moses tended to dismiss reports of civilian casualties. Villagers had been killed in the crossfire, he would say, or they made the mistake of locking themselves in their huts rather than running away when the shooting started. He believed that if people burned to death when tracers ignited thatch roofs as they cowered indoors, it was unfortunate, but their own fault.

I asked Moses if he had ever killed soldiers himself. Of course, he said, so many. "Some you cannot know if you are the one who shot them, but you see many dead," he said. "You cannot feel bad, you are doing your work, your duty. A soldier killing a soldier—it's not bad."

I later asked if he had killed civilians. He took a sip of water, looked at the floor for a moment, and said "No." But he knew plenty of people who had. "They were following orders—they told us to kill everything, every living thing—whether an old man or a young child, it was an order from Kony," he said. "They will tell you killing is not bad, even God was killing. Go to the Bible, this verse, even God was killing. According to how you are indoctrinated, you can find it's not bad."

There was the time his unit had sought shelter in an abandoned village. The inhabitants had ventured back to look for food and the rebels caught them, forced them to lie under a mango tree and smashed their heads with the long pestles used to grind millet. They died in silence. "When something bad's going to happen to you, you cannot do anything. You know for sure you are going to die now, so you cannot cry," explained Moses. The rebels were worried that the villagers would tell the soldiers where they were. In any case, it was a punishment for returning to their homes. As Kony had said, "When somebody does something bad, you have to kill."

I was more surprised to learn that the rebels sometimes reached a kind of accommodation with the locals, especially in remoter areas. Moses once likened the guerrillas to wild dogs—they inspired fear, but were capable of showing affection to the people they loved.

"A dog may even tend to bite you, but it will not bite deeply, it is showing a kind of solidarity—maybe it's playing with you. It is the same thing with the LRA," he said. "At times, we were friendly to civilians. You, the foreigner, you might not believe it, but what I say is real."

The rebels would ask people for food, explaining that they were trying to overthrow their persecutor Museveni. They would tell them to move away from the camps so they wouldn't get hurt during attacks on soldiers stationed nearby. Kony would sometimes broadcast instructions to his commanders to show restraint when dealing with peasants, saying they should give them a chance to learn from their mistakes instead of killing for a first offense. But if the "Chairman" was ever offended, the slaughter started.

The violence was extreme, but far from random. Villagers who were suspected of helping the army were punished with mutilation, while massacres taught people that it was pointless to mobilize against the rebels since Museveni could never protect them. As Kony had preached in his sermons: "If one Lord's Resistance Army soldier is killed, you have to kill at least a hundred enemies in return."

Moses had been a soldier—he was only doing his job.

When Kony gathered his people in his camp in southern Sudan in early 2002 and told them they would soon be receiving "visitors," everyone grasped it was bad news. The omens had been far from promising. Locusts had devoured much of the sorghum planted around the base a few weeks earlier. Moses had rushed out with other rebels in a futile effort to capture the insects in jerry cans. Much of their crop was lost, but they scavenged the remnants. Kony told them in his speech that it might not matter anyway: "You may eat the harvest, or you may not eat the harvest," he had said, "but don't be scared, because you are the children of God." His prediction came true in March. The "visitors" arrived in the form of the Ugandan army. Troops crawled up from the border by the truckload, nearing the Lord's Resistance Army strongholds on the road to Juba. Operation Iron Fist had started. Thousands of Kony's men, women, and children bundled up their belongings and began to march into the Imatong Mountains near the Sudan–Uganda border.

Moses trekked along with the rest as the column wound its way through mist and bamboo like a lost tribe in search of shelter. There was more fighting, more killing, hunger, and cold. Eventually, the order came for Moses's group to head south, back into Uganda, to form part of Kony's "counter-punch" against the Iron Fist. Kony himself remained holed up in the mountains, a fugitive guerrilla curiously reminiscent of Osama bin Laden hiding in his cave.

When November came, Moses found himself only a couple of days' walk from Gulu. He sent a message to his father, himself an ex-army officer who had, like many Acholi, served under Obote:

"This is to inform you that I'm still alive. WEF today I'm informing you that if possible you have to come and see me. I'm your son."

Moses had been unable to shake the habit of using the old army abbreviation WEF—With Effect From—even when writing to his father.

One night, both men made their way to an appointed spot. Father could barely recognize son. Not only was Moses seven years older, his face marked by the hardships of the bush, but he was wearing a uniform and carrying a gun. Worse still, he appeared to be the man in charge of the rebels keeping watch.

His father pleaded with him to come home, even bringing a photograph of his young daughter Nurah, born to his one-time girlfriend after he was seized from the dormitory. Moses refused. Kony's commanders had told their recruits they would be poisoned if they returned. He gave his father another letter.

Moses's father went back to his house and was unable to speak for three days, refusing food and tea. Eventually he handed over the message to his wife. Moses had written to his mother asking if she would also come and meet him, saying he had a child in his care who needed to be taken to safety. He wanted her to bring his older brother along too, as well as supply him with new Wellington boots, a smart shirt and a pair of trousers. The part about the infant was not strictly true, but Moses thought it might convince her to take the risk.

His mother tore up his letter and threw it into the latrine, afraid the army might hear about it. Suddenly she was angry with her husband for not bringing back her boy. For seven years she had heard only rumors: Moses had lost a leg, been sold into slavery in Sudan, or died. Now she knew her son was alive—alive, but out of reach.

A few months later, Moses met Father Carlos in the clearing. As he watched the priest talking to Kony on the radio, he realized he had been given another chance. He murmured a message to Carlos as the meeting ended, trying again to get word to his mother. Now that he was back in Uganda, thoughts of his family and the girl called Peace grew more intense—but so did the fighting.

The ceasefire Kony had promised Carlos never held, and the rebels advanced beyond their traditional areas in Acholiland, threatening neighboring Lango and Teso. Politicians assured the people there that the rebels were on the brink of defeat; Moses listened as one MP broadcast a radio message urging men to take up spears and women to wield knives to drive Kony's fighters back, assuring his listeners they only had a few bullets left: "Do you want to be killed like chickens?" he asked his audience. "We will defeat these rebels in a week!"

One of the commanders radioed back to Kony, reporting what the politician had said.

"Eh! That one is not good!" said Kony.

"And sir, a local man killed one of our sergeants."

"By what means?" asked Kony.

"Sir, they used a spear."

"Now, from this day on, don't use the primitive weapons they are talking about, like hitting people with these pestles," Kony said. "Now use guns—even if you see only one person, just fire at him, and if there are five to ten of them, use the bombs."

Moses's unit was ordered to stage an attack on one of the larger army bases, situated in the middle of one of the camps for displaced people in the Lango area. The grass had not yet grown as tall as it would at the height of the rainy season, and the army spotted their column advancing across the plain. There was nowhere to hide, so the rebels chose to fight.

"We made an L-shape," Moses said. "We have very many ambushes: U-shape, box-shape, extended, I know a lot of tactics!

They died and died. Now we gathered together, but still the plan remained the same, to go and attack the big defense."

But Moses had other ideas.

"By that time, I was making a plan to escape. I was not happy in that fighting, because I thought maybe I was going to die. I was now scared, and I remained at the back."

The rebels spread out in an attack formation and walked through the huts on the edge of the camp toward the army's positions in the middle. Groups of soldiers sat drinking outside their straw shelters, mistaking the intruders' green fatigues and gumboots for Ugandan military uniforms. Then one of the rebels shot an officer who was riding past on a bicycle, and everyone started firing.

Moses saw the soldiers putting up their hands and saying "Don't shoot," still unaware that they were facing Kony's men. Moses simply squeezed his trigger again and again. He ran forward with the other rebels, stabbing one man in the chest with his bayonet. As he began to remove the soldier's uniform, Moses saw that they were about the same age. He soon gave up on the clothing, realizing there was no time. Most of the camp's guards had fled, but there was still one man in a white shirt firing at them from a ditch. Moses raised his gun.

"Mistakenly, I find that all my bullets are gone now—*click*! Now I have to make my way back, using military tactics, or they will shoot at me straight away."

Moses jumped up and mimed firing, tricking the soldier into ducking back down into the ditch. He was able to step backward, pop up, then step backward again several times before the man caught on that he was bluffing.

"Then I tried to run, but I was shot down," said Moses, pulling down his collar to reveal a scar in his shoulder. The bullet had torn right through him, but he was still able to run back to his comrades. A woman rebel bound the gash.

A couple of days later, a helicopter gunship stalked their unit for almost three hours. They tried to hide but the canopy was too thin. Cannon fire killed dozens of his comrades.

"I prayed that if I survived that day, I would go back home," he said. "I'd go straight back to our home."

If only it were so simple.

7. "SHOCK THE WORLD"

On the road from Gulu to Nimule

rumor reached me at the Acholi Inn: Vincent Otti had appeared in a clearing and told members of the government of southern Sudan that the rebels wanted peace. It seemed unlikely, but there was speculation that Kony himself might put in an appearance. I had to get to Juba, the south's capital, to find out what was happening. The only problem was I had just caught malaria.

The attack began with a headache. At first I thought it might be down to one too many bottles of Bell at the Acholi Inn the night before, but that same morning I decided to visit a doctor's office on a corner in Gulu. A nurse pricked my finger and scrutinized the blood spot under a microscope. The doctor asked if I had been taking prophylactic drugs. I had to admit that I'd never bothered, assuming a full stomach would keep me safe. He gave me some pills and sent me home.

I swapped my tiny room at the Franklin for a house on the edge of town rented by Bob, the former colonel, who had gone away for a few weeks. In some ways, I was lucky. You could die from catching a drug-resistant form of malaria in Gulu, but my dose was not so bad. I lay on the sofa watching DVDs of *The Sopranos* between bouts of fever and mild hallucinations. Bob's dog was sick too and he had asked an Argentinean called Esteban who worked for the UN to look in and keep an eye on him. The visitor kindly kept me supplied with mineral water. The only downside was the smell as he chopped liver in the kitchen to try to cheer up the canine.

I noticed that my box of pills was stamped "Sample only—not for resale," but the contents worked. After a few days I began to think about how to get to Juba. The town lies about 300 kilometers [186 miles] north of Gulu, on the other side of the border. Virtually all the trucks, pickups, and buses heading to Sudan used a road that was far to the west and several days out of my way. I could see a more direct route on the map, but it seemed that virtually nobody used it. Once trodden by Arab slavers, it now went straight through what was known as the "LRA triangle."

Just a white space on the map of southern Sudan, the "triangle" was notorious for rebel attacks. The road cutting through it also traversed a series of minefields. Two men working to clear them— one Iraqi and one Sudanese—had been killed on the route some months before; Lord's Resistance Army fighters were the prime suspects. But for all the potential risks, it would have been impossible not to take this road. Touching the curves of the White Nile as it meandered north, the trail followed precisely in Kony's footsteps.

I knew from Moses that the Lord's Resistance Army's old bases in south Sudan were threaded along the road to Juba like beads on a necklace. I wanted to see them for myself, to try to grasp something of the isolation the abductees must have felt. And I hoped my journey might teach me something more about why the government in Khartoum had supported Kony for all those years. But transport was going to be a problem.

It looked as though my best bet would be to try and cross the border at a town called Nimule—pronounced "Nim-you-lay"—

that lay roughly halfway to Juba. From there onward I would have to improvise. I emailed a Dutch friend called Huub, who lived in Juba, to ask his advice. His reply was encouraging, though I wondered what "about two days" would mean:

"On Nimule transport, that's a rough road, not without danger as officially the road is not mine-free, nor bandit-free, but there are traders plying that road. Best is to contact someone called Bashir in Afroshop in Gulu. His friend or brother travels regularly by lorry from Gulu to Juba. For a fee he possibly can take you, and be prepared to pay some soldiers on the way. Take water as it's difficult to find while travelling. The journey might take about two days (one night in Nimule, then one in Juba), if there are no breakdowns, that is."

Later he added: "The route is not 'suicidal' but take care!"

I had managed to recruit one potential ally, an evangelical American preacher named Samuel Childers who had founded an orphanage in Nimule. Describing himself as a "non-educated hill-billy pastor," he was partial to dressing in US Marine Corps uniform and carrying an AK–47. I had heard he had repeatedly invited Kony to dinner, a prelude to a man-to-man fight. I imagined the duel—Kalashnikovs at dawn. Unfortunately for me, Kony had yet to take him up on the offer. Perhaps it was his cooking.

Childers had kindly offered me a bunk at his Shekinah Fellowship Children"s Village after I met him in Kampala. The orphanage was also host to his entourage of born-again Sudanese soldiers. I hoped they might help me find a way to Juba. I packed my bags, bought plenty of water and a few tins of sardines, and checked to be sure my Thuraya satellite phone was working. I traced the red line that headed north on the map and thought the journey looked straightforward enough.

Bashir had disappeared, but his colleague behind the counter at the Afroshop introduced me to a driver who was on his way to the border. He led me over to the bus parking lot, where touts hustled for passengers for ramshackle coaches with names like White Cock and Baby. Only lorries went to Nimule.

I clambered onto the back and found some space on a sack of salt, stowed alongside boxes of Chinese "Moon light" hurricane lamps, crates of soda, and boxes of flashlights. I was among the last of about a dozen passengers to board, squeezing in between a man with an earring and a piebald cockerel sheltering under a bicycle. I looked over to see a crowd scrambling onto one of the other trucks, and realized I had been lucky to find a place.

It was like watching panic-stricken passengers abandon a sinking ship, only in reverse. Following some unseen signal, a crowd of men, women, and children surged into a metal cage enclosing the back. A woman thrust her baby toward outstretched hands, before hoisting her own flip-flopped foot onto the side. Wrists and elbows flopped between the bars as the truck lumbered away.

My mobile gave a double beep. It was Daniel the Reuters reporter, texting from Kampala. He'd heard a report of oil workers being ambushed further up the road on the Sudanese side. I called and he said the details were still vague. There was no way I was going back to the Franklin.

The truck breezed out into the empty land surrounding Gulu. The man with the earring began munching a boiled egg, while behind me a woman crunched on a stick of sugar cane, spitting rind over the side. I decided to save my sardines for later, content to gaze at the wilderness. A solitary sunflower was the only dash of color against the green. I felt almost hypnotized, until the smell of mud brought me to my senses.

We had reached Pabbo, one of the biggest camps in the north. Once a center for upland rice farming, it was now dependent on food aid, like everywhere else around Gulu. A kite made of sticks and plastic bags floated on an invisible thread, defying the squalor below. Hawkers offered trays of biscuits, water, and more eggs. We stopped and waited.

A trio of soldiers clambered aboard our truck, taking turns to suck at the corner of a pouch of clear spirit. Either they were planning to enjoy the journey, or they needed a stiff drink before we set off. Soon a line of vehicles had formed a convoy. The soldiers sitting on top of the tanker marked "DANGER PETROL" driving in front of us had presumably drawn the short straw.

As the train of trucks, buses, and pickups rolled out of Pabbo, the foliage flanking the road seemed higher, the emptiness more profound. I spotted a man in uniform sprawled beneath a tree, certain he had been shot. It took me a second to realize he was dozing. When we halted again and the soldiers climbed down into the bush, I thought they were forming a perimeter. All that happened was an unzipping of flies so they could relieve themselves in the grass.

The convoy split at the next camp, a place called Atiak, scene of one of the worst massacres committed by Kony's forces. In April 1995, a group of rebels attacked a detachment of militiamen deployed to protect the trading center, then looted the market, killing more than a dozen people. Then they rounded up a large group of villagers, as well as teachers and students from a technical college and marched them to a river bank, separating the elderly and pregnant women and children under ten from the rest.

One of Kony's most senior commanders, a man named Alex Otti-Lagony, told the gathering: "You Acholi have refused to support us. We shall now teach you a lesson. You have been saying we hack people to death. Now we shall show you we have bullets." They shot dead more than 70 people. Otti-Lagony ordered the survivors to applaud, saying "clap your hands to thank us for eliminating these bad Acholi."

Reporters visiting the scene found the students' bloodstained exercise books and lecture notes scattered among the bodies. The slaughter did not end there. The *New Vision* said the rebels killed more than 250 people that day, the victims of the river-bank massacre among them. Kony's current deputy, Vincent Otti, came from Atiak. He had been among the supervisors of the slaughter.

Watching the other vehicles branch off, I deduced that our truck would make the riskiest part of the journey alone. A man in civilian clothes clicked a magazine into his AK-47 and leapt onto the back, and we began to roll again. Ruined huts littered the landscape like giant chimney pots. There were hardly any birds, apart from a pair of white-tailed pigeons flapping back toward Gulu. It began to rain.

We unfurled a tarpaulin over our heads, thorns stabbing through the gap around the sides as the truck lurched over potholes. Every few minutes, somebody's arm would tire and the tarpaulin sag, unleashing a torrent of pooled rainwater from the top, usually over my legs. Mud sucked at the tires, eventually bringing us to a halt. We climbed down and trudged alongside as the driver maneuvered around the craters. I envied the passengers in the cab.

Eventually we reached the border post on the Ugandan side, which comprised a collection of huts and a few mean shops. One of the passengers led me into a brick office where a man sat behind a table. A picture of Museveni meeting Bill Clinton while he was still US president hung on the wall behind him. The man asked for a few thousand shillings, wrote something on a scrap of paper in return, then stuffed the money I gave him into his pocket.

The truck drove on to another hut. Somebody had scrawled the words "Alian and Immigration" on a page from an exercise book and stuck it on the wall. I handed over my note and the officer took my passport. I declined his request for a bribe, but he stamped it anyway, giving me a good-natured smile. I began to walk down the track. There was no sign, but this had to be Nimule.

We had crossed an invisible border. Hills kneaded the horizon just as they did in northern Uganda, but this place felt different. The huts I passed were spread out under mango trees, looking a little like the Acholi villages described by Lloyd in the days before the camps. I passed a church, its enormous thatched roof drooping over low mud walls, and then climbed up a mound to what seemed like the only guest house. The White Nile swept past in a gentle arc, its surface shimmering.

I ordered some rice and stew in the dining area. A Sudanese truck driver ordered the same. I could not understand his Arabic, but managed to gather from his broken Kiswahili that he had just arrived from Juba. The road was open.

One of Reverend Childers' friends, a southern Sudanese soldier named Colonel Akol, collected me in his pickup the next day. We drove to the orphanage, finding children running around between the bunkhouses. A Sudanese camp manager called them over to greet me and ordered one boy to roll up his T-shirt to reveal the stump of his missing arm. The man said it was Kony's work, though there was no way to tell.

I was given a bunk in one of the rooms. Shelves contained the complete *Encyclopedia Britannica* and a volume called *Day of*

Devastation, Day of Contentment, along with *The History of the Sudanese Church across 2,000 Years*. A framed picture on a desk showed a group of southern Sudanese soldiers posing outside the orphanage, a white man among them. Well built, with a walrus moustache running down his jowls and a few flecks of gray in his hair, he stared straight at the camera. I recognized Childers immediately.

I had tracked down the Reverend through his Boyers Pond website some months before, and had ended up spending a few hours chatting with him at a flat he used when visiting Kampala. Photos of his family decorated the walls, among them a picture of him straddling his Harley Davidson on a road through snow-bound mountains back home in the United States. A couple of southern Sudanese orphans peered out from the kitchen. One was called Angela, the other Walter, and they were now being looked after with Childers' help.

I had wanted to know how a man who began his career mingling with drug dealers and biker gangs in America had ended up in a remote corner of Africa with a Bible in one hand and a gun in the other. I also wondered what he made of Kony. The answer to the first question took longer than the second.

Born to a half–Native American father, an ex-marine who made his living as an iron worker strolling girders at skyscraper construction sites, Childers went off the rails fast. There was plenty of marijuana to be had at the school near his home in Grand Rapids, Minnesota. He smoked his first joint aged eleven, and quickly discovered acid and crystal meth. When he was sixteen he rode a Greyhound bus to California with a sawn-off shotgun tucked in his jacket, soon ending up as a "shotgunner"— muscle hired to ensure drug deals went smoothly. Childers was waiting for one such deal when he unwittingly took his first step toward Nimule, by meeting his future wife in a bar in Orlando.

"I hung out at a lot of the strip joints, the dancing bars," he said. "In fact I met my wife at one of the drug deals. She come up to me and she said, 'Hey, I know you,' and I said 'No, you don't,' and I settled back in the corner. That day I had a sawn-off 12-gauge shotgun and then my other pistols with me.

"My wife's very attractive, you've seen a picture of her, she was really hot-looking then. I wanted her to get away from me, because if the guys come in and see me talking to her, they wouldn't take me so serious. Then I think two days later I met her, went to her house and we got hooked up. It was soon after that I kind of got out of the shotgun dealing."

Within a few years, Childers had cut his shoulder-length hair, was spending less time with biker gangs like the Iron Range Riders, and had found a career running a decorating business. He managed to restrict his drug dealing to purchases for personal use, though he still bore the skull and crossbones tattooed on his arm in a Florida jailhouse. Nimule was getting closer.

After his wife became a born-again Christian, Childers promised God he would forsake drink and drugs if they could overcome their difficulties conceiving a child. When they were blessed with a pregnancy, he decided to follow her example and embrace Jesus as his savior. "That night, I just kind of broke in the church, gave my heart to the Lord." When he went back the next night, he received more than a sermon.

"This guy comes up and he prophesied over me, that I would be in a war with him, and he prophesied that I was going to Africa. I was ready to beat this preacher right there in the church; I'd just got saved so I was still rough under the collar."

Despite his skepticism, Childers ended up joining a mission trip to south Sudan where he came across the body of a child who'd been killed by a landmine.

"I couldn't tell if it was a boy or a girl, it was gone from the waist down. I remember I stood over the body and I said 'Lord, I'll do anything I can do in order to help these people.'"

Before long, he was clearing the bush for his orphanage at Nimule, sleeping under a mosquito net hung under a tree. A few years later still, he was flying to Hollywood for talks with agents. His favorite working title for a proposed movie about his life was "One Man, One Power," perhaps starring Russell Crowe as himself, with Morgan Freeman as one of the Sudanese commanders. The slot to play Kony was still open. He was reluctant to go into too much detail, though I did glean a preview of a scene set in a place called Yei.

"When we got into town they said, 'Pastor, there's some witch-doctors here that's going to kill you.' And I said 'Well, I've been hearing that all my life.'"

"Anyways, that night I was sleeping in a round *tukul* about as big as this room and—this is the Gospel truth—my door was locked from the inside and something entered my room and woke me up from a dead sleep. I reached for my flashlight, and God said to me 'No, you begin to pray,' and I could just feel that something had entered my room, and God said 'No, you pray.' I prayed for a few hours in the spirit and kept praying and finally I went back to sleep.

"I woke up that morning and opened my eyes up, and I sat on the edge of the bed and as I was sitting there, rubbing my eyes, thinking about what happened, I looked down on the floor, and a perfect circle of gray ash was around my bed, *a perfect circle.* It was probably one inch wide, and a half-inch high, perfect gray ash. I started to cry. God spoke to me and said Satan come to kill me that night, but he could not cross the bloodline of Jesus Christ as I was praying.

"But I mean there's story after story like that," he said. "I had a witchdoctor one time come running up toward me in a village and one of my bodyguards went to shoot him and I said 'No! No! No! No!'

"He came right up close, maybe from here to the fridge," Childers gestured across the room, "and he threw down a bag of bones and he started chanting, and dancing. You know how the witchdoctors are in the movies? I took three steps and hit him with both hands in the chest. He flew, I'm not exaggerating, and I know this will sound like it's exaggerating, this man flew at least 25 to 30 feet, it was like a bus hit him, and he fell to the ground, and he rolled over and started crying, and started crawling away.

"There's no way I could have done it, to hit someone and make 'em literally fly like that. There's no way I could have done it. It was God.

"In the movie they'll probably add a few things, that might not be quite exactly how it happened, but everything'll be based on the truth, let's put it that way."

Some time before my visit, a television crew from the *Dateline* news show in the United States had filmed Childers carrying an AK-47 on his lap as he drove to the orphanage, but he was rather coy when I asked him whether he had shot anyone during his brushes with the Lord's Resistance Army. Given his rather unconventional activities, it was perhaps not surprising that his compatriots in Kampala had taken note. Childers said he had received a phone call from the US embassy about a year earlier and had been warned: "This is not your war—you need to just let it go."

"And I said, 'You know what, you're absolutely right, it's not your war, but it is mine,' and I hung the phone up on him."

I soon learned that Childers shared a view of Kony I had heard time and again in northern Uganda, from soldiers in Museveni's army to born-again aid workers from Europe. One of Uganda's generals had once said much the same thing: Kony was an agent of Satan.

"I believe as a Christian that the man is fully oppressed, depressed, demon-possessed, whatever you want to say," Childers said. "Maybe Satan himself has possessed him, maybe he is a Ruler of the Darkness."

There were advantages in blaming the Devil. It avoided having to ask questions about how the war started, and why it had lasted so long. But I was beginning to see that Kony was only part of the problem. The elders, religious leaders, and politicians in Acholiland had failed to tame their errant son, while donor countries had looked the other way for years, content to let the United Nations feed people in misery. Museveni had proved singularly unwilling or unable to end the war, as had his army. But the more time I spent in Nimule, the more it became clear that the trail of culpability led all the way down the White Nile, to Khartoum.

Fortunately, Childers was offering a solution—if only Kony had the guts.

"I've said this in many interviews and I know Kony has heard it," Childers told me. "If he thinks he's a man, he needs to come out and meet me face to face. We're gonna fight. Bottom line, we're gonna fight, and I will win."

Just before sunset, Childers' orphans began to kick around a partially deflated football. Dust and shrieks rose from the pitch as the crowd of barefoot youngsters hammered shots at the hapless goalie, the one-armed boy jostling with the best of them. I could not resist slamming a few shots past the diminutive keeper, still smarting from my humiliation in the pool hall in Patongo. Rapidly exhausted, I sat down with a group of southern Sudanese soldiers and enjoyed the last of the sun.

Several born-again members of the Sudan People's Liberation Army—known as the SPLA—would spend their evenings hanging around at Childers' place, including Colonel Akol. I found him rather taciturn, but I got to know one of his subordinates better, a young sergeant called Deng. He told me that Childers had baptized him in the pool of the Kampala Sheraton. Like the other soldiers who gathered at the orphanage each evening, he had spent years fighting in Sudan's civil war.

In crossing the border at Nimule, I had stepped into an entirely different conflict. Already I was feeling out of my depth. Just as my grasp of the Lord's Resistance Army had once been based on a couple of paragraphs that were constantly recycled in Reuters stories, so too was my knowledge of the history of southern Sudan:

"The Sudan People's Liberation Army (SPLA) rebels have been fighting the Arab-dominated government in Khartoum for greater autonomy since 1983. Religion, oil, ethnicity, and ideology have complicated the conflict."

Tagged on at the end was a line that had become almost bland through repetition: "An estimated two million people have died, mainly through hunger and disease." We might also have mentioned the extensive use of child soldiers, southern militias who killed more people than the government, and accusations that famine relief had helped fuel the conflict, but that made it too long.

Officially, the war had ended a year before my visit to Nimule. The Khartoum government had signed a peace agreement with the SPLA in Nairobi on 9 January 2005. The deal transformed the

SPLA rebels into the ruling party of a new government for the south, and Juba became their capital. Businessmen poured in from Kenya, Uganda, and further afield, all seeking a slice of the administration's oil money and the billions of dollars of aid promised by donor countries to help rebuild. There was even talk that somebody had opened south Sudan's first pizza parlor in the town, though I assumed it was a fantasy dreamed up by homesick Europeans. By 2011, the south was due to vote on whether to break away from Khartoum for good and declare independence; in a few years, a whole new country might be born.

Sudan's north–south civil war had generated far more international coverage than Kony had ever done. The scale of the conflict dwarfed anything taking place in Uganda, which Sudan, the biggest country in Africa, could swallow more than ten times over. For Western powers, the stakes were also higher. The war was often portrayed as a conflict between Islamists in the Khartoum government and Christians among the rebels— though in reality the religious dimension was more complex. In 1993, the United States had declared Khartoum a "state sponsor of terrorism." Human rights groups have accused companies from Canada, Sweden, China, America, Malaysia, and Austria of benefiting from the government's scorched-earth policy of clearing villagers from the oilfields. When a separate civil war broke out in the Darfur region in western Sudan in 2003, Washington would describe it as "genocide." With significant interests such as these on the table in Sudan, Museveni's failure to tackle Kony was easily overlooked by his allies.

Quietly, and almost unnoticed by the outside world, Kony exploited the conflict as a means of propelling him to the height of his career. Embraced by the government in Khartoum, who wanted a proxy to fight the SPLA, the young "healer" who led a handful of followers from his village became more powerful than anyone could have imagined. And although his heyday was not to last, his years in Sudan completed his transformation from village hero to devourer of his own people. As I was about to learn from the soldiers in Nimule, the eventual fate of Kony was one of the biggest questions clouding their newfound peace.

There was still no transport to Juba, so Colonel Akol and Deng took me sightseeing. As always, they wedged an AK-47 between the front seats of their pickup. We swung down the main track, passing a whitewashed building with a red, green, and yellow sign that read "Rocketball Bar." Everywhere I saw the words: "New Sudan," the name adopted by the rebels-turned-rulers in the southern government. There was just enough fresh paint to make it seem possible that, after more than twenty years of war, things might be improving.

The colonel drove us down a trail through a papyrus swamp bursting with umbrella-shaped flowers. We reached the rusted skeleton of a customs house. A wooden vessel named "Jesus Cares Nile Transporter" lay idle on the bank. Steamers had once plied the White Nile, but now only clumps of vegetation raced past in the current.

Reverend Lloyd had described seeing hundreds of hippos teeming in the river not far from Nimule, delighting his hosts by shooting four of them. A trail of men, women, and children had carted away the meat in baskets. The only thing I found resembling wildlife was a crocodile that lived in a cage near the orphanage. Deng said it was called "Kadogo"—"little one." I would have hated to encounter its mother.

Tourism over, our talk turned to the war. Akol said his men had seen one of the Sudanese government's Antonovs flying past only a few days earlier, and suspected they were still ferrying supplies to Kony's forces scattered in south Sudan. The rebels would light grass fires to guide the pilots. "They are still dropping food and ammunition to the LRA," Akol said. "That's no secret."

He was right—Sudan's security services had never completely cut off their support for Kony, but his stock in Khartoum had fallen in the past few years and supplies were delivered less regularly, if at all. The Sudanese had even allowed the Ugandan army to overrun Kony's bases during Operation Iron Fist, when he was forced to flee into the cold embrace of the Imatong Mountains. Sudan's rulers had made Kony, but when the relationship began to sour, they almost broke him.

In the early days of his uprising, Kony led just one of several Acholi rebel groups that emerged after Museveni seized power. The others soon dissolved: the government army defeated Alice Lakwena in late 1987, and a more conventional contingent led by renegade Acholi officers—known as the Uganda People's Democratic Army—accepted amnesty from the government less than a year later. A group of Acholi military men who were not prepared to trust Museveni threw in their lot with Kony. They brought a degree of military expertise, but his movement was increasingly isolated.

With the other rebel groups taken care of so swiftly, the government at first seemed to underestimate the threat that Kony posed. When Museveni did eventually take action, the army's heavy-handed tactics only deepened resentment among many Acholi toward their new rulers in Kampala. Some Acholi still write letters to newspapers recalling the atrocities committed by soldiers during "Operation North" in 1991, the forefather of a succession of offensives designed to crush Kony's rebellion.

Troops executed many civilians, rounded up hundreds of people for "screenings" in Pece Stadium in Gulu, and detained politicians without trial. Contemporary reports of abuses committed by the army read much like accounts of outrages perpetrated by the rebels years later. Museveni won few friends in those early years, but neither did Kony.

When the government began to organize Acholi peasants into self-defense militias known as "Arrow Brigades," Kony decided on an appropriate punishment. Young men carrying bows and spears could do little to prevent his fighters meting them out. Acholi men who dared take up arms against his rebels would have their hands removed; women who raised the alarm would have their lips chopped off; anyone who failed to listen to Kony's commands would lose their ears. In later years, he decreed that villagers caught riding bicycles would have their legs hacked away. While this appeared to be irrefutable evidence that Kony had lost his mind, in fact it made horrible sense—bicycles were the quickest means by which villagers could alert the army.

There was a time when a resolution seemed hopeful. Betty Bigombe, the Acholi politician who had worked at the World Bank, began her talks with Kony in 1993, long before a host of other initiatives (Father Carlos's efforts among them). While her initial job title—minister of state for pacification of northern Uganda, resident in Gulu—made her sound like a colonial official dispatched to crush restive natives, her peacemaking efforts turned her into a heroine for many Acholi. Others thought she was too close to Museveni, remembering that she had created the "Arrow Brigades" that so angered Kony. But she was perhaps the person who came closest to persuading him to come home.

Despite being a regular at the Acholi Inn during her trips to Gulu, Bigombe was remarkably difficult to pin down for a chat and her two mobiles never stopped ringing. When I finally managed to corner her, she gave a wry smile and said: "Joseph Kony has been the man in my life." As she told the story of her attempts to coax him out of the bush, I realized she was only half-joking.

As the wife of a Ugandan ambassador, Bigombe had been better acquainted with the diplomatic circuits in Tokyo and New York than with the rigors of the bush at the time she began her dialogue with the rebels. But venturing out with groups of elders, she quickly adapted to encounters with boys with guns, and on one occasion, a young girl with a machete.

"I tried to talk to her, she wouldn't say a word," Bigombe said. "All we got was a recorded message on a cassette."

The message was from Kony and said he was ready to talk. There were further trips to meet his followers. A choir of rebels singing "Holy Spirit" hymns entertained the delegation, while Kony's priests sprinkled them with holy water mixed with shea-nut oil, just as they would anoint Carlos years later. Eventually, the Chairman turned up in person, sporting braids in his hair, sunglasses, and a cowboy hat.

Bigombe explained that Kony's priority had been his personal safety. Some of the Acholi officers who had accepted amnesty had died in mysterious circumstances. He feared he might be killed if he ventured out of the bush.

"We went on talking," Bigombe explained, "and we agreed that on 2 January 1994, we would sign the peace agreement."

Kony's rebels emerged from their hideouts in anticipation of the deal and hung around at village shops, sharing meals with soldiers. The atmosphere across northern Uganda was electric. Kony even wrote to Bigombe to suggest they hold joint rallies in the towns of Kitgum and Gulu. He asked the government to give him six months to assemble his fighters so that they could be disarmed. Bigombe took the rebels' demands to the president, certain the war was over.

"He told me that I'd delayed this process, that he would finish the rebels militarily within two months."

It was the worst moment of Bigombe's life. Addressing a rally at Kaunda Ground in Gulu, Museveni issued an ultimatum. Unless the rebels surrendered within seven days he would use force to crush them. Kony was furious at what he considered another betrayal, but Bigombe did not give up hope, having already resisted repeated attempts from within the government to sabotage the talks. She contacted Kony on the radio each day at 11 a.m., desperate to salvage something. Then the army made good on Museveni's threat.

"After that attack, in the next radio communication Kony said, 'Listen very carefully, this will be my last communication with you: government is not serious about peace talks. I'm going to shut down my radio, don't try to call me anymore. I'm not angry with you because you have done your best. I thought you would be scared, but you came to all these meetings.'"

Kony's next words proved prophetic.

"'Unless we demonstrate to people that we are still here, the government will never accept peace talks. I'm going to do things that will shock the world. Many people are going to die.' These were his words," Bigombe told me, "these were his words. I pleaded with him and begged him, but he shut off the radio." The collapse only deepened the Acholi people's resentment toward Museveni. Many concluded the president had deliberately scuppered the negotiations; he was either too proud to talk to Kony, or he was trying to keep his enemies weak by allowing the war to continue. Memories were still raw of the "peace jokes" almost a decade earlier, when Museveni had signed an agreement with the Acholi generals who toppled Obote, and then marched into Kampala. But to lay the blame entirely on the president risks obscuring the role played by the Sudanese government.

Even before the talks failed, Khartoum's security chiefs appear to have promised Kony huge stocks of weapons to enable him to continue fighting Museveni. This raises questions as to whether Kony's request for six months to disarm was in fact buying him time to re-arm.

"Many people say that when Museveni gave the ultimatum the rebels went to Sudan because they had no choice, but it's clear they were receiving weapons from Sudan before," Carlos told me. "The government of Sudan was the real spoiler."

Whoever bears the greater responsibility, it is clear that the failure of the talks pushed the Acholi people further away from their president, and Kony deeper into the arms of Khartoum. The year 1994 marked a turning point in Sudan's relations with the Lord's Resistance Army. For the first time, the government gave Kony a safe haven in which to build his camps, and more guns than he knew what to do with. Now all he needed was recruits. His men crossed back into Uganda armed with two rifles each and plenty of rope, raiding captives just like the Arab slavers of the previous century. His army of a few hundred fighters in the early 1990s soon swelled into the thousands.

Khartoum's rationale for supporting Kony was simple. President Omar Hassan Ahmed al-Bashir's Islamist government was struggling to defeat the southern rebels, who were supported in various ways by Museveni. The Ugandan president had been at university in Dar-es-Salaam with the SPLA's leader, John Garang, and sympathized with his liberation struggle. Museveni had on various occasions sent troops across the border to help his Sudanese ally, although much less publicly than during Operation Iron Fist. Kony's growing force would not only fight the SPLA in the south, but also punish Museveni by destabilizing northern Uganda.

Sudan's army continued its time-honored method of fighting a war by sponsoring local militias to raze villages suspected of sheltering rebels. It was simple enough to harness Kony for the same task, turning his force into a semi-official branch of the military. Sudanese officers visited Kony's camps, feeding his sense of importance. He opened an office in Juba known as the "embassy," and another in Khartoum, flying to the Sudanese capital for consultations. Lavishly supplied by outsiders, he became increasingly blind to the antipathy he had earned among his own people. I could not shake the image of drug pusher and addict; Sudan pedaling guns and prestige, but only enough to keep Kony hooked. His sponsors knew he would never overthrow Museveni, but he could still cause enough chaos to be useful. Kony had addressed cheering crowds in the early days of his rebellion—now, the liberator had become a destroyer.

With the help of Sudan, Kony's promise to "shock the world" quickly became reality. His rebels staged the Atiak massacre in 1995, prompting Uganda to break off diplomatic relations with Khartoum. Rebel activity intensified, while Museveni's army was distracted by its interventions in Congo. It was only several years later that Uganda and Sudan began to patch things up, and in Nairobi in 1999, the two countries finally signed an agreement to stop supporting each other's rebels.

Although Khartoum never stuck to the deal, Kony again felt betrayed. His forces clashed with Sudanese troops, and he shunned Juba. When the Sudanese government gave the green light for the Ugandan army to roll across the border for Operation Iron Fist, it appeared for a time that Kony's dalliance with Sudan might have proved his undoing. But Sudanese military intelligence played a double game, sending him enough supplies to keep him going while simultaneously allowing the Ugandans to capture his camps. Even when Kony was forced to find a new home in Congo, the SPLA officers in Nimule were certain that his old friends in Khartoum had not forgotten him completely.

We took our usual chairs outside the orphanage that evening, and watched a brilliant moon climb above the hills. The children sang hymns before bed, their chorus drifting over the empty pitch. Deng told me an elaborate story of how his SPLA unit had used their trucks to run down giraffes during the war so they could roast the meat for dinner. After a while I began to lose track of what he was saying, until he made the announcement I had been waiting for:

"I am 100 percent sure that tomorrow you are going to Juba."

8. THE MOST DESOLATE SPOT ON EARTH

Flying from Juba to Khartoum

The old woman climbed off the back of the pickup, squatted on her haunches and lit a pipe. Puffing wisps of white smoke, she looked utterly at ease. I did not share her feelings. The last milestone had said Juba was another fifteen miles away and we were still surrounded by forest. I had no idea why we had stopped.

The two dozen passengers quickly settled into separate groups of men and women on the road. The driver—a gray-bearded old man in olive fatigues—got out and peered under the chassis. One of the rear wheels was leaning at a sickly angle. Our fate now rested in the hands of Lieutenant Thiop.

Colonel Akol had entrusted me into his care that morning in Nimule. Thiop, who had a shaved head and wore dark glasses, came up to the height of my shoulder. His upper incisors had been removed, and his remaining teeth looked like stubby fangs. I guessed the grenade that was perched handily on the dashboard belonged to him. He pulled out his Thuraya phone and began to chatter in a language I could not understand.

Chances of rescue looked slim. We had passed only a handful of vehicles during the seven-hour drive to Juba, and these were mostly burned-out tanks. Red skull-and-crossbones signs marked the minefields that lay along the route. In places the track was so narrow the pickup had brushed past the white tape that encircled the danger zone while our legs dangled over the side. Looking like robots in their blue armor, boots, and visors, de-miners knelt on the verge and swept squeaking metal detectors over the soil. When we'd stopped for a break, one of the older passengers had blundered into the bushes to relieve himself. Thiop had shouted a warning, and he ambled back in one piece.

We had even caught sight of Ugandan troops deployed at a place called Aru Junction; one of their Mambas was parked in the trees, and the men were camped in bivouacs. Four years after it had begun, Operation Iron Fist had acquired a certain air of permanence. The Ugandans must have felt a long way from home, but the place where we had just broken down seemed lonelier still.

I walked over to the cab and plugged my own Thuraya into a charger connected to the cigarette lighter. The screen showed the battery filling. I sat down on the road and Thiop joined me, balancing his AK-47 between his knees.

"Do you have a gun?" he asked.

I shook my head.

"A pistol?"

"No."

"You have a knife. Not even a knife?"

I shook my head again.

"Then if I run away with this gun, how will you defend yourself?"

He smiled, revealing his fangs. "You are a soldier," he said. "Why else are you traveling alone like this in southern Sudan?"

I told him.

"You want to meet Joseph Kony? Hah! He will slaughter you like a chicken! Green, young soldier, you are a solider!"

An engine growled in the trees. We looked round as a white four-wheel drive drove past with some European-looking men in the back, heading toward Nimule. I hesitated a moment too long to flag it down, though in any case it had been going in the wrong direction. I assumed they were relief workers on their way to visit a project site, although it was a little late to be driving around outside Juba. Thiop chuckled as the vehicle disappeared round a bend.

"Can you sleep out here?" he asked. "Can you drink this water?" He pointed at one of the puddles on the track.

"We'll make it to Juba," I said.

"There is no car!" he said. "Go and prepare your place to sleep!"

The driver squatted down next to us. Thiop shot him a knowing glance, then spoke again.

"You know, Aler will help us."

"Aler?"

"Yes, Aler," said Thiop. He picked up a stick and wrote A-L-E-R in the dirt. "Aler can do anything."

"Like what?" I said.

"At night he can make my teeth grow like this," Thiop thrust out his jaw and curled his lip. I imagined the missing incisors sprouting out of his gums.

The older man nodded, also smiling. I realized we had returned to the realm of the spirits.

"He can even make a woman pregnant," said Thiop. "He can move me from here to my village, right now."

The time had come to call Colonel Akol. We had waited an hour, and there was only one more hour of daylight left. I got through on the first try. "So you're telling me the car has not left Juba yet?"

"Don't worry, another one is coming," Akol said. "No problem."

I looked at the huddle of women and children, wondering how I could eat my sardines without anyone seeing. I still had some bottles of water in my rucksack, plus my sleeping bag, and a mosquito net. I just hoped the soldiers would stay awake.

Then I heard the engine again. I looked up and saw the white four-wheel drive returning, this time heading toward Juba. I took another look at the women and children, and at Thiop, then began to wave. The car stopped and the back door opened.

"Are you going to Juba?" I said.

The men in the back nodded.

"Can I come?"

I rushed back to the pickup, shooing away a kid who'd rested his head on my bag. In my haste I almost forgot my phone. As the car door closed I felt a pang of guilt. I should really have asked if my rescuers could spare room for some of the other passengers. I was about to tell the driver to stop so I could leave my water with the women and children, but I hesitated. I did not want to cause even the slightest delay for my new friends. They did not look anything like the aid workers I was used to seeing.

They were big guys with dark hair, all clutching Thurayas like mine, and they did not seem to speak much English. When I tried to strike up a conversation, one of them gestured to the man in the front passenger seat. I could only see the back of his head, but he introduced himself as Radu from Romania.

"So how are you traveling?" he said, craning his neck round. "You don't have car?"

"No, I'm just independent."

"Independent?" he laughed. "No. You are totally *de*pendent."

The men in the back laughed too.

"So," he said. "Do you know much about the security round here?"

"Well, I've just come up from the border. They said down there that the LRA killed seven people in Pagire a few weeks back, not far from Nimule."

"Seven people?" asked Radu, sounding surprised.

"That's what they said."

Radu whistled through his teeth and turned back to the road. I asked one of the passengers what business they were doing. One of them cocked his head at Radu. "Ask him."

I decided to save the question, barely taking in the view as we clanked onto an iron bridge over the White Nile and into Juba. The sight of so many people wandering the lanes between the huts was profoundly reassuring. We passed a set of defunct traffic lights by a roundabout draped with a banner that read: "SPLA— OUR LIBERATOR, OUR DEFENDER," then turned down an avenue lined with neem trees. The Romanians dropped me near a razor-wire compound filled with a fleet of UN cars. Radu fished out a business card that bore the address of a prospecting company in Bucharest.

"What are you looking for?" I asked.

"Oil," he said, and I could have sworn he winked.

I gave the name of my Dutch friend, Huub, to one of the Sudanese guards sitting behind a desk in the cabin that served as an entrance to the UN compound. He gestured for me to sit down on a sofa that was the perfect shade of United Nations blue. A procession of military officers and policeman with insignia from Peru and Sri Lanka to Canada and Ghana walked around a metal detector on their way out. I stepped outside and opened a tin of sardines, letting the sunflower oil drain into the earth. It was already dark. Where was Huub?

Half an hour later, a former Gurkha commander from the Indian army took pity on me and drove me to another compound, where green tents stood in rows as in an army camp. A large flat-screen television broadcast BBC World across a dining area where a mixed bunch of foreigners and Sudanese were eating. We had made it just in time for the buffet. I heaped my plate with salad, potatoes, and meat, filling a bowl with chocolate cake and custard, wondering what had become of Thiop.

The compound had at least 50 tents, each named after towns across Africa, but somehow I ended up in the one called Nimule. There was even electric light and a fan, which I'd not seen since I'd left Gulu. I plugged in my laptop and began to download my photos of Kony's former homes.

The pictures hardly did his camps justice. I had taken them from the back of the pickup as we sped past before the break-down; Lieutenant Thiop had been reluctant to linger for long. Kony had abandoned his positions on the Juba road some years earlier, but more recently they had been used by Khartoum's army. These latest occupants had left only a few weeks before my trip, burning anything they could not carry.

I wondered if Moses would even recognize his old prisons. Often he had spoken of a place called Jebelein, based on the Arabic for "two mountains." Now it was just a collection of charred stakes and squares of ash-blackened soil. "Life in jail was very difficult," he had said, "this military life." Kony had imprisoned thousands in his colonies, but when I saw them they were nothing but cinders.

Even shooting past them on a pickup, I thought I could catch a hint of the crushing sense of separation his camps must have ingrained. Young abductees were almost completely cut off from the outside, their world shaped by rumor. Kony by contrast was well informed about international affairs, sometimes finding a novel use for his radio. One escapee said he would listen to the news in secret, then miraculously "predict" the headlines of the next bulletin. Recruits must have felt as though they had been whisked onto another planet, where the commanders were kings of their own universe.

Surrounded by their wives, the senior officers lived in relative comfort. Dining on chicken and goat, they wore brand-new uniforms, drove pickup trucks donated by the Sudanese, and held parties, albeit with soft drinks. Rebels watched films on a screen powered by a generator. They all named Chuck Norris's *Missing in Action* movies as favorites, though Sylvester Stallone's *Rambo* series was also popular.

Yet, as in any dictatorship, the commanders lived in fear. Kony was unpredictable, sometimes sounding like a conventional leader: he lectured his officers on the need to set a good example in battle, to avoid delegating key responsibilities and to treat recruits with respect. At other times he would say "no eating of fish for a month," or "leave only the pregnant women and the children, but kill all the others," depending on his mood. Followers had to prove that their loyalty was beyond question, creating a kind of "Emperor's New Clothes" scenario where few dared to challenge the wisdom of Kony's orders.

One day in late 1999 Kony told his rebels he had dreamed of heavy rain pouring into a lake until the build up of waters caused a dam to burst. The dream seemed to contain a message: soon a close ally would betray him. Not long afterward, he ordered his men to shoot one of his most respected deputies, Chief of Operations and Training, Alex Otti-Lagony, the man who had led the Atiak massacre in 1995, alongside Vincent Otti. After the execution, Kony told his men: "You are going to be punished by God, because you have made your hands dirty with blood."

The killing of one of his strongest allies only reinforced the sense of paranoia that gripped his movement, weakening its battlefield strength. Ugandan journalist Billie O'Kadameri, who knew Lagony, told me his execution deprived the rebels of one of their most effective commanders:

"When you are with him, it's like he cannot kill a fly, yet he had a reputation as the deadliest of all the commanders. He would give orders to kill as if he was giving orders to serve food. The moment Kony killed him we knew that Kony was the most dangerous man in the world."

Pampered by the Sudanese military, his word imbued with the power of life or death—even if he seemed oblivious to the pain he was causing his people—I wondered if Kony really believed he would one day lead his "New Acholi" to a promised land in Uganda. Certainly, he had enough faith in the future of his movement to proceed with the education of its children. Back in Gulu, I had met one of the teachers.

After a few false starts, I found Wilson at the primary school on the edge of town where he'd worked since escaping from Kony. He sent one of his pupils to bring us a couple of chairs so we could sit in the shade of the eucalyptus trees. He spoke so softly that the rustle of their leaves almost drowned out his words.

Wilson had been teaching the addition of fractions one morning when rebels burst into the school and abducted his students, taking him along too. "Why do you go to school when it's time for war?" the commander had asked. After they reached the camps in Sudan, a rebel officer called him to a hut where he found his daughter, another captive, waiting for him.

"We just said 'hello'," Wilson said, "but in my heart I felt miserable."

If it hadn't been for his education, Wilson might not have lasted long in Sudan; he was already considered a weakling by his new masters and had fallen ill with worms. But his head for numbers had already proved useful as the rebels roamed northern Uganda, harvesting recruits. He counted the money when they ambushed a bus and murdered the passengers; he read the labels of the drugs they plundered from shops. He even prevented a young guerrilla from flinging away a tube with a red label—antiseptic cream—having mistaken it for the glue used to repair tires for bicycles, which were banned by Kony. Even the commander who abducted him called him *lapwony*—teacher—and one day Kony overhead the greeting.

"So we have a teacher?" Kony said, turning to Wilson. "We may end up staying here for a long time and our children won't learn anything. You will be our teacher."

Wilson founded Kony's first kindergarten, teaching 30 youngsters belonging to the senior commanders. Half of them were Kony's children. Choruses of "Bounce the ball, bounce the ball, bounce the ball high" and "She walks on her toes, she walks on her toes, where she is going, nobody knows," sometimes followed by a rendition of "Twinkle Twinkle Little Star" would drift across from the hut that served as a classroom. Pleased with his children's progress, Kony ordered his fighters to abduct more teachers.

When the rebels netted a headmaster, the school expanded to primary level, and so they ransacked schools for pens, notebooks, and Oxford English textbooks. Wilson was allowed to listen to the radio for the dates of the Ugandan school term, so they could mirror the timetable. The school soon grew to accommodate 60 pupils.

"Eventually, even the commanders who had wanted to kill me became friendly," Wilson said. "Their young ones came back from school talking English, saying 'Good morning' and 'How are you?'"

Kony rewarded Wilson with a wife, but his good work did not exempt him from forced labor in the fields. Once he was given 50 strokes for neglecting to hoe a corner of Kony's personal plot.

"They thought I was trying to rebuke them because I was a teacher, that I was a big-headed person," he said. "They hate learned people. You just had to say 'Thank you, thank you,' but should you hesitate in any way, they could kill you. Life was very hard at that time, all the commanders fixed their eyes on me."

The school thrived for a while, but Wilson decided he would prefer to die trying to escape than waste any more years in Sudan. He ran from the camp one night and made it to Juba, eventually reaching home. Some time later, his daughter also returned.

Wilson was relieved to be back, but he was not entirely satisfied with the way things had turned out. His daughter had decided to marry the commander she had lived with in the bush when he too returned, and he was not Wilson's first choice of son-in-law. To make matters worse, Wilson had just missed out on a job in a new school for former abductees funded by the Belgian government. The secretary had given him the wrong form, and now the deadline had passed so it was too late to apply. I muttered my sympathy and he nodded, then walked away clutching his battered satchel.

I only stayed one night in the tent, which was just as well; at $60 it had cost about ten times the fare for my entire journey from Gulu to Juba. Huub picked me up the next morning and took me to his house near the old cholera hospital. Goats wandered around an abandoned truck in the yard that was riddled with bullet holes. A discarded safe lay nearby, supposedly lugged across the border by Ugandan soldiers as they fled one of the upheavals in their homeland many years before. Like most of the town, the house had electricity extremely rarely. In the evenings, we chatted by candlelight. In the mornings, we took turns washing using a bucket of cold water and a tin cup.

Celebrations to mark the anniversary of the start of the SPLA's uprising were due to begin in a few days' time, and Huub suggested that this might be a good occasion to locate the officials who had met Vincent Otti. One name in particular kept surfacing—Riek Machar. A former guerrilla leader with a PhD from Bradford University in strategic planning in industry using vector space methods, Riek was now vice president of the new southern government. His marriage to British aid worker Emma McCune during his bush days was about to be chronicled in a film based on a book called *Emma's War* by journalist Deborah Scroggins. Nicole Kidman was supposed to be playing McCune, who had died in a car crash in Nairobi in 1993. I had no idea what Riek made of the idea of a movie about his love life, but I hoped he would connect me to Kony.

First, I needed cash. In Nimule people use Uganda shillings, but Juba runs on Sudanese dinars. I left the house and walked to the dirt road that cuts through town. I had to look twice when a minibus with Ugandan plates rolled past, exactly the same kind as in Kampala. Ever since the Sudan peace deal was signed in early 2005, Ugandans have been flooding into Juba to make their fortune. All I needed to do was find one who would change some dollars.

I jumped onto one of the buses and we juddered up the rutted track that serves as a high street, passing a sign with red stenciled letters that read "ARMED CONFLICT IS HEALTH RISK." I kept an eye out for the pizza parlor I had heard about, but instead I saw young boys sitting in the shade selling petrol in Coke bottles.

We passed the abandoned campus of Juba University and a spanking new sign pointing down a lane toward the "New Tokyo Internet Café," which was surrounded by more mud huts. Then I saw the corrugated-iron stalls of the Custom Market, the place where the Arab world collides with East Africa.

The bus stopped near a shop where a trader in white robes sipped a glass of sugary tea, an electric fan battling with the heat. Tins of condensed milk, boxes of biscuits and Foster Clark's mango juice powder formed a wall behind him, while the scent of sweet incense wafted from some unseen source. Around the corner, Ugandan traders unloaded green bunches of *matooke* from a truck, while porters heaved crates of Nile Special and Bell lager into a shed. Traders from Khartoum to Kampala were competing for a piece of the action now that peace had ended Juba's isolation. Those that did not come by truck came by bike. Aloro was one of them.

He sat with a group of other young Ugandan men on a row of chairs outside the Arab's shop. They wore the skewed baseball caps and string vests of hip-hop stars, slapping wads of cash into their palms as if to complete the look. Keying the exchange rate into a calculator, Aloro explained how he had loaded his bike with four crates of beer at the Ugandan border and cycled all the way to Juba, sleeping by the roadside at night. He had sold the bottles for a huge mark-up and then become a money changer, never looking back. I handed him a couple of hundred-dollar bills and he gave me a wedge of dinars and a grin.

When I first set out to find Kony, I never imagined I would spend quite so much time listening to speeches. It was 16 May 2006, the 23rd anniversary of the day in 1983 when the southern rebels started their war against the government in Khartoum. As I sat surrounded by uniformed soldiers, wilting on my plastic chair, it was like being back at Army Day in Uganda where Museveni had paraded Kony's boy soldiers. The big difference was that in Juba the man who dominated the occasion was dead.

With his domed head, whitish beard, and penetrating eyes, John Garang stared out from a framed photograph propped up in front of the empty lectern. His remains lay interred just a few steps behind the podium. Purple and red plastic blossoms lay strewn over the grave, while a strand of tinsel looped its way around a wooden cross. It looked more like a shrine than a tomb.

This should have been Garang's day. After leading the SPLA's long struggle against the Sudanese government, he had signed the peace agreement to end the war. Millions turned out when he came to Khartoum to be sworn in as first vice president of Sudan in July 2005, part of the deal's complex formula for sharing wealth and power between north and south more fairly. Three weeks after taking office, however, the helicopter ferrying him home from Uganda ran into bad weather.

Rumors began to filter out of Kampala that something had gone wrong. A few hours later, Sudanese state television broadcast a report assuring the population that Garang's helicopter had landed safely. In reality, the wreckage of the fuselage was strewn over a hilltop, along with the bodies of passengers and crew. There were no survivors.

Riots convulsed Khartoum as southerners confined to shanties on the fringes of the city attacked shops owned by Arabs, certain the government had assassinated their hero. Some northerners formed vigilante groups in response. More than 100 people were killed in three days of clashes before security forces restored order. Disturbances also broke out in Juba—I saw the gutted remains of buildings that had been torched by the mobs.

Had he not been a teetotaller, Kony would no doubt have opened a bottle of something and toasted his old foe's demise. Garang had been en route from Museveni's cattle ranch at Rwakitura, scene of many of the Ugandan president's most important meetings. I had visited once. The house was modest by presidential standards, and soldiers bivouacked near a green helicopter gave it a military flavor reminiscent of Museveni's guerrilla days. The two men had agreed to launch a fresh offensive against the Lord's Resistance Army, hoping a joint operation would succeed where Operation Iron Fist had failed. Kampala's diplomatic circles buzzed with talk that a US intelligence official had attended the planning session. When the meeting was over, Museveni lent his old friend a helicopter to fly him home.

Just as Kony seemed about to face a more deadly onslaught than anything he had survived in the past, fate handed him a way out. Garang's death gave southern leaders a much more pressing issue to tackle than any fugitive Ugandan rebel.

Garang had been a talisman; when he died people wondered whether the peace deal he had forged would crack, and they feared a repeat of the infighting that had torn the SPLA apart in the past. To widespread relief, Garang's deputy and SPLA chief-of-staff emerged to take his place. Salva Kiir was the man we were waiting for now.

Having secured a seat in the VIP pavilion, I noticed a man named Samson Kwaje sitting in the front row. In his gray suit he looked just as he had during his days as the SPLA's spokesman in Nairobi when Garang was still a guerrilla. His messengers always seemed to deliver press releases to the Reuters office just as I was about to lock up, necessitating even later nights than usual. I maneuvered my way through the chairs to shake his hand. Now no longer spokesman, but information minister of the southern government, he promised to introduce me to Riek after the ceremony.

A pickup crammed with soldiers drew up, followed by a four-by-four. Salva stepped out of the car and walked toward the podium. Wearing a thick black beard and matching black broad-brimmed hat and suit, with a ring glinting on his middle finger, he reminded me ever so slightly of a sheriff in a Western. He began with a eulogy to the man who stared out of the portrait in front of him and I wondered if I would stay awake. Then I almost fell out of my chair.

Kony had been captured—on film.

Salva announced that his representatives had not only met Vincent Otti, but Kony himself. He had shown a video of the encounter to Museveni, who had given his blessing to a new attempt at talks. Kony had been filmed saying he was committed to ending the war in his homeland. If he did not, Salva said, the SPLA would drive him from Sudan. The audience broke into applause. In a few sentences, Salva had turned a distant hope of peace in northern Uganda into a possibility.

Samson led me through the crush toward Riek. Soldiers and spectators danced in conga lines past an antiquated tank, cheering and kicking up dust. Being a bulky man who seemed to wear a perpetual grin, Riek was a hard man to miss, but the press of bodies was too dense. I saw his head bob above the crowd, then disappear. When I caught another glimpse he was ducking into a white car, and a moment later he was gone.

Riek's office lay in a complex of ministries near the parade ground that accommodated Garang's grave. The buildings were concrete blocks built by Yugoslav engineers in the mid-1970s, and they echoed with sawing and hammering as the new government made itself at home. Mostly you could just wander into rooms where a receptionist sat behind a desk telling visitors that the minister was out. In Riek's case, I could not get past the gate.

A guard told me to fill in a slip, but when I came back the next morning I was not on the list of appointments. UN officials, European Union envoys, Asian investors, and an American human rights researcher had taken priority. I came back again the next day and was told Riek had left for Khartoum. Nobody knew for how long.

I was beginning to wonder whether tracking him down would be worth it. Kony's video seemed to be a sign of progress toward talks, but Juba was sapping my enthusiasm for the chase. Lacking the hundred dollars I would need to hire a car for the day, I found myself trudging through the crushing heat from one missed appointment to another. Soon I resorted to hitching rides, flagging down a car from Congo, a truck from Uganda, and a sewage wagon from Sudan. But the one lift I really wanted was to Khartoum.

I had heard numerous reports of sightings of Kony in the city over the years, whether in the military sports complex, the officer's club, or just walking the sandy streets. I was keen to see his adopted city first hand, but I also wanted to tease out more of his story. Kony's association with the Sudanese government had embroiled him in a much bigger war than the conflict in northern Uganda. A few months after hijacked jetliners slammed into New York's Twin Towers on 11 September 2001, the United States branded Kony an official enemy as it sorted the world into friend and foe. I wanted to know how the spirit medium from Odek had earned the ire of President George W. Bush. Most of all, I wanted to make the journey to Khartoum for free.

Filling in a few forms, I applied for a place as a journalist on the plane that ferried UN staff between Juba and Khartoum. I presented myself at Juba's small airport with my paperwork in hand, only to find my name had been left off the manifest. A British nun lingered by the counter, trying to catch the attention of the officer checking in the passengers. I thought for a moment she had managed to get the last place, until I saw the man scrawl my name at the end of the list in ballpoint pen. I found a seat near a passenger reading a book about aid workers called *Emergency Sex.*

The plane followed the White Nile north, the river braiding into channels then untangling itself like a thing alive. The Reverend Albert B. Lloyd spent six days braving the mosquitoes, marshy odors, and endless weeds of the enormous Sudd swamp on the steamer *Dal*, describing it as "the most desolate spot on earth." The flight would only take a few hours, leapfrogging the "dead sea of green" that had so maddened the missionary.

The land below soon turned gray as ash. Wadis coiled over the plain like dropped spaghetti. Villages appeared on the banks of the pewter-colored Nile, minarets gleaming through the haze. The pilot announced that we had arrived in the middle of a sandstorm. A terracotta mist obscured the grid of streets emerging from the desert, but I felt a wave of satisfaction as the plane began to descend. I had made it, all the way from Kampala to Khartoum, where the White and Blue Niles merged. I didn't know it then, but I was going in precisely the wrong direction.

9. MR. DUSTY

Abou-Shouk camp in Darfur

Robed men clustered around a counter, waving sheaves of paper in a vain effort to catch the eye of officials sitting behind glass panes. I waited in line before a teenage boy with a moustache led me through to a room occupied by a large man in a blue uniform. He flicked through my passport.

"You have entered the country illegally," he said. "This is out of my hands."

He exhaled deeply, jammed his beret on his head and beckoned me to follow. My heart sank as we walked along a corridor and climbed a flight of steps to another office. His superior sat behind a desk wearing a navy headscarf to match her uniform. Gold rings gleamed on fingers patterned with henna tattoos. She scrawled something on my form in red cursive script.

"You go to the immigration police," the policeman translated. "You must make a statement about how you got here, then you come back and we will give you an exit stamp to go back to Uganda."

After I'd waited for two days on the cream-colored plastic chairs of the Aliens Control Department in Khartoum, the prospect of being sent back to Kampala did not seem quite so awful. Somehow I had failed to get a stamp in my passport between Nimule and the capital, and sorting out this omission seemed like it might take longer than the journey itself. I was tempted to head straight back to Juba, but I was loath to leave before I'd met the one man who might tell me something about Kony's ill-starred alliance with Sudan's rulers.

His name was Hassan al-Turabi, and he was renowned as one of the most influential Islamic scholars of his generation. With a career in Sudanese politics spanning decades, Turabi was credited with revolutionizing theories of Islamic government, although his attempt to impose his ideal in Sudan quickly became mired in tyranny and seemingly endless civil war. Kony's relationship with Sudan began in the years when Turabi was still in the ascendant, ultimately sucking the Ugandan guerrilla into a much wider conflict—the United States' "war on terror." I was hoping the philosopher who did so much to shape Sudan's destiny could help me unravel Kony's marriage of convenience with Khartoum.

The breakthrough with immigration came on the fourth day. The policeman took another look at my papers, stamped my passport and offered me breakfast, gesturing to a tray laden with freshly baked rolls and dishes of sliced carrots, chopped onions, and appetizing sauces. I thanked him, but I could not bear the thought of spending another minute in the building. "Don't mention it," the policeman said, and went back to his meal. As I walked back past the cream-colored seats, my phone rang. My luck had turned—Turabi would see me right away.

I took a taxi down a street running parallel to the Blue Nile. Flowing fast and brown, the river merged with its White twin a little further downstream. The city center was still laid out in the Union Jack pattern that had so fascinated Lloyd; it had been designed by British officers to enable a small unit of artillery to defend the whole town. He had watched Englishmen play cricket and polo before taking tea with a certain Lady Wingate, remarking on the pleasures of the city's gardens after the perils of the bush. I was more worried about the traffic.

More men in turbans weaved among yellow taxis as they crossed between the colonnaded shop fronts, the cloth of their white robes dazzling in the sun. A young waterseller clinked tin mugs to attract customers, and I caught sight of the minarets of the Kabir mosque in the central square. Further away, construction had begun on a tower that resembled a stripy blue Easter egg. Sudan was pumping more and more oil, luring millions of dollars of investment into the capital despite the conflict consuming the Darfur region in the west.

Turabi occupied the kind of flat-roofed villa in the Manshia district typically owned by Khartoum's wealthier inhabitants. Palm leaves drooped over a high wall, and an aide greeted me at the entrance, leading me to a room that was sparsely but expensively furnished. I took a seat and scribbled ideas for questions in my notebook, suddenly feeling a little nervous. A Sudanese student I had met some years before had always referred to Turabi as "Mr. Dusty." He spoke of him with a mixture of loathing and terror, though I could never work out the nickname. Only years later did I learn that *turab* is Arabic for "dust."

Turabi was seen as the mastermind behind the 1989 coup that brought the current government to power, with a mission to turn Sudan into an Islamic state before exporting the model all over Africa. In addition, he had been tremendously influential in the years when Sudan's government adopted Kony and his Lord's Resistance Army. Since then, Turabi's fortunes had proved mixed; he had fallen out with the president and spent time under house arrest. Now that he was in opposition, I wondered if he might be a little more frank about the regime's associations with Kony.

Several Acholi talked about Turabi and Kony as if the pair had been friends, though it was hard to imagine a greater contrast than that between the wandering warlord and a lawyer with a doctorate from the Sorbonne, who was equally at home discussing the finer points of Islamic political theory as he was American politics. A Sudanese friend summed him up with a warning: "Your problem won't be getting Turabi to talk, it will be getting him to shut up."

The scholar appeared in a robe just a shade paler than peach, and wore a snow-white headdress and neatly trimmed beard. I immediately felt scruffy in my shirt and jeans. His skin was much more youthful than his 74 years, and his smile infectious. He spoke with an accent at once exotic and aristocratic, and he used the word "actually" a lot. Chuckling from time to time, he seemed privy to some cosmic joke that the rest of humanity could not possibly understand. In an instant I realized he would run rings around me.

Turabi began by denying that he had ever even met Kony. He had not been involved in security matters, he said, and in any case, it was only natural that the Sudanese government had sought allies to fight Museveni, who was backing Garang's SPLA rebels. I knew I sounded naïve even as I said it, but I wanted to know if Sudan's government felt in any way responsible for the suffering their adopted Ugandan had caused.

"People in Europe think that these girls are kidnapped and so on and so forth," Turabi said. "You know, in this part of the world, actually, these are just females; people don't *kidnap* them, they take them as wives. It's almost a customary thing in tribal areas, you can go and . . ." he chuckled, ". . . grab a girl and take her and she's your wife and then later on you're discovered and you send some cows and that settles it. It's not a crime, kidnapping and so forth."

"But at the same time," I said, "the LRA did kidnap a lot of very young people to turn them into soldiers and wives for their commanders."

"Yes, soldiers, because even Museveni himself, this was his theory," Turabi said, "and John Garang's. Both of them from the beginning, they said the best thing is to recruit young people," he chuckled again. "Kidnap and recruit young people—because if you recruit old people, they'll have their own memories and their own associations, you can't trust them that much."

"So this tactic wasn't an original tactic?"

"John Garang did the same thing, by the way, Museveni did the same thing, actually. They think it's a good idea, because the children are blank, the blackboard is yours, you can write whatever you like on it, actually."

"That's a pretty cynical way of looking at it, isn't it?"

"It's not cynical, this is the state of Africa. Museveni did it first!"

Turabi described how he had watched the Ugandan president's young fighters marching at an Independence Day parade shortly after Museveni took power. "I told him 'These people are too young!' None of them was as tall as the gun and the bayonet, because, you know, in a parade, you have to carry the bayonet as well. The commander in chief," Turabi chuckled, "he was about 27 or thereabouts, definitely below 30."

"One might argue that two wrongs don't make a right . . ."

"What is right, what is wrong? I mean, values, where do they come from? These are your values, and my values as well, actually. Locally, of course, custom was the value, actually."

"You don't think the people in the army who were essentially supplying the LRA and giving them the remit to go and abduct thousands of young people . . ."

Turabi cut in: "The army probably supported them simply to provide them with a buffer to fight against John Garang, who was supported by the Ugandans."

"I can see the military logic," I said, "but there's a question about the tactics. If you've got a group of allies who are going off and abducting children to turn them into soldiers, isn't it wrong to support those people?"

"Do armies ever care about these things?" Turabi asked.

"I'm asking you," I replied.

"Have you read about armies in the world? Even in Europe, actually, there was the First World War, Second World War, actually. What about the atomic bomb?" Turabi chuckled. "It's the worst crime humanity has ever known, actually, but people never say that. Look at German towns, actually."

I found myself nodding in spite of myself. "Dresden?" I offered.

"Completely!" he said. "All military people in the world do bad things."

He recalled how US troops used earthmoving equipment to attack trenches occupied by Iraqi forces during the liberation of Kuwait.

"What happened in the Gulf War? It's a desert, you have to have tunnels. The Americans marched on them, then they brought in bulldozers and just buried them, tens of thousands of soldiers, and nobody said a word. Armies are awful."

He repeated the phrase with an almost melancholy tone: "Armies are awful."

One of Turabi's aides brought a glass of freshly squeezed orange juice and a tiny cup of bitter black coffee. I realized that if I had come to find some hint of contrition for the Sudanese government's support of Kony, I was looking in the wrong place.

Turabi's conscience was clear. I asked if I could take a picture. He nodded, and I snapped away.

"People will think you have a portrait of a terrorist," he said, and gave another one of his chuckles.

Following Kony's fortunes from reports that filtered into the Nairobi newsroom, it was easy to assume that the war was driven mainly by the prophetic voices in his head. Viewed from Khartoum, the picture looked rather different. The more I talked to people in Sudan, the more I began to realize that Kony was a bit player in a much bigger drama. The conflict had divided Africa, put the United States on a collision course with Khartoum, and embroiled characters from Osama bin Laden to Monica Lewinsky. Kony was cast very much in a non-speaking role.

The origins of the rebels' rise and fall in Sudan can be traced back to a broadcast on Radio Omdurman on the night of Friday 30 June 1989. An ex-paratrooper named Brigadier-General Omar Hassan Ahmed al-Bashir announced that a group of officers had overthrown the government, naming himself as the new leader. Martial music played on the radio, tanks took up positions around the presidential palace, and soldiers barricaded bridges over the Blue and White Niles. After years of infiltrating the government and military with his Islamist supporters, Turabi's hour had come.

Working as the hidden power behind the new administration, Turabi orchestrated a project to transform Sudan into an Islamic state. The government declared "jihad" against its enemies in the south, and began to look for allies. Even before the coup, the Sudanese army had enlisted the help of Arab Baggara militia to loot, rape, and take slaves in rebel areas. Kony might have been a foreigner, but he too fitted the bill (his commitment to the biblical Ten Commandments aside). The government was already backing a militia, known as the Equatoria Defense Force (EDF), that counted many Sudanese Acholi in its ranks. It was a small step to bring Kony on board, particularly after the collapse of Betty Bigombe's peace initiative in early 1994. The Lord's Resistance Army played a vital role in defending the southern approach to Juba and causing havoc in Uganda in retaliation for Museveni's support for the SPLA. It seemed that Kony's hour had also come.

Now on Khartoum's payroll, Kony joined a list featuring some of the most notorious international terrorists. The British academic Alex de Waal describes in his book *Islamism and its Enemies in the Horn of Africa* how Turabi attempted to turn Khartoum into a global center for militant Islam by inviting revolutionaries from Palestine to Chechnya to set up shop in the capital. Osama bin Laden lived there in the early 1990s, running construction and agricultural schemes and expanding his al-Qaeda network. A host of terrorists including Ilich Ramírez Sánchez, alias "Carlos the Jackal," helped run training camps. Turabi's insistence on supporting Saddam Hussein during the 1991 Gulf War set the tone for the regime—it was rapidly becoming a pariah.

Buoyed by initial successes on the battlefield against the SPLA, the leaders in Khartoum sought to spread Islamic revolutions throughout neighboring countries. Sudan's security forces backed armed opposition groups with Islamist leanings in Ethiopia, Eritrea, and Uganda, including the Allied Democratic Forces that fought in the Ruwenzori Mountains in the west and staged bombings in Kampala. The Ugandan army insisted the group had received training from al-Qaeda. The Sudanese government's alliance with Kony's Lord's Resistance Army was purely opportunistic, but even his fighters acquired a smattering of Islam. I remembered Moses shouting *"Allah Akhbar!"* when the rebels knocked out the tank at Achol-Pii, and how Kony had ordered people to be killed for raising pigs.

Quite apart from the fact that they were backing rebels in the region, high-ranking Sudanese officials were themselves accused of sponsoring terrorist attacks. Investigations into the bombing of the World Trade Center in 1993 led to Khartoum, and Washington declared Sudan a "state sponsor of terror." Sudanese officials helped orchestrate a failed attempt to assassinate the Egyptian president Hosni Mubarak in Ethiopia in 1995. The UN imposed sanctions.

Perhaps not surprisingly, the Sudanese government's activities rapidly earned it the enmity of its neighbors. Alex de Waal writes that by late 1996 an "undeclared regional war" had broken out between Sudan and a short-lived alliance of Uganda, Rwanda, Ethiopia, and Eritrea. By this time, Kony was just one counter in a battle entangling a myriad militias, rebel groups, and armies, all divided roughly along pro- and anti-Khartoum lines. Uganda played a pivotal role, sending troops into Sudan to fight the Sudanese army alongside the SPLA, with support from Ethiopia and Eritrea. Some people even argued that Museveni was happy for the war in northern Uganda to continue because it served as a smokescreen for the weapons and troops being shipped into the Sudan border region. Behind the scenes, the United States was the biggest player of all. Washington financed its allies in the so-called "frontline states" in their efforts to contain Khartoum, with Museveni center stage. During a visit to Kampala, US Secretary of State Madeleine Albright called him a "beacon of hope," prompting one frustrated opposition politician to say "She's a witch."

I thought back to the picture I had seen at the border post at Nimule of Museveni shaking hands with Clinton. You could still order a Clinton Pizza in the Speke Hotel in Kampala in commemoration of his visit in March 1998. Museveni was not only a key bulwark against Sudan, but also occupied an important strategic position. A French minister once dubbed Uganda America's "aircraft carrier" in Africa—US forces used Entebbe airport as a base for their "Operation Support Hope" mission to help Rwandan refugees who fled to Congo after the 1994 genocide. American troops trained Ugandan counterparts.

Washington even dispensed some public praise for Museveni's conduct of the war in the north. The then Assistant Secretary of State for African Affairs Susan Rice told Congress in July 1998 that she believed the Ugandan government was trying to respect the human rights of noncombatants and deal as "humanely as possible" with abductees in the rebel ranks, though she said more had to be done on those fronts. Looking back, I wondered if she might not have been a tad harder on the army, who tended to list captured rebels as "rescued children" while the abducted youngsters they sometimes shot were added to the body count as "terrorists." Recognizing the difficulties Uganda faced in defeating the rebels, Rice also said the United States was encouraging efforts to talk. But she added the caveat: "It is, frankly, difficult to imagine a negotiated settlement with a group like the LRA." Fairly or otherwise, her words were taken by some Acholi as evidence that America was happy to endorse Museveni's preference for using force to crush Kony, however futile.

Rice also said the United States would put pressure on Khartoum to end support for the rebels, echoing a pledge made by Hillary Clinton during a speech at Makerere University in Kampala four months earlier. "The LRA call themselves soldiers," Clinton had said, "but they are cowards, for only cowards would hide behind children in battle." Museveni's past use of child soldiers was conveniently ignored.

The United States' relations with Sudan reached a nadir in 1998, when suspected members of al-Qaeda blew up American embassies in Kenya and Tanzania. President Clinton retaliated by firing cruise missiles at suspected al-Qaeda training camps in Afghanistan and flattening the al-Shifa pharmaceuticals factory in Khartoum, claiming it was owned by Osama bin Laden and used to manufacture ingredients for VX nerve gas. In an interview with Reuters, Turabi accused Clinton of destroying the plant to provide a distraction from the Monica Lewinsky sex scandal. Unable to strike back with missiles, the government organized marches where protesters shouted "Down, Down USA!" Sudanese television flashed up pictures of Clinton with crudely drawn vampire fangs.

By the late 1990s Sudan's international isolation was beginning to take its toll. The regional alliance opposing Khartoum collapsed in 1998 when Ethiopia and Eritrea went to war, but the regime had already been shaken by the coalition that had gathered against it. Sanctions were complicating efforts to exploit oil, a source of wealth for the Khartoum elite. A simmering power struggle between Turabi and Bashir burst out into the open when Bashir stripped the former of his powerful position as speaker of parliament, then had him arrested. Sudan began trying to patch things up with neighboring leaders, including Museveni. Kony was looking more and more like damaged goods.

The 9/11 attacks turned the Ugandan rebel into even more of a liability. I was in the Nairobi newsroom shortly afterward when the US State Department issued a "terrorist exclusion" list of groups in Africa. I scanned the line-up: Rwandan rebels blamed for the genocide, the limb-chopping Revolutionary United Front in Sierra Leone, and Kony's Lord's Resistance Army. Given the time he had spent in Khartoum, and his status as an enemy of

Uganda—one of America's closest allies in the region—it was no surprise he had been blacklisted.

The "terrorist" tag did not go unnoticed in Sudan, whose leaders became increasingly anxious to clean their tainted image. Even before 11 September 2001, the Sudanese intelligence agencies had begun to share files on their old friends in the world of Islamic militancy with their new friends in the CIA. Six months after the Twin Towers fell, Sudan authorized Operation Iron Fist. As Father Carlos put it to me once: "Sudan was anxious to do something to prove they were not supporting terrorist groups while Uganda thought 'Let's go for the final solution.'"

But Sudan's government never cut off all its support for Kony, and the Ugandans would often protest that the Sudanese were allowing him to shelter behind a "red line" in the south that they themselves were banned from crossing. A Ugandan intelligence chief who attended liaison meetings between the two armies described how the Sudanese officers would take tea, then discreetly disappear for a glass of whisky; he always suspected them of tipping off Kony before the Ugandan forces launched their attacks.

Kony's old friends in Khartoum had not forsaken him completely, but he was in a far more precarious position than during his zenith as king of those camps I had seen on the road to Juba. His Faustian pact with Khartoum had made him vulnerable to events half a world away in Washington.

While President Clinton had sought to contain Sudan's Islamist influence in the region, President George W. Bush took a much more proactive stance in seeking to end Khartoum's war with the SPLA. Compelled partly by the religious right, human rights groups, and African-American lobbyists who wanted an end to what they saw as Sudan's persecution of black, southern Christians, Bush brought unprecedented pressure on both sides to come to an agreement. The peace deal signed in Kenya in early 2005 declared that all foreign forces had to leave. Now that the SPLA were the official rulers of the south, they wanted both Kony and the Ugandan army out.

For all his comebacks in the past, it was tempting to conclude that Kony had been cornered in his new home in Garamba National Park. He might have eluded the Iron Fist, but the offensive had cost him more of his commanders over the past few years than he had lost in the entire course of his rebellion. In addition, Museveni had referred the rebels to the International Criminal Court in the Hague in December 2003, so Kony and his key commanders were wanted men. Branded an enemy in the "war on terror" and reviled around the world, Kony appeared to be very short of friends. It looked more and more as though the rebel leader, never more than a pawn to Khartoum, might finally be sacrificed.

But one man was willing to offer Kony a way out. Riek Machar was having more success coaxing him from the shadows than many had thought possible. In late May 2006, Africa's most-wanted man made it onto CNN.

The cameraman's shooting style reminded me of an amateur horror film, but the images were clear enough. Riek was seated on a chair in a forest flanked by soldiers and officials. Jerking back and forth around the clearing, the camera picked out figures standing among the trees. Bright sunlight turned the men into silhouettes, but you could clearly make out the spiky outlines of their dreadlocks.

The view panned back to Riek. He reached down into a leather briefcase next to his chair and fished out two thick wads of dollars tied with rubber bands.

"I wanted to solve problems," he said. "Besides the food I brought, my president asked me to deliver this to you. It's also food, for you to buy food. No arms."

He gave one of his winning grins as he waved the stack of notes. "No ammunition," he said. "Food."

He put the cash into a brown envelope.

"No ammunition," he said again. "No arms. He says I must deliver this to you to buy food, $20,000."

Riek handed the envelope to the man sitting opposite him, who wore green Wellington boots, smartly pressed olive fatigues and a blue beret, with a lanyard looped under his arm. He had a thin moustache and a puzzled expression, and he must have been in his early forties. I couldn't see a gun, but instead he clutched a brown, bound diary with a blue ballpoint pen tucked inside. He gave the faintest of smiles as he took the money and passed it to an older-looking officer sitting on his left, who barely looked at it before handing it to an even more elderly comrade.

The camera stayed steady as Riek bade the visitors farewell.

"Thank you very much," Riek said to the man in the blue beret, shaking his hand. "Nice meeting you, Joseph."

A Reuters video journalist had managed to obtain a copy of the film through a contact in the Ugandan army. A producer edited the pictures in Nairobi, then transmitted them to the Reuters television bureau in London. Before long, the footage of Joseph Kony accepting a brown envelope stuffed with cash was playing on television screens all over the world.

Newspapers printed fuzzy images of Kony extracted from the tape. There was no more "Born to be Wild" T-shirt, no more dreadlocks, just a blue beret, Wellingtons, and a ledger. He looked smart if bewildered, though relieved to take the money.

Not everyone was impressed at the idea of handing $20,000 to the International Criminal Court's number-one suspect, least of all the court itself. The chief prosecutor, an Argentinean human rights lawyer called Luis Moreno-Ocampo, reiterated that Sudan, as well as Congo and Uganda, 'had a duty to arrest the accused. Riek later said that he could not have apprehended Kony even if he'd wanted to.

I went to an internet café in Khartoum and read the Reuters story based on the video. "I am not a terrorist," Kony had said. "I want peace."

The fact that the video had surfaced should have warned me that things were moving faster than I realized, but I felt in no great rush to leave Khartoum just yet. Besides, I had just been commissioned to write a story for the *Times* that would improve my finances, provided I could take a day trip to Darfur.

Ambassadors from five continents filed into a room at the Khartoum Hilton and took their places for the news conference. Britain, the United States, France, China, and Russia formed the nucleus of the group, and they were joined by representatives from countries such as Argentina, Slovakia, and Tanzania. Fifteen in all, they had come to talk about the slaughter in Darfur.

Under normal circumstances they would be meeting in a chamber in the United Nations skyscraper overlooking the East River in New York. But things were not getting any better in Darfur, so the Security Council had decided to meet Sudan's president in person. Their visit to Khartoum was just one stopover in a crisis roadshow that was to take in south Sudan, Ethiopia, Chad, and Congo's capital, Kinshasa. A pack of correspondents from the United States had tagged along for the whole trip; I just wanted to hitch a lift for part of the way.

When the venerable British diplomat chairing the group opened the floor for questions, it was not surprising that Kony barely merited a mention. Everyone wanted to know about their plan for Darfur. For more than two years, coverage of the conflict in western Sudan had dominated news from Africa. The Sudanese government had repeated its trusted technique from the civil war in the south by arming militias to attack villages, and supporting them with helicopter gunships and Antonov bombers. In Darfur, they called the militias Janjaweed, the "Devils on Horseback." I had heard that several of Kony's commanders had been spotted in the region, presumably passing on tips.

Northern Uganda had never created anything like as much furor, even though the numbers of civilians uprooted from their homes was comparable. The sheer brutality of the Sudanese government's response in Darfur, and the murder of many thousands of its own people, eclipsed the slow-motion suffering in the camps around Gulu. And Museveni was an ally of the Western powers, Sudan was not.

As I jotted down notes from the briefing, I could not avoid a prickly sensation that I was getting distracted from my mission to meet Kony. But I had been asked by the *Times* to accompany the ambassadors on their quick touchdown in Darfur, and it would only take a day. The press conference had also been an excuse to visit the Hilton, a brown lump of a building overlooking the meeting point of the White and Blue Niles. A few years earlier, some rather different visitors had turned up in the lobby on a peace mission of their own.

In July 1999, Kony's mother, father, and brother had flown to Khartoum to try to convince their son to come home. The Carter Center in America, named after its founder, former president Jimmy Carter, had attempted to organize a reunion to encourage

Kony to open negotiations. The meeting never happened, but the parents did manage to speak to their son in southern Sudan by telephone from a room in the hotel. It was the first time they had talked in more than ten years, and all Nora could do was plead with Kony to return.

I never managed to meet Nora during my time in Uganda, but an Associated Press journalist who interviewed her later reported that Kony was the fifth of her twelve children. Only four were still alive.

Sitting in the Sunset Lounge, I felt almost sorry for the elderly couple as I pictured them wandering around the building with its dated decor and globe-shaped lamps. It was a world away from their home in Odek. The menu offered a Hilton Pizza "with a bit of everything and a lot of love," while a sign asked patrons to refrain from smoking cigars in the buffet area. I wondered if Kony himself had ever wandered through the reception, remembering something a southern Sudanese journalist had told me a few days before: "Even now you cannot say that Kony is not in Khartoum. How do you know? He's not living in foxholes; he's traveling like any president in the world."

I waited in Khartoum while the delegation made an afternoon trip down to Juba. When they returned, one of the journalists told me that Kony's representatives had already arrived in the town, though he had not managed to meet them. The rebel delegation was apparently holed up in one of the tented camps, waiting to start talks with the Ugandan government. There were rumors that Vincent Otti might even turn up, and perhaps his boss would not be far behind. My first reaction was to panic.

I called a car and we negotiated our way through the traffic to an airline office, where I shelled out a couple of hundred dollars on a ticket to Juba. I would just have to skip Darfur and let the *Times* down. The woman serving me filled in the flight time on my ticket. The plane would leave at first light.

But as the cab headed back into town, I began to have second thoughts. I was reluctant to disappoint the paper by ditching the Darfur trip, especially as there was no guarantee that Kony would appear in Juba anytime soon. I made a few calls and established that his representatives there were not in fact commanders from the bush, but sympathizers from the Acholi diaspora who had flown in from Britain, the United States, and Kenya. I reckoned that if they had turned up for peace negotiations then they were bound to be around for a while. I decided to go to Darfur the next day as planned, and then fly to Juba as soon as I got back. I would only lose 24 hours. In any case, a friend had invited me round for drinks at her flat that night, and it was a long time since I had been to a party.

A DJ played soul from decks set up on the flat roof, a warm desert wind blowing across the city. Glo-sticks fashioned into luminous orange and blue wristbands shone in the darkness. I had once met a Sudanese man who was given 40 lashes for breaking Sudan's sharia law by drinking *aragi* spirits brewed from dates, though the authorities tended to take a more lenient approach with foreigners. I had heard tales of expats serving beer in teapots to confuse prying eyes, but the aid workers and UN staff who trooped up the stairs had smuggled enough bottles of red wine and gin to get the dance floor going. I chatted to a Sudanese girl in a black dress called Siham, and she gave me her number.

I was still up when the muezzin's dawn cry began to drone across the rooftops. I took a car to the airport and joined the ambassadors on their flight across the desert to a town called El-

Fasher in north Darfur. Sudanese attack helicopters stood on the airport runway with drooping blades, presumably taking a break from strafing villages. We drove in the standard large UN cars to a garden where a chief in a turban served the diplomats tea and assured them everything was fine. I slipped away for an hour to the Abou-Shouk camp on the edge of town, which housed tens of thousands of people who had fled the fighting. Families lived under tarpaulins that flapped in the breeze, the women's shawls blazing blue and pink against the sand. The desert dwellings looked different from the muddy squalor of the camps in northern Uganda, but the sense of waiting was the same.

We returned to the airport and the ambassadors boarded a plane heading west to Chad, to where so many of Darfur's refugees had fled. I took the eastbound plane to Khartoum, double checking with the Ethiopian pilot just to be sure. I had a flight booked for Juba the next morning, and the last thing I wanted was to miss it. But as the plane took off, I wondered whether spending just one more day in Khartoum would make any difference, especially since I could then spend an evening with Siham.

I ended up postponing my flight back to Juba and the next day worked on my Darfur story in a friend's flat. I gave Siham a call, but she said she had plans. I told her I was leaving for Juba the next day, but she was certain she was busy. Feeling a little aggrieved, I called a Norwegian I knew who worked for the UN, and she invited me to join her at an Italian restaurant where she was meeting some people for dinner. The best part was that she knew the owner, guaranteeing a glug of gin in our tonics with no questions asked.

As I walked into the restaurant's garden I caught site of a Dutch man I'd met in Juba who also worked for the UN. He waved me over to his table, but the look on his face told me he had bad news:

"We were trying to call you," he said. "Some journalists have just gone to meet Kony."

10. THE SECOND COMING

Juba

A sandstorm howled through Khartoum that night, though I would not have slept anyway. I rushed to the airport before dawn and found a seat on the first plane heading south. We followed the White Nile upstream until Juba's tin roofs flashed on the plain. I tried to keep calm by playing classical music on my iPod, skipping over Otti's voice when he popped up between Beethoven and Bach.

Standing in the doorway of his house, Huub greeted me with a shrug and a smile. He explained that a group of journalists had left Juba the previous morning to accompany Riek for his latest meeting with Kony. He knew all the details because two of them had been staying with him—a Dutch newspaper correspondent named Koert Lindijer, and his friend Petterik Wiggers, a photographer. By now they would be hundreds of miles away, perhaps already waiting in the clearing.

I paced around the bullet-riddled truck in the yard, trying to work out a way to catch up. Riek's entourage of advisers and bodyguards, together with Kony's representatives from the diaspora and the journalists, had taken a chartered plane from Juba to the small town of Maridi in southern Sudan. From there they would have spent hours driving to a village somewhere in the forest that spanned the border with Congo. All I could do was send Koert a text on his Thuraya, pleading with him to let me know what was happening. I knew him a little from Nairobi, and I had a feeling he would help. I sat down in the yard to watch the goats browsing around the rusting lorry. My Thuraya gave a double beep.

"We are in the clearing," Koert's message read. "It's a nice adventure, but until Kony shows up, it's not a story."

Ashamed as I was to admit it, I desperately hoped he would not appear. I told myself it was perfectly possible that he had sent a deputy to meet Riek while remaining closeted in the forest, in which case I wouldn't have to feel like such a failure. If I had stuck to my plan and rushed back to Juba from Darfur I could have been in the clearing myself, instead of relying on updates by text. It was impossible to stop agonizing over how I had strayed so far off course. In retrospect, the warnings seemed obvious: Salva Kiir's speech announcing the peace initiative; the appearance of Kony in the video; the arrival of his delegates in Juba. I had been blind to the portents. A few hours later, my phone beeped again: "We have met Kony and Otti, heading back tomorrow."

Koert called me the next day with even worse news. Apart from his photographer friend, Koert said a German TV journalist working with a British cameraman had also joined Riek's trip. The pair had been invited into the bush for an audience with Kony, returning the next morning with a tape containing an interview. I called my mother and asked her to record *Newsnight* on the BBC. It seemed like she would see more of Kony than I would, just by watching television in the living room of a house in the London suburbs.

The journalists who shot the interview flew straight back to Nairobi, and then on to London to edit their scoop. Koert had been introduced to Kony, but he had not had a chance to ask him anything. He said Otti had done most of the talking during the meeting, complaining to Riek about the exorbitant prices the locals were charging for goats. Kony had assured Riek that his representatives in Juba would reflect his true wishes when the talks began. Then he disappeared back into the forest. Listening to the story by the light of a kerosene lamp in Huub's living room, I still could not quite believe I had missed my chance.

With my time and money running low, I was growing increasingly exasperated with Juba. It should have been a pleasure to sit by the White Nile in the evening, a bottle of Bell in hand, watching a giant moon rise above the mango trees. Nights spent drinking in the tented camps were rarely boring, spiced with tales of the quirks of life in town: the SPLA soldier who blew himself up with a hand grenade; another who'd been eaten by a crocodile the day before that; the white Zimbabwean who came to build roads after losing everything back home; the French oil executive in search of a stolen oilfield. A cowboy-hatted South African prospector called Fritz even asked if he could borrow my Thuraya to try to find his missing helicopter. But I was indifferent to the drama; everything seemed tainted with failure. I promised myself I would head back to Nairobi as soon as I had made contact with Kony's delegates, just in case another chance to visit the bush unexpectedly presented itself somewhere down the line. Unfortunately, they were proving almost as hard to find as he was.

Kony's people were staying at a compound called the RA International hotel, a gathering of Portakabins not far from the row of crumbling whitewashed shops and mosques that populate Juba's main street. A marquee served as a dining area in the camp, the lingering buffet odor of fried cabbage transported me back to the Acholi Inn. There was a continual low hum of air conditioning, and a constant traffic of four-by-fours. It was perhaps understandable that the man working at reception denied any knowledge of the Lord's Resistance Army.

I watched a queue of Sudanese and foreigners troop into the dining tent for lunch. Contractors and aid workers held out plates for dollops of pasta sauce, but I had no idea what Kony's officers might look like—there were no Wellingtons or dreadlocks. My only consolation was a huge screen that treated diners to either MTV or the build-up to the football World Cup in Germany. One of the Sudanese staff wore a yellow T-shirt that read "World Cup 2006—I support Sudan," the slogan cheerfully defiant despite the fact that the national team, the Desert Hawks, hadn't even qualified for the African Nations Cup in 30 years. I was beginning to lose hope of finding my quarry when Koert called me. Kony's proxies were holding their first press conference.

The irony was that I might have passed one of Kony's friends in the street back home in London and been none the wiser. The Acholi who had dabbled in the Lord's Resistance Army from afar tended to keep a low profile, especially after Kony's designation as a terrorist. But I had managed to locate one of them before I made my way to Uganda. After several phone calls, and a few postponed appointments, he agreed to meet me one evening in December, in a hotel bar in Croydon, south London.

It was already dark when I boarded the train in the wintry west of the city, passing terraced streets and desolate supermarket car parks. As we hurtled through frozen stations, I considered how I would approach the key question: why would anybody in their right mind consent to work with somebody like Kony? The man had once been one of his spokesmen, regularly calling BBC radio to deny reports of atrocities and representing the rebels at conferences. After I'd waited for fifteen minutes in the lobby of the Croydon Park Hotel, I began to wonder whether he would even turn up.

Kony's former frontman breezed through the sliding doors in a navy blue fleece and shook my hand as though I were an old friend. We ordered a couple of pints in the bar. Red and gold baubles glinted above rows of bottles behind the counter, while clusters of office workers traded gossip at the surrounding tables. I hoped my contact would keep his voice down, but he had a habit of leaping to his feet at crucial moments in his story, especially at the part where Kony orders his execution. Despite the years that had passed since his association had come to an end, he insisted I did not take notes, or use his name.

My new friend explained that he had been a man of some wealth and status before Museveni marched into Kampala. But after the atrocities committed by the army and its Acholi troops in Luwero, all Acholi people were under suspicion. He described how soldiers burst into his house one night and dragged him off to a cell, where prosecutors accused him of grand-scale tax evasion.

"I told them, 'You don't ask me stupid questions. If you want my head just take it, but don't ask me stupid questions,'" he remembered, laughing. "I gave those lawyers a rough time. They kept calling for advice, but they knew they had no case."

Soon afterward a friend warned him he was on a death list drawn up by Museveni's men. He had just boarded a twin-prop Fokker Friendship at Entebbe when he saw two security men dashing toward the plane, their pistols drawn. They climbed aboard, but the furious captain ordered them out. My contact landed in Nairobi without the money for a taxi.

"The others, the ones who said they would stay in Uganda and fight on, they are all dead now," he said, folding his glasses and placing them on the table.

His face seemed to slacken for a moment, but soon he was wagging his finger in the air again, grinning as he reminisced about joining Kony. In Nairobi he had contacted other Acholi who had fled after Museveni's takeover. They kept in touch with the rebels via radio from a house near the Ngong Hills outside the city. One day, a call came whispering over the airwaves:

"The Teacher wants to speak to you."

"I knew it was Kony," he told me. "He said he wanted somebody who could help them on the outside, abroad, and so I said 'Yes.'"

The government of Sudan gave him so many passports he sometimes missed the last call for passengers because he had forgotten which name he was supposed to be using. A military plane flew him from Khartoum to Juba, and he would travel on to the Lord's Resistance Army camps outside the town. He would spend evenings discussing the movement's agenda with Kony and his officers.

"There was no way we could base it on the Ten Commandments," he said. "I nearly left them at that point."

I did my best to nod along, but all the time I was desperate to ask how he could possibly have devoted himself to a group that abducted thousands of children, hacked villagers to death by the dozen, and chopped off people's lips. When I finally managed to put the question, he insisted that he had tried to persuade the rebels to clean up their act. I wondered if his anger with Museveni had blinded him to what Kony's men were doing. He was by no means alone in his rage.

As I looked back through the *New Vision* archives in Kampala, I came across stories of a host of Acholi exiles in Britain, Kenya,

Germany, and the United States who had helped Kony. Rebel sympathizers seemed most active in London, where they occasionally called press conferences in cheap hotels in suburbs like Crystal Palace, or issued statements from an address in Earls Court. One of Kony's most prominent associates was said to go by the nickname of "Mr. Don't Care." The *New Vision* reported that he had been arrested in Britain in a joint operation by the FBI and Scotland Yard on charges of embezzling $4 million from the city of Clovis in New Mexico in a series of bogus deals starting in 1996. Ugandan officials suspected the funds would be used to buy arms and uniforms for Kony's rebels. The charges were eventually dropped in 2002 after a key witness for the prosecution committed suicide, according to a story in the *Daily Monitor*. Little had been heard of "Mr. Don't Care" since then, but my new friend blamed this man for having turned Kony against him.

"It was that fucker who set me up," he said, angry again. "I introduced him to Kony and I said this guy is a conman, a liar, and a thief, but we need his money," he said. "That guy is a real fucking bastard."

He had almost been killed during his last visit to Kony's camp, before he turned his back on the rebels for good. I offered him a third beer and after a moment's hesitation he accepted.

"Now that is the last one, my brother."

I bought another couple of pints and he lifted his glass.

"When Museveni goes, in Acholi it will be like the second coming! No, better even than the second coming!" he grinned. "I will get on the first plane, if I have to climb into the engine compartment, I will go."

We shook hands, and I headed out into the icy streets, my head spinning. From what he had told me, there were a whole range of reasons why Acholi abroad might support Kony. Some had lost relatives to Museveni's soldiers at the time of his takeover, fleeing comfortable lives in Uganda for the uncertainties of asylum. Others had more calculated motives, seeing the movement as a chance to extend their political influence, or even make money by collecting funds from various organizations trying to mediate between government and rebels. Not all were so cynical—there were members of the diaspora who genuinely wanted to help end the war. But what would stay with me from our meeting was the heat of anger, smoldering in exile, and the desire for revenge.

I called my contact a few days later to try to arrange another meeting, but he kept changing the appointment. I never saw him again, though Kony seemed to have had no trouble finding new representatives.

The pair of middle-aged Acholi men who strolled in to address the journalists waiting on the inevitable plastic chairs in the RA International compound in Juba reminded me a little of my Christmastime encounter. One, a former colonel in Obote's army, had flown to Juba from his home in west London. He had hard eyes and a reserved manner. His companion was a teacher who worked in Nairobi, and had a softer, fuller face. Taking their seats behind a table covered with microphones, they insisted Kony was ready for peace.

Sudanese journalists working for local papers like the *Juba Post* and *Southern Eye*, or the town's FM radio stations, fired angry questions. They wanted to know why the rebels had inflicted so much suffering on the Sudanese, and what compensation they would offer. Kony's representatives simply blamed the atrocities on the Ugandan army, saying they had slaughtered people to tarnish his image:

"There is a unit from the UPDF from Uganda that plays a double game. By night, in plain clothes, they pretend to be LRA," said the teacher, projecting his voice as if addressing a classroom. "That's what the UPDF have done, right from the time they started their guerrilla warfare."

Even though they insisted that Kony wanted to end the war, I once again had to fight the urge to ask them about the abductions, the mutilations, the massacres. But these men had been among the group who had visited the rebels in the bush just a few days previously. If anyone could lead me to Kony, they could, so the last thing I wanted was to antagonize them. I bowled the teacher a deliberately soft question, asking him about the rebels' vision for Uganda, and I carefully noted down the answer.

"Our vision for Uganda," he said, "is of a country in which the citizens are united. There's a part of Uganda which is prosperous and another part where people are dying in camps. We want a country with justice, where people work together, where people can participate in a democratic process of government."

After the briefing ended I chatted to the former colonel, named Wilson Owiny. He told me he lived in East Sheen, a rather well-to-do suburb near where I grew up. We exchanged a few pleasantries about the joys of walking in the Royal Parks near the Thames, and the miseries of commuting to central London. I could not help picturing him riding into town on the District Line, passing through underground stops at Turnham Green and Barons Court, with thoughts of Kony racing through his head. For all the polite chit-chat, there was something controlled in his manner.

The teacher seemed more approachable. He showed me his badge from the school he worked at in Nairobi. It bore his name, Obonyo Olweny. We took a seat at a table under a mango tree and I told him I had been traveling around northern Uganda. He asked if I had any pictures of his home area in Patongo, telling me he had left it twenty years earlier.

I opened up my laptop and showed him photographs of crowded mud huts, ragged kids, and the half-built Kurnget Hotel with its crooked sign. He stared intently at the screen, and drew a hand across his eyes. He seemed to be wiping away tears.

A few days after the press conference, the Kony interview aired on BBC television and radio. His picture graced the front page of the *Times*. The World Service crackled from a radio on a windowsill in the house. Kony was the top story:

"The conflict between the LRA and the Ugandan government has killed thousands, forced well over a million people to leave their homes and repeatedly been described by the UN as one of the world's worst humanitarian crises.

"Joseph Kony claims to be under the influence of spirits and has called for Uganda to be governed according to the Ten Commandments.

"There have been other claimed interviews with Kony, but he says this is the first time he's met a journalist.

"He uses the interview to dismiss survivors' stories of having their ears or lips cut off by the LRA as propaganda, alleging that government troops mutilated people then blamed it on his group."

Kony's voice, a little reedy, took over.

"That one is not true, that is propaganda which Museveni has made."

The interviewer broke in: "I've seen photos . . ." It was hard to hear properly, but it sounded like he was saying ". . . of people with no noses."

"That is propaganda which Museveni made," Kony repeated. "Let me tell you clear, that thing which happened in Uganda,

Museveni he went into the village and he cut the ear of the people, pretending to the people that that thing was done by LRA, it is not true, I cannot cut the ear of my brother . . . I cannot kill my brother, that is not true."

"Although many children have now told of being coerced to fight for the LRA after being abducted, Joseph Kony claims this is more propaganda. The interview took place as the south Sudanese vice president Riek Machar was pursuing a peace initiative, meeting Kony himself. Whether he will get closer than previous peace brokers is not yet clear."

I listened for a while longer.

"Now for some music, let's go to Senegal . . ."

I switched off.

I decided to make one final attempt to meet Riek, though I knew I would have to head back to Nairobi soon. My time off from Reuters was running out, my money was fast going the same way, and I had reached the limit of my tolerance for Juba's heat, dust, and constant disappointments. Above all, I could not shake the feeling that I had missed my big chance purely through my own incompetence. After I'd met Riek, I would cut my losses.

I eventually managed to get past the gate and into the outer office, where a former rebel colonel called Deng Deng sat behind a desk in a Kaunda-style suit and marshaled the visitors. More officials from the United Nations and European Union missions in Juba waited on the sofas, alongside Indian businessmen and Sudanese journalists. The door would open, giving the occasional glimpse of Riek as the next batch of visitors shuffled inside. After five hours, he summoned me into his office.

From what I had read, Riek had an intriguing past. He had initially fought alongside John Garang in the SPLA, but was

among a group of commanders who broke away from the movement in 1991, splitting the southern rebellion. According to
Human Rights Watch, Riek's forces resorted to "increasingly
bloody and ethnically motivated attacks against civilians" as they
fought the SPLA with covert help from Khartoum. Riek eventually joined the Sudanese government, even working as an
assistant to President Bashir, before returning to the ranks of the
SPLA in 2002. Given his contacts in the north and south, and his
own guerrilla credentials, he seemed well placed to deal with a
man like Kony.

There was of course one major snag. Riek had already been
criticized by human rights organizations for talking to Kony and
his Lord's Resistance Army commanders rather than sticking
them in a cell at the International Criminal Court.

"I don't think I had the capability to arrest those guys in the
forest," Riek told me. "If the ICC came out to say that they would
give the peace process a chance before the legal process is done,
then we would resolve the conflict."

It was a tricky circle to square. Kony and his commanders
refused to emerge without guarantees of immunity. At the same
time, the prosecutors were loath to back down on their first case.
Under the court's statutes, the warrants could not be withdrawn,
though there might be a way to delay proceedings indefinitely if it
was deemed in the victims' interest. Many people in northern
Uganda believed the court had been wrong to intervene at all.
Some elders wanted to revive a reconciliation ritual known as
mato oput, in which both parties share a drink made from a bitter
root. The idea was to pursue a different kind of justice from the
brand on offer at the International Criminal Court through a
process of truth telling, forgiveness, and compensation that would
still hold rebel leaders to account. Moses was a fan of the scheme,

but others wondered how relevant the rituals were in the age of the AK-47.

As we talked, Riek's television showed images from CNN of Charles Taylor being extradited to the Hague. The former president of Liberia would face charges in a special court set up to try suspected perpetrators of war crimes in neighboring Sierra Leone, where guerrillas specialized in chopping off hands in a way not dissimilar to the Lord's Resistance Army. Famous for his white suits, dark glasses, and devout Christianity, Taylor had agreed to go into a comfortable exile in Nigeria after rebels drove him from power only three years earlier. Now the man known to his young fighters as "Papay" was being carted off to jail. I imagined Kony would be following his fate with interest, but Riek was optimistic:

"I think he wants to reach a peaceful settlement to the conflict," Riek said, turning from the screen. "He's beginning to be concerned about the suffering of his people."

I asked him whether he had any plans to go back to the bush for another meeting with Kony. All I got was a "maybe" and one of his enigmatic grins.

A couple more weeks dragged by in Juba with no sign of either another trip to see Kony, or the Ugandan government delegation turning up to start talks. The only high point was that I met the woman who had interviewed Kony, a documentary maker and academic researcher from Germany by the name of Mareike Schomerus. The rebels called her "Malaika," blurring the pronunciation of her name into the Kiswahili for "angel."

Mareike showed me the *Newsnight* report on her laptop at Huub's house. The worst part of it was that despite her achievement in landing the interview, she was horrified by the version screened by the BBC. She thought the editors had opted for a clichéd story of an "intrepid" reporter going into the jungle to meet a sinister rebel, glossing over the complexities of the war and missing a chance to remind viewers of the suffering caused by the Ugandan government's encampment policy. I was a lot more impressed with the story than she was, amazed to see a "Kony special" on prime-time news. The rebel leader had predictably denied committing atrocities, although he had said, "Only God knows a clean war." Mareike had even spotted a copy of the book *On War* by Carl von Clausewitz kicking around the rebel camp. I would have given anything to know who was studying his dialectical approach to military analysis.

Getting the interview had involved almost a year of painstaking and sometimes risky work, which made me feel a little better. Mareike explained that she had been approached by rebel representatives while she was conducting research in Gulu for a report on the plight of former abductees. (The report was called "A Hard Homecoming," aimed at relief agencies to help them improve their support for those who had returned from Kony's war, and I had already come across a copy.) It seemed Kony and Otti were keen to find out more about the charges against them at the International Criminal Court, and Mareike had earned a reputation for trustworthiness among the former combatants with whom she had been talking.

As the months went by, Mareike built up enough of a rapport with the Lord's Resistance Army to ask for a television interview with Kony himself. Eventually she got the call. She had also thought to take Kony and Otti copies of the warrants out for their arrest. Apparently, they had no idea that they would get some of the best defense lawyers money could buy if they ever ended up in the dock. Otti had assumed he would face the death penalty, which the court cannot give. It was no wonder the rebels were now seeking legal advice.

Fascinating though it was, Mareike's account only served to disappoint me further. I was reluctant to give up, but I decided the time had come to concede defeat. She had done a far better job of tracking down Kony than I had, and it seemed unlikely I would get another chance in the near future. I called the Eagle Air office and reserved my ticket to fly back to Nairobi. First, though, I would have a last supper.

I walked down the main street toward the restaurant, passing a boy with a bell tied around his ankle leading a blind woman with a stick. Teenagers hawked bundles of twigs for cleaning teeth, while a secondhand bookseller laid out sun-faded copies of *Gulliver's Travels* by the roadside. An Arab shopkeeper had taken off his sandals and was sloshing water from a plastic kettle between his toes. The Café de Paris lay just around the corner.

We could have been in France. Tucked into a tiny courtyard, the pizzeria offered everything from croque-monsieurs to succulent steaks and avocado in a vinaigrette dressing. When I went back in the evening, I found European visitors clustered around a handful of tables with neat cloths, sipping glasses of red wine or ordering espressos. The French owner sat in the corner, puffing clouds of apple-scented smoke from a hubble-bubble pipe. There were a thousand ways to make money in Juba's gold rush. For a moment I even entertained the notion of importing pool tables, but by then I was glad to be leaving.

Before long we'd touched down at Jomo Kenyatta International Airport in Nairobi. A woman with one of the tourist companies smiled and asked if I needed a taxi, and a few minutes later I was speeding toward the city with a young driver called Jeff. We chatted a little about Kenya, but he seemed irked to talk politics—corruption, he said, the same old story. I took his mobile number just in case, though the last thing I wanted to do was go back to the airport. I was looking forward to the big city.

I found a flat to stay in for a few months in a suburb called Hurlingham. There was a supermarket nearby, a bar called Sippers and a casino with a flashing neon sign of pyramids and a palm tree. It was the perfect place to rest up for a while and put my disappointment behind me. I was sitting down to do some work one Friday evening before heading out to meet a Reuters colleague at the Havana bar in Westlands when my mobile phone vibrated, rattling on the glass tabletop. I guessed it was a message from my friend.

"Have just been told that i might be going back into the bush tomorrow. bit surprising. not sure it will happen. Keep you posted."

It was Mareike, texting me on her Thuraya from Juba.

It was happening again.

I stepped onto the lawn in front of my flat, pulled out the antenna of my phone and waited for it to lock onto the satellite. I tried calling Obonyo, the teacher, but his phone was off. I then tapped in the number of the head of Kony's delegation in Juba, a man named Martin, who told me I was welcome to come and see the Chairman. All I had to do was meet them in Juba at 9 a.m. to catch a plane for the first leg of the journey. I had roughly twelve hours. I knew it would be impossible.

"No problem," I said, "I'll be there."

I called the travel agent's emergency number, but booking offices were closed on Fridays. I knew Eagle Air would fly a small plane up to Juba from Entebbe airport near Kampala early the next morning, but that was a whole country away. The travel agent rang back—there were no flights available for Uganda. I had only one more option.

I searched my flat for a map. If I were able to reach Entebbe by land, then I could grab the Eagle Air flight and just about make it to Juba on time. The road plunged into the Rift Valley, shot up through the tea estates in western Kenya, crossed the Ugandan border, and then skirted the edge of Lake Victoria for the final stretch. I would have to drive through the night, but with luck I might get to Entebbe just after dawn. I dialed Jeff's number.

He was having dinner at his girlfriend's house, but he said he would be happy to run me to the airport. The price increased significantly when I explained that the airport in question was in another country. I hardly bothered to bargain. The plane would leave a couple of hours after sunrise, and I needed him to drive as fast as he could. I was banking on a clear run, no traffic, and no police.

As Jeff was on his way to the flat, I scoured the kitchen for food. I had only just moved in and the cupboards were almost bare. I found two cans of baked beans and a couple of tins of kippers. I was throwing them into my bag along with a sleeping bag, mosquito net, and some spare socks when Jeff arrived.

We sped up Waiyaki Way, the concrete barrier dividing the lanes making it feel like a racing track. Streetlights gave way to blackness, cars swooshing past on the opposite side blinding us with their headlights. A lorry lumbered by with one headlamp, a motorized Cyclops. We overtook a coach with a dolphin logo on the back, then passed a broken-down truck. A man wearing a hood waved a flashlight, but we just flashed past. I could smell smoke as we raced through a patch of forest, passing a sign saying: "Speed that thrills, kills. Drive safely."

"These roads are very funny at night," said Jeff. "If you don't take care, you find yourself in Hell."

He seemed to relish the challenge, skimming down into the Rift Valley past Suswa and Longonot, the sacred peaks of the

Masai. The volcanoes looked even more majestic silhouetted against the stars.

I willed the glowing needle on the speedometer to creep higher. Jeff chuckled with exhilaration as the dial touched 140 kph [87 mph], hovering there for a few seconds before he slammed on the brakes and we swerved into a diversion. I would never have seen the warning, propped up by a mound of earth that blocked the way. The needle sank down to 30 as we fell in behind a lorry grinding over the dirt.

We soon veered back onto the road, weaved between rows of spikes, and then hit the outskirts of Nakuru town. Jeff stopped in the yellow glow of a Shell garage. I yanked two coffees from the waitress's hands, ladled in sugar, waved away milk. We were striding back to the car when two men in long coats appeared, brandishing guns.

11. "WE WANT TO SEE YOUR CHAIRMAN"

Vincent Otti in a clearing in Nabanga

"What do you want from me?" asked Jeff, throwing up his hands. "What do you people want from me?" "You ran over our roadblock," said one of the men. "We followed you."

"How can I have run over your roadblock? Look at the tires!" Jeff pointed at one of the front wheels. Not a scratch.

"You have tubeless tires," said the man, as if that explained everything. "We followed you here, my friend. You just come with us."

I tried to catch Jeff's eye, but he was staring at the officers. Then he opened the car door and got back in. The policemen climbed into the back. One of them unclipped the magazine from his submachine gun, revealing a glinting brass shell. He snapped the magazine back in place, a not altogether friendly gesture. I tried again to catch Jeff's attention, but he was fuming, focused on the road, so I got in beside him.

We reached the twin rows of spikes and climbed out of the car. More police appeared from the darkness, wearing long raincoats and berets, clutching G-3 rifles. They did not have numbers. One nudged the barrier with his boot, pointing out where a couple of the six-inch barbs had been crushed.

"Look, you have damaged this roadblock," he said. "This is a serious matter."

"How can that be?" said Jeff. "Look at the car—there's nothing."

The policeman shone his flashlight. The tires were clearly untouched, but he found a tiny scratch on the paint beneath the bumper.

"There," he said, pointing his flashlight. "Look. How can we mistake that license plate?"

Another policeman nodded at me. "*Safari usiku si poa*," he said. I knew enough Kiswahili to understand: "It's not cool to travel at night."

"You said you followed us after we hit the roadblock," I said to the officers. "So how come you had to come back here in our car? Where's yours?"

"We followed you," said one of them, "in a bus."

Jeff shook his head. I wished they would just drop the pantomime and ask for the bribe. I raised my eyebrows and cocked my head ever so slightly, once again trying to let Jeff know that I wanted to pay and go, but he would not give in so easily.

"Let us hear what story they have," he said. "We shall wait for their bosses."

Drizzle pattered the windscreen as we sat waiting in the car. I knew by now there was no chance of reaching Entebbe in time. When the traffic police finally arrived in a Land Rover, they let us go. Even for the Kenyan police, this was a scam too far. "It's human nature to make mistakes," the traffic officer said, "human nature." Jeff had won, and I felt rather ashamed for having been so willing to pay. We drove back toward Nairobi at a more sensible speed and Jeff dropped me at the airport. He only charged me about $300, half the price we'd agreed. At a moment when everything seemed to be going wrong, his gesture meant a lot.

The horizon was turning an eggshell color. Just after sunrise I called Eagle Air on my mobile.

"How much would it cost to charter a plane to Juba?" I asked.

"That would be around . . ." the man considered for a moment, "$2,900."

"You said $2,900? US?"

"Yessir."

"Do you accept cards?"

"We only take cash."

I hung up and headed off to look for a bank.

I was walking toward the Barclays in the international arrivals hall when it occurred to me that there was no way I'd get that much money over the counter with my Visa card. My best bet seemed to be to check if there might be an early plane heading to Entebbe, and to try to persuade Eagle Air to hold the Juba flight until I arrived.

The Kenya Airways office opened before dawn. I was the only customer. I asked the man behind the desk when I'd be able to fly to Entebbe, and he told me there was a flight leaving at 7:30 a.m., arriving in Entebbe 45 minutes later. I visualized the airport. If I ran off the plane and across the tarmac, I could jump straight onto the Eagle flight. That was the beauty of small airlines—there was always room to negotiate. For the first time since I received the text from Mareike, I felt my mood lifting.

I called Eagle Air back and was told that if the Kenya Airways flight was on time, they would hold their Juba flight for fifteen minutes so I could make the connection. But he stressed that it had to be on time, there was no way he could wait any longer. I thanked him profusely, whipped out my card and bought a ticket to Entebbe. The only seat left was in business class, setting me back more than $300 for a one-way ticket, on top of the money I had given to Jeff, but I was past caring.

I joined the queue at the Kenya Airways desk, hoping to squeeze on board carrying my rucksack with its tins of kippers and other essentials. I was worried that if I checked my bag in I might still miss the Eagle Air flight as I waited for it to turn up on the carousel in Entebbe. I handed my ticket to the young woman behind the counter. A badge on her red jacket told me her name was Phoebe.

I flashed my best smile, but she insisted I check in my rucksack. If I couldn't persuade Eagle Air to wait, it would just have to be abandoned. I didn't much like the idea of heading into the bush minus sleeping bag and spare clothes, but I salvaged what I could, fishing out my mosquito net and a roll of spare socks and stuffing them into my jacket pockets. Bag or no bag, I couldn't miss this trip. Not again.

"Is the flight on time?" I asked, trying not to sound anxious.

"I'm sorry, sir," she smiled. "We're actually going to depart about forty-five minutes late." My jaw dropped. "We're waiting for connecting passengers from Johannesburg."

I asked her to repeat what she had just told me before swearing loudly, feeling the eyes of the whole queue on me. I apologized to Phoebe. Her smile was no more. I called Eagle Air again, but there was no way they would be able to hold that long. The man sounded genuinely disappointed, though not as much as I did.

I demanded my rucksack, but the conveyor belt had already sucked it into the airport's innards. Phoebe told me I'd have to walk around to the arrivals hall and reclaim it when her colleague had managed to extract it from the machine. I grabbed my ticket and passport from the counter and stalked toward the exit.

"Excuse me!"

I turned around to see a British man in a blazer dragging a suit-case on wheels. He was not smiling either. He stretched out an open hand.

"You've taken my passport."

I looked down, realizing I had grabbed his documents by mistake. I handed them over, suddenly aware of how disheveled I looked. I had no flight, no bag, and had just wasted another 300 bucks. Juba was not getting any closer.

Eventually the system regurgitated my rucksack and I trekked off to the East African desk. It was my last card. They flew to Juba most mornings, though the flight only left after ten, too late for me to join the expedition to the bush. Several passengers had already lined up at the window. I contemplated waving a $100 bill and announcing that I would give it to anyone who would offer me their place. I was not sure what would be worse: not making it to Juba at all, or arriving to find I had just missed the trip. Luckily there was still space, and I laid down another sheaf of $100 bills.

"Green," said a deep, Sudanese voice. "How are you?"

I turned to see Samson Kwaje, south Sudan's information min-ister and the man who had tried to help me find Riek at the SPLA day. He was waiting for the same plane.

"You're heading to Juba?" he asked. In his suit, he looked a lot sharper than I did.

"That's right, I'm hoping to get on this trip to the bush," I said. "But I'm not sure I'm going to make it."

"Oh, don't you worry," he said. "You'll get there."

His blithe tone soothed my anxiety. I took a seat in the depar-ture lounge and began sending texts to Martin and Obonyo. If there was any way they could hold their departure until I arrived then I promised them coverage in every newspaper, television, and radio station in the world. There were no replies.

The airliner soared above Kenya, tracking the path of the Rift Valley, the vista of canyons and volcanoes rolling beneath us in painfully slow motion. The White Nile looked like a hairline fracture running the length of the continent, the only flaw in the perfect expanse of green. A giant Ilyushin cargo plane had just left Juba. Framed by the plane window, it looked tiny as a toy.

We circled once and then swooped in to land, shooting past a wrecked fighter jet that languished by the runway. I scanned the apron for any sign of a waiting plane. There was only one possible candidate, an old twin-prop that could have starred in a World War II film. I wondered if the white car parked nearby was the same one that had whisked Riek away from the SPLA celebrations a few weeks before.

I elbowed my way through the crush surrounding two policemen who were stamping passports in arrivals, and scanned the crowd for anyone who looked as though they might be on their way to meet Africa's most-wanted man. It was a hard category to discern at the best of times, and all I could see was the usual crowd of Bangladeshi UN soldiers, Sudanese troops, and families trailing suitcases and daughters.

More minutes ticked by before I managed to retrieve my rucksack. Driven now by desperation, I jostled through the crowd toward the VIP lounge. A guard cradling an AK-47 simply stepped aside as I bustled through the entrance. I searched the faces of the men and women sitting on the sofas until one man caught my eye. Wearing the loudest tropical shirt in the room, he was talking animatedly to a Sudanese colleague, a hand placed on his knee to hold his attention. I interrupted:

"Mr. Vice President, do you mind if I come with you to the bush?"

"Of course, you are welcome," Riek said, as if it was the most natural request in the world. He smiled his gap-toothed grin. "We are leaving anytime now."

I slumped onto a sofa, overwhelmed by a flood of exhaustion and relief. Of course they were late, things always moved slowly when it came to the rebels. As long as I managed to secure a seat on the plane I would finally meet Joseph Kony. Feeling rather pleased with myself, I reached into my bag for my Thuraya so that I could let Obonyo know where I was. I patted my pockets and looked through my rucksack again, but the phone had gone. My warm feelings vanished with it.

I tried to tell myself that the Thuraya was not important. Losing it might mean another $1,200 down the drain, but at least I was here. I decided to check at the immigration desk, just in case. One of the policemen had left it standing on the table for somebody to claim. I could not think of many other countries where a phone lost in an airport wouldn't have disappeared into somebody's pocket.

I staggered back to the VIP lounge, where a young member of the rebel delegation wearing shades and a camouflage baseball cap was handing around a list for people to sign. A few Ugandan journalists had arrived, as well as a couple of American reporters, a Sudanese television crew from al-Jazeera in Khartoum, and Mareike. I began to write down my name.

"Who are you? Who said you could come?" The young man looked me up and down through his shades. I explained that Martin, the delegation leader, had given me permission, and I added my name.

We walked across the apron and began to board the vintage Hawker Siddeley I had seen earlier. There was a go-faster stripe painted along its white fuselage in orange, red, and yellow. I made sure I was among the first to get a seat, before Riek's bodyguards clattered inside. One squeezed along the aisle carrying a machine gun with a belt of ammunition coiled in a black box, chipped paint revealing the metal beneath.

Next came a dozen or so of Kony's representatives, dressed as if they were about to tour a national park, which, in a sense, they were. Martin wore a brand-new bush hat and carried a video camera, another man tucked a green umbrella under his arm. A pair of Italian mediators from the Community of Sant'Egidio in Rome, who had come to help Riek, sported a similar look. One wore a hat saying "Save the Elephants."

The faded purple seats were filling rapidly, and just as I was beginning to wonder whether everybody would squeeze on board, I heard a dispute developing at the rear.

"We need to get four off," said a voice.

"OK," said another. "You remove your *mzungus*."

I sank low into my seat. *Remove your mzungus*—in other words, "remove your 'whites'." All I could do was sit there and hope nobody would try to haul me off at the last minute. Somebody passed around a clipboard, and we wrote our names down for the manifest. The metal fuselage heated up like an oven.

"Everybody's sweating, huh?" Riek said, as he finally boarded the plane, drawing a murmur of laughter. I could see between the headrests as he sat down and unfolded a copy of the *International Herald Tribune*, with a headline that read: "China Vows Broad New Censorship Measures."

At last the door closed and the propellers blurred. The faintest of tremors shivered through the airframe and we were airborne, on our way to the border.

My ears popped as the plane began to descend, banking toward a dirt airstrip torn out of the wilderness. We skimmed over palm trees, square huts, and deserted fields. Somewhere below lay the town of Maridi, but all I could see was a cloud bank building on the horizon. The passengers stirred, packing away headphones from MP3 players, squinting through the windows.

Kony felt close now. I pictured him bivouacked in the forest, surrounded by a circle of teenage guards, with one or two wives in silent attendance. Otti would be wading through the foliage in his Wellingtons with a Thuraya clamped to his ear, making arrangements for the meeting. The rebels might have to trek for days to the rendezvous on the frontier between Congo and Sudan, but they could not afford to disappoint Riek.

Considering the time I had devoted to studying Kony, I realized I had given very little thought to what I would actually ask him when he emerged. I sat in the plane jotting questions in my notebook: *What kind of person are you? . . . Tell us about your early life . . . Which leaders do you admire the most?* None of them would come anywhere near to what I really wanted to know: *Joseph, where did it all go wrong?*

The plane touched down, lurched up, and then settled, white wings skimming over the long grass that flanked the runway. A crewman opened the rear door and lowered a set of steps onto the airstrip, where soldiers from the town had lined up to greet Riek. A tall SPLA officer in crisp fatigues, with an ebony cross tucked into his webbing belt, stepped forward to greet us. His eye was covered in a milky blue film.

"Welcome to Maridi," he said. "I am Major Paul."

We walked for a few minutes to a compound run by the CARE aid agency on the edge of town. A Filipina lady wearing a T-shirt saying "Let Girls Finish Their Education" served rolls and mugs of milky tea under a mango tree while Riek's men assembled the convoy. He called for a cob of roast maize.

"The French team are murderous," he said. "I begin to pity the Italians before the game."

A member of the rebel delegation chimed in: "The French team is very balanced, but the Italians have a lot of lapses." He munched on a half-cob of maize clasped between his thumb and forefinger. In his V-neck pullover and Wellingtons he looked like a country squire visiting his estate.

"You know why Indians can't play football?" he said. "Because whenever they take a corner they put a shop there."

I wondered what the conversation would be like after a few more days—discussing the World Cup might be our only hope of salvation.

It was only in Maridi that I learned the true purpose of the trip. Riek was intending to persuade one of the five suspects wanted by the International Criminal Court to attend the opening of the peace talks in Juba. He knew Kony would not venture out, but he thought he might tempt Otti. Bringing one of the top commanders to Juba would be a huge coup, and it would force the outside world to take his peace initiative seriously. Radiating confidence, he always managed to give the impression he knew something the rest of us did not.

Rumors persisted in Juba that he had first met the Lord's Resistance Army leader a decade earlier, when they were both fighting the SPLA. Riek later denied this. He told me he first set eyes on Kony on 3 May 2006—the encounter I had seen on the video—although he conceded that an officer in a guerrilla movement he had led, working for Khartoum, had helped link Kony to the Sudanese army. Riek's varied career had gained him a rather mercurial reputation in the eyes of some, but cutting a peace deal would earn him considerable prestige. Judging by the length of time we'd already been waiting, it would also require patience.

I took a picture of our driver, a young Sudanese man named Joseph, as he clambered up onto the roof of our car to lash down some bags. One of Kony's delegates approached me, saying: "We don't encourage taking pictures." His tone was polite but faintly menacing.

It was dark by the time the convoy began rolling. Riek rode in a GX-R Toyota Land Cruiser in racing green with tinted windows. A decorative tissue box perched on the dashboard gave the car a rather ladylike air, which was quickly dispelled by the pickup full of soldiers manning a heavy machine gun that provided his escort. We followed in more four-by-fours.

Admittedly, it was not the best of gambits, but after about five minutes I asked "Are we nearly there?" in a feeble attempt to lighten the atmosphere in the rebel car, drawing a brief ripple of laughter. But mostly we rode in silence, each of us alone with our thoughts about the man at the end of the trail. A wall of undergrowth enclosed the road, and the headlights picked out enormous potholes. Joseph splashed through them with abandon, spraying chocolate-colored mud.

After a few hours we stopped at a place called Ibba, a halfway point on the way to the border with Congo. A wooden sign said "WELCOME TO JESO GUEST HOUS." Another bowl of roast maize cobs appeared, burnt and cold. A boy of about twelve lit a candle in one of the huts where we were to sleep. Slipping into teacher mode, Obonyo asked him his name. He was called Repent.

We left Ibba early the next morning, passing a broken-down truck with Congolese licence plates and one or two barefoot villagers who were hacking at the giant grasses by the roadside with machetes. Obonyo explained that they were Zande people, and pointed out the stone mounds clustered near their huts. "These are graves," he said. "They bury their dead in a sitting position."

I made another feeble attempt at a joke and there was more polite laughter, swallowed once again by silence. Embarking on small talk with the rebel delegation was like trying to light damp kindling, but I had a flash of inspiration. I dusted off my tale of the *muok*—the monster I had seen in pictures in Patongo—and asked if anyone had any idea what it was. The conversation reverted to Acholi as one of the younger members mimed a mole-like digging motion with both hands. When he told me its name was "ant bear" in English I felt a touch of disappointment. The *muok* was perhaps not as mysterious as I had thought.

Jolting over the craters, I tried to think of more questions for Kony: *Why has this war gone on for so long? How would you describe yourself? How would you like to be remembered? What do you see as your achievements? What prompted you to start fighting?* I suspected a hostile question might make him clam up, but nothing on my list seemed quite right.

The convoy finally pulled up in a circle of thatched huts. Riek stepped out of his car, immaculate in polished black shoes, pressed russet shirt and matching trousers, and ducked into the largest shack. I thought of a medieval prince, visiting one of his most distant outposts. His bodyguards waited outside in the drizzle, blowing out plumes of cigarette smoke that misted in the damp air. A couple of rebel delegates huddled under their green umbrella, looking rather sorry for themselves. Rain turned the mud into a giant brown mirror.

We had reached Nabanga. There was no sign, but this outpost marked the frontier. On the other side lay Congo, and the forest of the Garamba National Park. Somewhere out there the Guatemalan soldiers had met their deaths hunting for Otti a few months before. I could see nothing but huge teak trees and head-high grass. It felt like the edge of the world.

I followed a path past a derelict school. A boy leaned against a bicycle waiting for customers who might be interested in the tin of coffee beans placed on a sack at his feet. A metallic braying sound drifted through the forest as someone drew water from a hand pump. I walked back to the school and unrolled my sleeping mat in a classroom. Flat stones lay on the cracked floor in place of desks. Someone had scratched stick soldiers on the wall with charcoal, scrawling graffiti in looping handwriting: "*Mr Moses has two beautiful looking girls. I love them very much.*" I slumped down in a corner, wondering how long we would have to hang around in this place. More importantly, what would we eat?

One of the rebel delegation eventually procured a jerry can full of honey, apparently the only commodity Nabanga could boast in abundance. I poured a glob into the ripped-off base of a plastic water bottle and took a sip. The rush of sugar after a day of roast maize cobs made my head tingle. But though it was delicious, it was not exactly filling. I had a couple of tins of kippers, baked beans, and some biscuits, but that was it. Selfish though it was, I felt too hungry to share. Thankfully, others were more resourceful; I watched transfixed through the classroom window as the Sudanese cameraman from al-Jazeera gripped a goat in a headlock, then drew a blade across its throat. The beast collapsed onto its knees and then keeled over, slaughtered halal style.

A man shinned barefoot into a mango tree and looped a rope over a branch. Joseph the driver attached the animal's hind legs to the rope and pulled it taut, hoisting the carcass off the ground. A soldier chopped off its head and placed it on a large leaf, the tongue lolling. The blade flicked again, and the hide slipped off like an overcoat, exposing wobbling meat. Martin wrung out the steaming contents of the intestine into a plastic basin. I confined my assistance to gathering firewood.

When it got dark, the dozen or so rebel delegates gathered around the fire, chattering away in Acholi. Two more Acholi had come all the way from London: there was a woman called Josephine from Hackney, equipped with her sleeping bag from Blacks outdoor shop, and Justin, a man with a shaved head from Enfield. Another man had come from Las Vegas, where he worked in the construction industry. Only one or two members of the group seemed to have any experience of the bush, a man known as Captain Sunday in particular. His years with Kony seemed to have left their mark. Sometimes he favored you with a shrill laugh, before his face tightened with anger. Like his boss, he was unpredictable.

I still felt awkward around the rebel representatives, sensing they were wary of me. I could not tell how much of this was down to my nervousness, or how much they wanted to keep quiet. I had heard talk that some had lost relatives at the hands of Museveni's soldiers twenty years earlier, but it was a hard topic to broach. One of them called Museveni a fascist, and rehearsed an oft-repeated remark ascribed to one of his supporters who had supposedly referred to the Acholi as "biological substances," but I learned little about the concessions they hoped to win in Juba. I concentrated instead on the flames licking the pot, and enjoyed the aroma of bubbling chunks of goat. I reached for a piece of intestine roasting on a stick and chewed it for a long time.

At last I got to chatting to one of the delegates from southern Sudan who had come to help Riek mediate. He sat down on a log next to me and produced a bottle of single-malt whisky, apparently less inhibited than the rebels about talking to a journalist. I listened again to many of the criticisms of Museveni I had heard in Uganda: worsening corruption and a bias toward his Banyankole kinsmen in the army, cabinet, and privatized companies. Perhaps most contemptible of all, the man said, was the rewriting of the constitution to allow him to run again in the elections, a move that cost him many former admirers.

"Now he has shown his claws, Western countries are beginning to realize they have backed the wrong horse," he said. "The diplomats should say something about all this discrimination; they are the ones bankrolling the country. Tribalism is the key problem— we have to build a country where everyone feels equal."

He sipped from his plastic beaker.

"Western powers have been supporting the system that supports the war. They give aid but they don't want to look at what is happening. We need a catharsis, we need to get out all the bitterness, we need to tell the truth about what happened," he said. "Maybe now the West will see what has been happening here, the rebels will get their side of the story across. You have to see both sides of the coin."

The man took another slug of whisky. "I'm coming to the bush, I may get shot," he chuckled. "I have to enjoy myself." It was dark, but I knew he was smiling.

I bedded down in the darkened classroom, listening to the rebel from Las Vegas tell an involved story about a teenager who took ecstasy and drove his father's Porsche at 200 miles an hour down the freeway, chased by a police helicopter. To him Nabanga must have felt a very long way from home.

We ate breakfast in Riek's hut, gobbling down fried donuts glistening with oil. Immaculate as ever, the vice president chatted to the pair of Italian mediators about the tribulations of their football league as if we were in a restaurant in Rome. His Thuraya rang and I wondered if it might be Kony, but it was Kuwaiti investors seeking a place in Sudan's new El Dorado in Juba. They would have to wait. There was still no time set for our meeting, although Kony had to be close.

I was already tingling with anticipation, a slight pressure building beneath my diaphragm as on the day before exams. I expected the call to come at any moment, but perhaps I should have taken a hint from Riek's men. One dozed in a wooden chair, while another two sat absorbed in a game of chess. I thought of my trip to Khartoum; from that perspective Kony had looked like a pawn in a much bigger war. But out in the bush he was the king, keeping the one man with the power to help him waiting for days, while journalists, mediators, even his own people hung on his every word. I hated to admit it, but I knew I would feel a strange sense of privilege if he finally materialized. For all his crimes, Kony commanded a perverse celebrity.

I walked back into one of the classrooms and ate a can of kippers, confident nobody would see. Finishing my snack, I wandered into another one of the rooms. Sacks unloaded from the roof racks had spilled open to reveal a trove of medical supplies. Now I knew why the rebel delegates had been reluctant for me to take pictures. They had brought boxes labeled "Infusion solution 10 x 500 ml" from Pharmaceutical Solutions Industries Ltd., Jeddah, and bottles of Dettol antiseptic, along with shrink-wrapped Stim apple drinks and jars of Foster Clark's powdered pineapple juice. I peered into one of the bags and spotted a rather demure pink body lotion called Girlfriend. I wondered if it was for Kony or Otti.

The following day looked as though it would go much the same way, until Riek climbed into his car just before dusk. Soldiers scrambled into their pickup and gave chase. I joined the scrum to find a place in the last vehicle along with the other journalists. Squeezed knee-to-knee into the back, we watched the other cars disappear down a track that led to the border. Joseph was still rummaging through the cab in search of the ignition key.

I climbed back out, chewing my clenched fist in frustration. Kony could have been only a mile away, but we were marooned. There was no way the rebels would stay in the clearing for long. After all the waiting in Juba, the dash to the airport, the drive to Nabanga, this was the worst part. I found myself crouched on the ground, gnawing at my fingernails, unable to think straight. Five minutes passed, ten, then half an hour. The light was fading fast.

Joseph finally retrieved the keys and we raced down the mud track, finding the other cars parked in a clearing. A path disappeared into the undergrowth. I began to walk, convinced we would discover that Kony had been and gone.

Grass towered over our heads, until after a few moments we emerged in another, larger clearing. Branches meshed high above us, and a beehive made from a log dangled from the boughs. Riek and his entourage sat on a row of chairs, just as they had in the video of his earlier meeting with Kony. He thrust out his bulk, giving the same gap-toothed half smile, the same knowing look. Opposite him there stood an empty chair.

Carlos's words came back to me, his descriptions of twelve-year-old boys with machetes, young girls with guns, the splashing of holy water, consultations with the spirit: *"For me, the man is a psychopath. He may be laughing with you and very cordial, saying that he really wants peace, but the next minute he's very angry and shouting and making threats and saying he's going to give orders to kill everybody."*

Riek's bodyguards fanned out around the clearing; even Joseph had a gun. The forest felt supremely peaceful in the evening light. We waited in silence until the tall grass quivered and Kony's fighters strode into the clearing.

A young rebel wearing a trench coat buttoned up to the neck and a pork-pie hat wedged over his dreadlocks walked toward us, eyes hard, face blank. Another wore a ski jacket, another a polo shirt, and each carried a rifle. Their expressions were all like masks. I thought of Moses. He had once told me he had worn a "military face" in the bush. These young men were the same. They were used to keeping their feelings hidden and their personalities locked away, like all good soldiers.

The rebels formed a guard mirroring the perimeter set up by Riek's entourage, and a group of older men walked toward the chairs. One of them looked considerably more aged than the others, his face long and solemn, eyelids heavy. He wore a clean set of slightly baggy fatigues, shiny brown Wellingtons, and a forage cap over his graying hair. The man looked every inch an officer, the only ornamentation a single gold ring.

He shook hands with Riek and they all sat down.

"We want to see your Chairman," said Riek.

"He's still with the delegates," said the man. "We still have some talking to do."

Riek's smile vanished.

"I'm here to represent him," the man offered. He spoke so softly he was barely audible, but I could recognize his gravely voice from the radio show I had recorded on my iPod—*Joseph Kony is a prophet.*

Riek leaned forward in his chair, wagging his finger.

"I know you represent him, but since he's around I have to talk to him."

"Tomorrow then?" asked the man.

Riek sighed. "You guys! The world is running fast, you have to catch up with the rest."

The man looked down, fiddling with a leaf as he tapped his right leg up and down.

"From my side, I think we are faster than you," he said. "You travel by plane. We walked for three days. Now on the fourth day we reached here."

"Let's make it at nine o'clock," said Riek.

They shook hands, and Vincent Otti, the second in command of the Lord's Resistance Army, one of the five suspects wanted by the International Criminal Court, turned and walked away. The rebels followed him back into the bush.

The next morning Riek sat outside his hut listening to the BBC World Service and joking at the idea of Kony not turning up for his nine o'clock appointment. "Breaking news," he said, imagining the headlines generated by a no-show. "Kony chickens out of peace talks." He chuckled, though after waiting for three days on the border, the laughter was beginning to sound a little hollow. I wanted to ask him a few questions, but he told me to wait. "Not now," he said, "when I'm through with business, then I can brag." Even the mediators seemed confident. Kony could only have been a couple of miles away, hidden in the forest.

The radio crackled with the African headlines. One of Museveni's ministers had flown to the Hague for meetings at the International Criminal Court to discuss the peace talks. Already, people were wondering whether the warrants could be suspended to try to encourage Kony to negotiate.

Riek took another call on his Thuraya. "Juba airport has been taken over by Ugandan press," he said, smiling again. If Riek had his way, we would bear Otti back to Juba like a prize. Skeptics would be proved wrong, and there would be mounting pressure on Museveni to take the negotiations seriously. Assuming he could be coaxed, Otti's presence would be the biggest step toward peace for years.

We drove back to the clearing. Riek sat down on a wooden chair and opened a copy of *A Brief History of Time* by Stephen Hawking. It was not the kind of reading material you would generally find in Nabanga, but the book's exploration of the secrets of the universe seemed to help while away the hours waiting for Kony. A soldier lay back in the grass enjoying a less taxing distraction, experimenting with the various polyphonic ringtones on his mobile. I recognized one from my iPod, "Dilemma" by Nelly and Kelly Rowland, strangely soothing in the circumstances. I looked at my Thuraya; sometimes the screen said we were in Sudan, sometimes the Democratic Republic of Congo. We must have been right on the border.

"The worst things are these chairs," said Riek, shifting in his seat. "You know, part of the reason why peace talks fail is because of this waiting. You can get angry and leave." He massaged the bridge of his nose between thumb and forefinger, pushing his glasses up onto his forehead, letting the book close.

Three hours later, Captain Sunday stalked into the clearing in his baggy fatigues and green beret, looking like a bit player in a 1970s action film.

"Sunday," said Riek. "Are you guys all right? You don't know the time?"

"No, we know the time," said Sunday, unsmiling.

I felt a sharp pain in my thigh, a burning sensation that spread rapidly over my stomach. Something was crawling over my skin. I began to tear at my shirt, dimly aware of the soldiers laughing. The hairy culprit dropped wriggling to the ground, a huge brown caterpillar covered in spines. One of the Sudanese journalists crushed it with his boot. I was inspecting the angry welt it left behind as Otti strode into the clearing. If Kony's deputy wondered why a British man had been getting undressed at the start of a peace meeting, he did not show it.

More rebels accompanied Otti this time, including a young man who carried an American M-16 rifle with a grenade launcher attached under the barrel. Such weapons were a rare sight in central Africa, where virtually every gun was a variant of the old Soviet-designed AK-47 Kalashnikov. I sidled over to take a closer look, and he shoved it round behind his back without meeting my eyes. One guy with dreadlocks carried a much bigger machine gun, the shells looped around his neck like a scarf. Another taller rebel with a moustache wore a black hat with a pen tucked into the top. I risked a smile, and he grinned back.

"Chairman is not coming now," Otti said to Riek in his soft voice. "He talked today too much, he's now tired."

Riek was perhaps even more frustrated than I was.

"People's patience does not last that long, you understand that? You'll not get someone else spending five days in the bush like me. Don't take that for granted."

Otti glowered. "Do you think I myself can go up to Juba?"

"If you love your country you will risk it."

"I will come," Otti said, "but not at this time."

"What stops you from going to Juba now?"

Otti gave a humorless laugh. "I will come."

"We defied the whole world so that you have a chance to give your viewpoint. You're missing it."

"Peace cannot come in one day," said Otti, leaning forward in his chair. "We fought for twenty years—how can I go in as the first delegate?"

Losing patience with Otti's excuses, Betty Achan Ogwaro, a southern Sudanese member of parliament who had joined Riek's mission, began to berate him in Acholi. She wanted an apology for what the rebels had done to her people. Otti stared back with sullen eyes. When he answered in his mother tongue, his voice transformed from the murmur he used in English into an angry torrent. He sat up in his chair and squared his shoulders, the hands that had fiddled with a leaf while he'd talked to Riek suddenly coming to life. Pointing an accusing finger, then spreading his palms as if to say "*What have I done?,*" he looked like a man who would have a hard time admitting a mistake. His posture radiated a sense of entitlement, as if he were the victim. Still he refused to come.

Instead, Otti wanted Riek to bring elders from northern Uganda to meet them at their camp in Congo. In spite of all the atrocities they had committed, the leaders of the Lord's Resistance Army seemed to feel wronged themselves. As far as Otti was concerned, the Acholi elders had asked Kony to take up arms to defend their people against Museveni twenty years earlier, but then abandoned them to fight alone.

"We are their children," said Otti. "They are the fathers of this war."

Prompted by Obonyo, he took a couple of questions from the journalists. Thinking of Moses and his friend Christine, I asked Otti what he would say to people who had been abducted. He simply denied the rebels had kidnapped anybody, fixing us with a scowl. Then he walked away, back into the long grass.

I asked Betty what Otti had been saying when he became so animated. Apparently, he had compared the rebels' attempts to make peace in the past to a patient reaching for medicine to treat a bad case of malaria—each time they reached, Otti said, the government kicked away the cup.

As we traveled back toward Juba, I felt torn. Throughout my journey, I had always felt there was a chance of meeting the rebels, however unlikely it seemed. But to come within a few hundred meters of Kony and not even see him was almost worse than not meeting them at all. I decided to spend a couple more weeks in Juba, at least until the start of the peace talks. Even though I'd missed Kony twice, I had a feeling I might get a third—and final—chance.

Journalists hoisted cameras above their heads, jostling for a place at the back of the hall. Diplomats, UN staff, and members of the SPLA crowded the benches of the lecture theater in the national assembly building in Juba, which could have done with a lick of paint and a few more fans. I could see Father Carlos sitting toward the front, and ahead of him, the shaved dome of Colonel Otema's head. The owner of the Acholi Inn was wearing his sunglasses, even indoors. More Ugandan officers and officials sat next to him. After weeks of waiting, the talks were about to begin.

The hubbub ceased as a Ugandan minister wearing a suit stood up and made a speech saying how committed the government was to ending the war, offering to grant amnesty and education to all those who laid down their arms. It was clear they had come to discuss one thing: Kony's surrender. Then Obonyo's turn came. Wearing his blazer and yellow tie, he took the microphone.

In his best schoolteacher's diction, Obonyo launched into a tirade against Museveni's government, first outlining the abuses committed when the army headed north after Kampala fell two decades earlier, then conveying the graft and venality blighting the present. Now that the rebels had the world's ear, they were desperate to portray themselves as freedom fighters with a just cause. His tone as he described the military's past crimes was less than conciliatory:

"Scores of young men, both former soldiers and even those who had not been in the army, were arrested, tortured, and either killed or dumped in prison cells, without trial, under the most squalid conditions. They were sarcastically referred to as 'lodgers,'" Obonyo said, reading from a sheet of white paper.

"Our mothers, sisters, and wives were raped in front of us, and in some extreme cases men were sodomized in public, and in front of their family members. The NRA soldiers went to the extent of cutting men's anuses with razor blades and pouring paraffin therein to enlarge them to fit their sex organs."

The bitterness poured out, the same bitterness I had heard so many times against Museveni and his soldiers during my journey through northern Uganda.

"Northerners, some of whom had worked so hard to bring not only independence to Uganda, but the liberation of Africa, were repeatedly insulted, ridiculed, and variously referred to as ghosts, primitive idiots, backward and politically bankrupt fools, barbarians, killers, swine, rapists, etc. It became the deliberate policy of the NRM/A [National Resistance Movement/Army] to paint the whole of our ethnic group as evil."

Obonyo criticized the conditions in the camps, the ethnic bias in the army, the invasions of Congo, the theft of funds sent by donors to fight AIDS—the list went on. He did not apologize for the rebels' massacres, abductions, and mutilations. The Ugandan minister betrayed no hint of emotion during the speech, his head cocked up toward the ceiling, palms flat on the desk. Colonel Otema was less able to contain himself, almost bursting out laughing at Obonyo's parting shot.

"Should the regime in Kampala choose the path of violence and militarism, in the belief that they can defeat them, then they are in for a rude shock," Obonyo said. "The LRA has come of age."

People began to get up, cameras flashed, and the minister and Martin managed an awkward handshake. I worked my way down the aisle to greet Carlos. He was wearing a gray shirt with his white priest's collar and a wooden cross, and his usual slightly pensive expression. I asked him what he thought of Obonyo's speech. All he said was, "I don't know when that man was last in Uganda."

A few days later, I ran into Colonel Otema at the tented camp where I had spent my first night in Juba. He was sitting with Colonel Kyanda, the head of Ugandan military intelligence, a polished man who wore his beret folded under his epaulette. They were both fascinated by the pictures I had shot of the meetings on the border, the lineup of rebel officers revealing familiar faces from Obote's army of twenty years before. I later learned that one of the gray-hairs in Kony's ranks went by the *nom de guerre* of "tortoise," for reasons that never became clear, but Kyanda was more intrigued by the M-16 carried by one of the rebels. He guessed it had been retrieved from the body of one of the Guatemalan soldiers.

"After all these years in the bush," Otema said, "they are like animals."

"They're cowards," said Kyanda, examining the pictures of the young fighters in long coats and pork-pie hats. "They don't even know how to hold their guns properly."

Kyanda seemed intelligent and charming, yet he was reluctant to accept that the conflict's persistence might point to a deeper divide in Uganda. When I raised the question, he simply said: "Don't become a spokesman for the LRA."

As we parted he gestured at my Thuraya, knowing it would have the location of the clearing registered in its global positioning system.

"How about you give us those coordinates?" he said, smiling.

I just shook my head, and smiled back. We shook hands and he walked away, then turned once more, opening his palm in a final gesture of appeal.

"The coordinates?"

12. A GIRL CALLED PEACE

Moses and his mother at home in Gulu

oses's bodyguard broke the news: two of his *ting ting* had escaped. Commanders gathered around a campfire listened as the boy explained how the young girls had gone to the well half an hour earlier, but had not returned. The superior turned to Moses and remarked that captives usually ran away from less lenient masters. Moses's face creased with worry.

"I'll go and get them," he said, and went to grab his gun.

Moses snatched up his AK-47 and stuffed five magazines into his pouches. He had already put on his newest uniform and best Wellington boots. He tucked the blue-and-green lanyard he had found at Achol-Pii into his pocket, along with a slingshot made from a Y-shaped stick and a strip of inner tube. He also made sure to take his best epaulettes, the ones with two black diamonds and UGANDA stitched underneath. When he put them on, he looked just like an officer in the army.

He set off into the forest with his bodyguard, sweeping his flashlight through the trees. His companion, a teenager called Tabu, stalked along in front with his rifle, scanning the undergrowth for any trace of the girls. Moses wondered when he should tell him.

It was almost a year to the day since Moses met Father Carlos in the clearing. He thought of the man in the white shirt who had shot him at the army base, of the attack by the helicopter gunship that had killed so many of his comrades. They were now only a few hours' walk from a small village in Pader district called Lira-Palwo. To stay or to go—the odds of being killed were finely balanced.

Moses had confided in nobody, and especially not in his pregnant wife, who might not take kindly to the thought of him leaving. Like him, she was an "original"—she had been with the rebels for almost as long as his eight years. Since she had spent all that time in the bush, there was the risk that she might report him. But Tabu was different.

Moses watched him walking ahead, still dutifully looking for the girls. Tabu was a relatively new recruit, aged about fifteen, and he had been assigned to Moses as an escort. Moses imagined that he must spend his nights thinking about home, just as he too had thought about his own parents, and dreamed of the girl called Peace.

Moses knew the commanders would send dozens of men to hunt him down as soon as they realized he had tricked them. If they caught him, he would most likely be told to lie down while one of them smashed the back of his skull with a log. Tabu might suffer the same fate. After a few more minutes, Moses told him to stop walking.

"I'm fed up with fighting," Moses said. "I've fought for eight years, I've been wounded. I'm going back home now. Do you understand?"

For a second he was not sure if Tabu believed him. His eyes were suspicious. Moses explained that he had ordered the *ting ting* to run away a few hours before, telling them to cross a swamp and make their way to the trading center at Lira-Palwo. The boy nodded. Moses told him to shoot anybody who approached, still uncertain whether Tabu trusted him. Perhaps he thought Moses was testing him. Perhaps he would run back to the camp and tell the commanders. They found a place to rest.

When dawn broke, Moses took Tabu's gun and told him to report to the local councillor in Lira-Palwo. He hung the slingshot around the teenager's neck. It was the kind children fashioned to kill birds. The more boyish he looked, the better. Then he sent him down the road that led toward the village.

Moses walked some distance away, put on his blue-and-green lanyard and his shoulder pips and climbed a tree. He waited until he saw Tabu return with a much older man. The pair looked for him in the bushes. When they gave up, he clambered down and introduced himself. The trio began to walk down the road, Moses still clutching his gun.

They passed a contingent of a couple hundred soldiers, many wearing ragged uniforms and torn Wellington boots. Some carried firewood on their heads, others bags of maize flour. A few of them saw his smart new uniform, the lanyard, and the two black diamonds on his shoulder. "*Afande*," they barked, the greeting army men use for their superiors. The trick was working.

As the three passed the entrance to the camp, two soldiers stationed there saluted Moses, and they kept on walking until they reached the councillor's office. The two *ting ting* were sitting on chairs, having arrived just a few minutes earlier.

Moses unclipped the magazine from his gun and racked back the cocking handle to eject the remaining round from the chamber. He pressed the bullet back into the top of the magazine, then placed it together with the gun on the councillor's desk.

As I listened to Moses telling this story in the Franklin over a glass of milk, it was easy to overlook the risk he had taken.

"I was not feeling anything," he said. "In the bush, there is death, at home there is death, and if I have to die going home then fine, no problem."

He explained how an army truck had arrived and taken him to headquarters in Pader town.

"They asked me for secrets," he said. "They asked 'Can you go and shoot those rebels, do you know where they were going?' I'm a trained soldier, go back to them again? No way, my luck will run out! If I go there, I'll be the first person to be shot!"

Army intelligence officers eavesdropping on the rebel frequencies said they had heard Kony berating Moses's commander for losing such an able, loyal, and well-trained adjutant: *"He has not run away!"* Kony had said. *"You did something wrong to him! If you do not get him back you must return to Sudan and report to me!"*

Then the rebels decided to come looking for him. About a hundred of them attacked the village, killing several soldiers and civilians. The army officers took Moses up in a gunship to repel the raiders. A pair of the helicopters circled over the canopy, and Moses directed the gunners where to shoot.

"Because I know how we hide, I know everything. I told them, 'Don't shoot there, leave the big tree, shoot the small one.'"

The rebels fled back into the forest bearing a bloodstained uniform. They claimed it belonged to Moses, saying he had been killed. Knowing it was a lie, and inspired by Moses's audacity, other abductees began to escape from the same group over the next few days. They reported that any recruit caught mentioning Moses's name was to be killed.

After a week he told the army officers he had a splinter in his eye and that he needed treatment in Gulu. Once again, Moses boarded a helicopter.

One Sunday, when I had known Moses for a few months, he invited me to meet his mother. We walked past the pitch where Museveni had given his Army Day speech, past the white tents housing UN food for the camps, and along a track known as the Juba Road. Just as I was beginning to wish we had taken bicycle taxis we finally reached the house, a brick cottage with a corrugated iron roof.

Moses's mother was sitting on a sofa wearing a silver dress with puffy shoulders and a necklace of plastic beads. She greeted me with a smile and a little Acholi curtsy. Moses's young daughter Nurah wore an equally spectacular ivory-colored frock, giggling at the sight of their visitor. Looking serious again, she turned to her grandmother and began to stroke her hair. A younger boy, Oscar, played on the floor.

I sometimes lost track of Moses's various relationships, but I had established that Nurah had been born just after his abduction. Moses's mother had raised her and he had only met her when she was eight. The boy, Oscar, belonged to his late older brother. The children took their places on the floor to eat beans and cabbage, dining separately from the visitors as dictated by Acholi custom. Moses's mother chatted to her son as he prepared rolls and milky tea. She still wore the wedding ring of her late husband.

As the pair talked in Acholi, I looked around the room. Moses's salmon-pink tie hung from a string that looped from the ceiling, opposite a framed photograph of him mounted on the wall. A hand-painted wooden sign read: "Forget the Past, Enjoy the Present." Lost in conversation, Moses and his mother were laughing a lot. I asked what had happened when her son had returned.

"I was going to commit suicide," she said, with Moses translating her Acholi. "I saved up extra pills from the nurse, just a few each week, until I had enough. I gave myself one more week before I would take them."

Moses's mother had spent the eight years since he was abducted watching her loved ones die. First, the rebels had beaten to death Moses's half-brother, Baptist, just after their abduction. His other half-brother, Francis, had died of cholera some time later in one of the rebel camps. Moses's father had succumbed to a heart condition just a few months after meeting him in the bush. Moses's older brother, whom he had so admired for pursuing his studies to become a doctor, had died some time later of "sickness." Moses was convinced he had been poisoned by jealous Baganda students in his class. It seemed to Moses's mother that she had lost everyone. A group known as the Acholi Religious Leaders Peace Initiative had published a report called *War of Words* on the role of media in the conflict, and she had spotted Moses in a photograph, standing next to Carlos in the clearing where he'd spoken to Kony on the radio. But when more months passed without news, grief swallowed hope.

She withdrew to a shack on the edge of town, surviving on the charity of neighbors. Frequently sick, she began to hoard her tablets. Her mind was made up. She would swallow them all as soon as she had performed the final funeral rites for her eldest son; these were generally held some years after a death in Acholiland.

She was walking into Gulu to collect the typed invitations for the ceremony, due to take place a week later, when a friend came up and told her there was someone who wanted to see her. At first she was reluctant to follow, but finally relented.

A crowd was celebrating outside a small shop, men and women drinking sodas or beers, and everyone fussing over a young man in smart fatigues. Her friend led her through the throng and the man turned to face her.

"Is it you?" she asked. "Is it you?"

"Yes," he said. "It's me."

She repeated the question three times, and then she started to cry.

"I went and hugged her," Moses said. "She was shocked. Me, I have a strong heart, I cannot cry."

For a long time she could not speak. Moses told her to rest, saying he would explain everything later. Well-wishers thrust bottles of Nile Special into his hand, the first beer he had tasted in eight years. Born-again Christians thanked God, while old friends shouted greetings above the Lingala music that blared from the shop. They looked so much older, lives fast-forwarded in the moment he stepped from the time warp of the bush. As more and more people arrived, he scanned the crowd for the one other woman he wanted to see.

"They kept asking, 'How did you escape? Why have you stayed so long in the bush?' I explained to them that escaping is very risky; what we are hearing in the bush is different from what is happening at home. You are told that if you try to come home you will be killed, or there is a slow poison which is given to you, so after a period of time you will die."

Somebody handed Moses a mobile phone and he spoke to Geoffrey, the boy who had borrowed his bike a few hours before he was abducted. Geoffrey was studying at Makerere University in Kampala. He could not believe his old friend had returned. Moses scanned the crowd again. There was still no sign of Peace.

That night, Moses went to the studios of MegaFM radio in Gulu, appearing as a guest on the *"Dwog Paco"* show—"Come Home." The station broadcast appeals by former rebels for their comrades to return, doing much to dispel the fear of being killed that prevented so many of Kony's fighters from deserting him. Moses assured any members of the Lord's Resistance Army who might be listening that they would be treated well. That night he slept at his friend's place above the shop; Acholi custom decreed that he could not return to his mother's house after his long journey until he had undergone a cleansing ceremony, which involved stepping on an egg to symbolize new life. Early in the morning, he received a visitor.

Peace made her way up the stairs. She had been listening to MegaFM the previous night, and heard Moses's voice. She was carrying a baby girl. She handed the child to him, and he pressed the infant against his chest.

"I used to dream that we were together," Moses said, telling me about their meeting. "She was the only girl I dreamed about—I'd forgotten all my other girlfriends. Even when I was abducted, she used to visit my mother, bringing some photos, asking about me, the rumors about me. She loved me very much, so she was close to our family."

Peace had waited for him for years, but had eventually found a husband. She had given birth to their daughter at the time when Moses was still planning his escape.

"She insisted that she would leave that man and come back to me," Moses said. "I told her 'No, I don't want to bring conflict. You, as a girl, cannot stay for eight years without a man, so it's not bad. We'll keep on being friendly but you have to stay with that man.'"

He paused, reliving the memory.

"I told her 'You may feel somehow sad, but you have to forget it, because you know that it had to happen. You did not do it on purpose; it was nature, you had to do it. You have not to be sad.'"

Before I left his house, I took a closer look at the framed photograph on the wall. Moses had been wearing a blazer and a polka-dot tie, his right palm clasped over his heart, his expression like iron. He explained the picture had been taken shortly after his return, and said, "That was my military face."

When I visited Moses's house again, he handed me an old washing-powder tub filled with *simsim* paste, the Acholi delicacy made from sesame seeds that he'd promised me to take home to my family. I dipped my finger in—it tasted like super-enriched peanut butter. There was a radio playing next door, Jennifer Lopez's "Love Don't Cost a Thing." As we chatted, it became clear to me that his homecoming had been a lot more difficult than I'd imagined.

Considered a "FAP"—Formerly Abducted Person—in the jargon of the aid agencies, Moses was put through one of the several reception centers set up for ex-rebels. I had visited one some years before, where I'd met Anthony, the kid who had helped bludgeon five other people during his brief period in the bush. Some girls told stories of being forced to bite would-be escapees to death. These children related their tales quietly, while others played football or hobbled around on crutches, queuing with red and blue bowls for porridge.

Looking back, Moses felt the center had largely been a waste of time. Sitting in groups with youngsters who had been abducted for a few weeks, he had been encouraged to share his feelings. But he felt he had nothing in common with these children. He had been a commander, learned to fight, given orders, led by example. He had been wounded in battle, but it was a long time since he had been beaten.

"I became a leader of those people who abducted me," he said. "I was proud of being a leader—if you didn't have my recommendation, then you wouldn't be promoted. Life had turned upside down, but I was leading them in a good way. I was not biased to any side, that's why people loved me, nobody hated me. Those who joined the army, they respect me up to now."

At the center, he was just another FAP. It felt like a demotion.

"They claim that they are counseling you, but according to me that is not counseling, just group counseling—someone who has stayed for years is treated just the same as someone who has stayed two weeks or one month," he said. "But we have different levels of madness."

There was one consolation. Moses was once again given the job of health prefect, which involved taking sick people to the dispensary. And he made friends with Christine, the girl I'd met on his birthday, another abductee who had spent years in the bush. Talking together, they began to think about how they might help others who had ended up in their predicament. But after six weeks, Moses left the center with more pressing problems: how would he provide for his destitute mother?

"We, the abductees, come back, and there's no help for us," he said. "If you are a man, you can't get anything, not even a single spoon, or a mattress. Women get mattresses; we boys, we go barehanded, just like that."

Passing by the Acholi Inn, I would see former Lord's Resistance Army leaders like Kolo and Banya lounging around drinking Red Bull and watching the English football premiership on television at the Ugandan government's expense. All Moses got was a package from the state's Amnesty Commission, which provided pardons for rebels, to help him restart his life. This comprised the equivalent of about $130, a mattress, two saucepans, a blanket, a machete, and some seeds. As an old boy of the prestigious Sir Samuel Baker School, Moses did not think much of the deal, aspiring to more than a career as a subsistence farmer. When he gathered his relatives to ask for advice on how he might get going again, they pointed to an obvious solution.

"I said to them, 'You see, I'm your child, as I've returned back home I need your advice.' I'd found that my dad was dead, my brother was dead, the house was empty, my mum was alone and very weak, so what else could I do?

"The majority of the people were saying, 'Go back to the army, you have a big rank, you are a lieutenant, you will get a lot of salary.'"

The 105th Battalion would have welcomed him with open arms. Set up by the army to cater for former rebels, the contingent counted hundreds of Kony's ex-fighters among its ranks. Some advocacy groups worried that the military pressured returnees to join, but Moses would have felt at home among the battalion's members—they spoke Acholi and knew the rebels' ways. Some of Kony's youthful followers who chose not to join the battalion returned to the camps, where they still ended up serving in militias working alongside the army, risking their lives for a pittance to fight the rebels. Other escapees had more ambitious ideas. I once met a pair who wanted to apply to join the British Army via its website, though I never found out how far they got. For Moses, fighting—whether on behalf of the "rebels" or the "army"—would amount to much the same thing. His relatives asked what he had decided.

"When they finished talking, I told them: 'I'm not going to join the army. I've served with the army for eight years now. One of the reasons I came back is that I was tired. I got a lot of wounds. I will bear with the situation at home. Even if people are starving or sleeping without food, I will also do that, I'm not special.'"

The next day Moses walked past the Acholi Inn to an old colonial building which housed the army's Child Protection Unit, established to receive captured or escaped abductees. He handed in his uniform and walked back home.

Moses planted cabbages, onions, okra and aubergines on a little plot of land his father had left him, next to Severino's New World Meltar Jerusalem temple. "If I rewind back my life," he told me once, "if I had not been abducted, I would have been a big person." Instead he was earning his living with a hoe. I wondered how much anger and sadness went into the soil each time the blade struck. Gradually though, he began to raise some money. He even thought about clearing the water hyacinth from his father's old fishponds. Father Carlos helped him pay his mother's hospital fees and attend a computer course in Gulu where he was taught the basics of Microsoft Word and Excel. He still hoped to complete his education. Moses always seemed to have his notes on "Case Studies and Parables" from a peace studies course tucked under his arm like a talisman.

He often spent time with Christine, their friendship rooted in the affinity of veterans, though they were never more than friends. She survived by knitting woollen doilies. Sponsors helped put the daughter she brought back from the bush through school. Christine was one of the sunniest people I had met north of the Nile, but she was less forthcoming about what had happened to her than Moses had been. Eventually, he persuaded her to talk.

We took a couple of motorbike taxis past the Pece Stadium and reached the hut where she lived with her four younger sisters. One of them was doing her math homework at a rickety table. A sheet decorated with cartoons of footballs and rugby balls, shuttlecocks, and baseball gloves screened off Christine's bed; her sisters would sleep on mats on the floor. A sign said: "Let them talk but time will come," another read: "Never listen to all rumors." Christine laughed a lot, and today was no exception, until Moses began to translate her story.

Christine had been twelve years old the night the rebels came. She hid behind the hut door, but it was a poor choice and they found her in seconds. Kony's men dragged her into the bush where she was given to Vincent Otti as a *ting ting*. Christine said Otti treated her relatively well, calling her "my daughter," but soon she was deemed old enough to marry one of his bodyguards. She became the youngest of his seven wives. Moses asked her what happened next, but she covered her face with her hands. When she let them fall, I saw her eyes glisten. Her cheerful mask had slipped. Moses murmured something to her in Acholi, but she spoke to me directly in English.

"It's difficult . . . I can't recover," she said. "The scar is already there, it cannot be rubbed out. If somebody reminds me again, or mistreats me . . . I just recall . . ."

Somehow, Christine was smiling and laughing again by the time we left, making me feel only slightly less ashamed. I hadn't heard the details of what she had experienced, but the way her face had changed had been more telling than words. Moses walked me back toward the Franklin. Bicycles creaked past us and I could smell the scent of cooking fires in the evening air. Kids sang *"muno muno"* as I passed, cheeping like birds. I had never seen Moses so upset.

"I'm scared," he said eventually. "All the returnees are scared."

It took me some moments to realize he was afraid he would be hauled before the International Criminal Court. Maybe the conversation with Christine had triggered off more of his own memories. It was only afterward that I remembered how Moses had once been forced to participate in abducting girls just like his friend.

We had discussed the court before. I had tried to reassure him that there was no chance he would be arrested; the lawyers were only interested in the people at the very top of the command chain, Kony, Otti, and three of their senior officers. There were hundreds, perhaps thousands of former abductees like Moses who stood zero chance of being charged.

But disturbing stories swirled around the camps, transmitted by what the Acholi call *radio kabir*—"radio sorghum." The phrase comes from the toy radios children make out of mud using a stalk of sorghum as an aerial, a ready symbol for the rumors that spread so fast in the north. It was as if the hundreds of silent clay speakers were babbling out tales of their own. One of a thousand mythical bulletins had said the men from the Hague would come for all the former commanders, not just the top five. Moses never believed my assurances that it was just hearsay.

His dread of the court was mixed with something close to contempt. Like many Acholi, Moses worried that the arrest warrants would make it more difficult to convince Kony to come out of the bush. There was some suggestion that this fear of international justice had been one of the main factors that had encouraged the rebels to start negotiating, in the hope that a peace deal would get them off the hook. But Moses could not understand why powerful countries, including Britain, had gone to all the trouble of setting up a court that didn't even have a police force to arrest its suspects. Millions of dollars had been spent in the Hague, while he had nothing.

As we walked back toward the Franklin, I felt his mask was as fragile as Christine's. He was usually so good-humored, laughing about his rebel days, parodying Kony as an almost ridiculous figure, so it was all the more unnerving when he became angry. He gave a short, bitter laugh, and for a moment I caught a glimpse of his military face.

"I am not afraid of death. I could take ten pills and leave this world just like that. It would be better to die," he said, "or go back to the bush."

13. A STRANGE KIND OF WIZARD

Joseph Kony in Garamba National Park

A twin-prop plane named *Princess Tezita* taxied to a halt by the VIP lounge at Juba airport. The cabin door opened and passengers picked their way down the steps. Men in polyester suits clutched new-looking suitcases, their hair flecked with gray. Women in their best dresses wore stoic expressions, their babies on their backs. Waiting reporters searched their faces, wondering which could be Kony's mother, Nora.

There was only one candidate. A white-haired lady wearing a baggy blue sweater stepped onto the tarmac in her flip-flop sandals. She stood by one of the motionless propellers, staring into space. Photographers blazed away, ignoring the other arrivals. Sam Kolo descended from the cabin, looking extremely pleased with himself. Kenneth Banya followed in his usual khaki waist-coat with the Camel logo. I found myself taking his bags. I should have used the Heathrow Airport trolley I had seen clattering around outside the terminal.

Riek had invited them all to participate in his masterstroke. He would fly Kony's mother, his sister, and three of his wives with children in tow to meet him on the border. Another twenty or so relatives belonging to other commanders would join them, accompanied by Acholi elders, from the paramount chief to the archbishop of Gulu, along with dozens of other notables from across northern Uganda and southern Sudan. More than 200 people would deliver one message: "Time to come home."

Kony *had* to appear. The promise of being reunited with relatives seemed to exert a magnetic pull over rebels of every rank. Father Carlos had described how the first fighters he met had asked to see their parents. Moses too had risked his life to come home. Perhaps, by taking home to the rebels, Riek might convince Kony there was a real possibility of peace. Reuters had no spare reporters for the trip, so I had agreed to cover it to earn some extra cash. It was not quite my fantasy of stepping alone into a clearing for a chat around the campfire with Kony, but it was clear to me by now that my only hope of meeting him lay in joining Riek's flying circus.

Ugandan officials and army officers representing Museveni greeted the relatives, Kolo, and Banya in the VIP lounge like long-lost friends, slapping hands and embracing as though they were at a wedding. Kony's three wives sank into the beige sofas, though one older lady sat on the carpet, more accustomed to the ground. I recognized Margaret, one of Kony's wives, carrying his young son Okeny on her back. I had met her in Gulu some months before. She wore her usual survivor's expression, but she returned my smile.

I wondered how she felt about meeting her husband again. After she'd been abducted at the age of sixteen, Margaret had spent more than ten years with Kony. When we had talked back in Gulu she hadn't had a bad word to say about him, describing how he had always brought biscuits, soap, and clothes for his children, and admonished his commanders to treat recruits with kindness. Another wife cradled one of Kony's daughters, looking similarly stoic. I asked her how she felt about seeing him again.

"I love him so," she said. "He's very kind to me, he's the father of my children. I want him to come back because I'm sad that we never stay together."

Kony's daughter waddled around at her feet, reaching out toward a vase full of plastic flowers on a glass table.

"He always taught us how to behave well," the woman continued, "and he taught us how to pray, we prayed to God."

I was scribbling down her quotes for a quick story for Reuters when Frank Nyakairu, a Ugandan journalist with the *Daily Monitor*, brought me up to date. The lady in the baggy sweater was not Kony's mother after all, but another relative requested by the rebels. Apparently Nora, now in her mid-eighties, was sick. Not to worry, Frank said. The Ugandan army had promised to fly her in by helicopter.

We left Juba a couple of days later. Riek had chartered three aircraft this time, flying them in rotation to transport the multitude. His bodyguards summoned the journalists into the back of an Antonov 32-B cargo plane crewed by Moldovan pilots. I strapped myself into a seat on the bench, opposite the three wives. Little Okeny lay dozing in the crook of his mother's arm as the plane took off, heading once more to the border.

A buffet lunch was served in Nabanga just as the rebels arrived. After a sleepless overnight drive through mud and rain, the sight of more dreadlocked child soldiers milling around with bayonets was a lot less enticing than the onion and tomato salad. I broke open the cellophane covering the plate, and when I'd helped myself to a liberal serving I went to stand by a hut to watch the show.

Kony had no qualms about keeping visitors waiting for days, but he had lost no time in dispatching an advance party to scoop up his women and children. Photographers snapped their shutters as if a dinosaur had just blundered out of the jungle, struggling to keep each other out of their shots. The young rebels seemed to enjoy the attention, posing with stern faces then breaking into smiles when they were shown images of themselves on the backs of the cameras.

"I've never seen the LRA treating me like this before," Frank muttered, in between taking snaps of his own. "In the past they barked and shouted; this time they've been ordered to be human beings."

Wilson Owiny, the hard-eyed former colonel from East Sheen, drew up in a car along with other Acholi from the diaspora. He got out and shook hands with some of the teenage gunmen, but I had a feeling the pictures would not be ending up on his mantel-piece back in London. One of the rebels had the words "Education is Light" emblazoned across his T-shirt, and I wondered how it had found its way into Kony's camp. After a minute, I noticed a girl among them. Her blue basketball top bore the slogan "Only the Brave," and an AK-47 dangled from a sling over her shoulder. She looked about twelve.

I recognized one of the rebels from my last trip, a taciturn lad by the name of Okot. He wore a mop of dreadlocks like many of the others, and a plastic rosary hung round his neck. I asked him where he was from in the north and he mentioned Corner Kilak, a place I had passed through on my way to Patongo for Egeland's visit. Hoping to improve our rapport, I told him I had visited his home a few months before. He spoke enough English to tell me: "You're a liar."

Rebels gathered round as I opened my laptop and began to flick through my pictures, suddenly wondering if I had not made some horrendous mistake. Then I found it, a photo of the main road running through Corner Kilak. The shot showed a dog lying asleep by a sign that read: "*Lwok cingi inge limo coron pi gengo two*," or "Wash your hands after visiting the latrine to prevent diseases." My new friend nodded, and I felt a disproportionate thrill of vindication.

A car arrived to drive the relatives to the clearing, their final stop before the trek into Kony's camp. Kony's wives had been waiting outside the classrooms at Nabanga's derelict-looking school, where local women had been helping them do their hair. They now walked over with their three children to the circle of soldiers' huts where the rebels were waiting for them. Okot picked up one of Kony's sons, a boy named George Bush, and loaded him into the back. Acholi sometimes name their children after famous people who are making news at the time they are born. Was it possible Kony had been paying an ironic tribute to the American president? Another rebel picked up the little boy Okeny, popping his forage cap onto the youngster's head. Kony's son disappeared for a second under the oversized hat, before emerging puzzled into the sun. Enjoying the game, his new child-minder broke into a huge grin.

The rest of the relatives joined Kony's three wives and sister in the back of the vehicle, ready for their reunion. Mostly they had been kept away from the journalists, but I had managed to chat to a man named Walter, one of the commanders' uncles. He had held funeral rites for his missing nephew many years before.

"I will take some minutes to recognize him," Walter had told me. "He went when he was twelve and a half, now he's thirty-something. His appearance has changed, but I remember he has a broad face and bulging eyes."

The cars drove down the track toward the clearing, bearing their cargo to Kony.

Kony summoned the rest of his visitors a few days later. Riek's men had slashed the grass to form a huge circle on the border near Nabanga, pulling together straw huts and setting up a marquee to shelter the elders. Mediators from the Community of Sant'Egidio in Italy and Pax Christi in the Netherlands stood under an umbrella conferring with Riek, while journalists milled around beneath a canopy that kept off most of the rain. After several days of waiting, tempers were beginning to fray. One reporter chain-smoked, another just stared into the bush. There was still no sign of the one man we had come to see.

"Right, I'm giving him until 1:30, then I'm giving up hope," I said to nobody in particular. The clock on my Thuraya phone said it was fourteen minutes past.

At 1:28 another figure emerged from the path, a rebel officer in fatigues and beret. The press pack surged forward for a better look and I recognized the man as Captain Sunday. I had never been able to look at him in quite the same way since the Ugandan team in Juba had accused one of the rebel delegation of roasting people alive during the notorious killings outside Patongo—captured in the photo I'd seen of a leg sticking out of a pot. The rebels responded by reminding journalists of a documented incident in which one of the Ugandan officers had ordered soldiers to drag a suspect from Gulu prison. His head was later chopped off. "Whether or not it was cooked," the rebels said, "is anybody's guess."

Captain Sunday was leading a boy of about fourteen who wore a pair of Wellingtons. He paraded him past the journalists, then ushered him into the pavilion to meet the elders. We rushed inside, jostling to get a shot. The boy stared into the cameras with wide eyes and a quivering lip, a rivulet of sweat running down his forehead.

"This is Kony's son," Sunday said. "Kony will come next time."

Kony had named the boy Salim Saleh after Museveni's half-brother, a hard-living general who had been in charge of various offensives to crush the Lord's Resistance Army, as well as attempts to negotiate. He had also grabbed headlines for his involvement in the purchase of two Mi-24 attack helicopters from Belarus, the so-called "Junk Copters" that had the dubious distinction of being unfit to fly. Perhaps Kony felt some kind of affinity for a maverick who thought he was James Bond, as Museveni had once said. Captain Sunday offered the boy some water from an orange flask, and then led him back down the trail.

I shook my head, feeling that creeping sense of despair I recognized from my last visit to Nabanga. Perhaps sensing my frustration, a Sudanese captain from Riek's guard muttered encouragement. "That is a sign," he said. "In our culture, you cannot send your son and not come yourself. He will come tomorrow."

On the fourth day, I saw something slithering across the ground toward my feet. One of the policemen accompanying the mission shouted at me to jump up, then smashed down the stock of his rifle. A blue snake twitched and died, though apparently there was nothing to worry about. The Sudanese MP, Betty Achan Ogwaro, assured me that only the brown ones that fell from trees were really dangerous.

By now I was more worried about my personal hygiene. I had managed to collect some water from the borehole and sluice myself down in the bushes using a plastic bottle. I also tried to scrub my clothes using an old maize cob, as Frank had shown me. But it was risky to stray too far; the rebels would summon us to the clearing without warning, causing a mad scramble for seats in the cars. Eventually I found a man selling secondhand clothes out of a cardboard box in the shade of the teak trees. The pink sweat-shirt with a logo from Disney's *Pocahontas* looked too small, but I did get some jeans.

The major difference from my last trip was the food. A generator thrummed in the center of the soldiers' camp, its cable snaking to Riek's hut, where freezers cooled bottles of Coke and frozen meat. A team of Kenyan caterers chopped, boiled, and fried over charcoal stoves to serve three buffet meals a day. Long queues always formed for breakfast, where conversation revolved around the likelihood of a Kony sighting. Waiting for my sausage one morning, I got to chatting to a Sudanese elder in heavy glasses and cowboy hat named Clement. He explained how the rebels had once chopped off several heads and used them to prop a pot over a cooking fire.

"Later on they burned the bodies," he said, as we neared the trestle table stacked with basins full of donuts. "If you mention this to them they know it but they will not accept they are the people doing it."

In Sudan people nicknamed Kony's fighters *"otong-tong,"* meaning "chop chop." Sudanese chiefs had compiled a list of more than 3,000 of their people who had been killed by the rebels over the past few years, including dozens they said had been boiled and eaten; many thousands of others had been driven from their farmsteads. The rebels' predations in northern Uganda were widely known, but the chaos they caused while raiding for food in Sudan was often forgotten. The Sudanese elders also accused Ugandan troops deployed during Operation Iron Fist of raping, beating, and shooting civilians, though on a smaller scale. None of them quite understood why a Ugandan war was being fought on their turf.

Like supplicants barred from the Elizabethan court, locals loitered on the edge of the feast. Only their kids dared to venture inside the circle of huts, intrigued by the sight of the French manager of Juba's first pizzeria wearing a floppy hat and blowing richly scented smoke from his pipe. He was also a radio journalist who hoped to capture Kony on tape; the restaurant was only a sideline. When not marveling at these apparitions in Nabanga's midst, the kids busied themselves scavenging the hundreds of plastic bottles we discarded. A man who might have been one of their grandfathers stood and watched us from a safer distance, wearing a brown T-shirt with the slogan "Got Crabs?" The villagers must have been able to smell the buffet from their huts, and they had little food of their own—fear of the rebels had kept them from their fields.

As I walked back to the school, I met a young man with lonely eyes and an ivory ring on his finger. He asked if I could help him—he had walked for five days from his village in southern Sudan to find out what had happened to his sister, seized by the Lord's Resistance Army during a raid some months before. Kony had swiftly retrieved his own relatives, but had neglected to return the favor.

It was just beginning to look like another wasted day when Captain Sunday beckoned the reporters to the start of the trail, waving his Thuraya like a wand.

"Journalists, this side," he said, directing us with his outstretched arm. "You're going to meet the Chairman."

I exchanged a glance with Frank. An excited murmur spread among the journalists, and the photographers began to check their cameras. Captain Sunday was so unpredictable that I half expected him to change his mind. He had spent the morning poking about under the chairs in the pavilion to check for landmines. I watched his face for any sign of hesitation, but his brow remained locked in its customary frown.

We followed the trail into the forest in single file. Young rebels jogged past with stacks of pink plastic chairs balanced on their heads, picking their way over fallen logs. Major Paul from Maridi made his way to the head of the procession, giving a French photographer's hand a comradely squeeze as he passed. I felt the tingling breathlessness you get when climbing a steep hill, exertion and anticipation making me dizzy. I asked the rebel officer striding along in front of me if Kony was really waiting.

"You will see him," he said. "He's there, where we are going."

"So we're in Congo now?" I asked.

"Yes, this is the border."

We had gone a few steps further when he pointed up at a silver trunk covered in knobbles. I wondered how many similar trees had been accorded the honor of marking the frontier, although the display on my Thuraya agreed that we were now in Congo. The world's last northern white rhinos were wandering around somewhere in the Garamba National Park. Some said Kony had been dining on elephant meat of late, though from the look of the trail, all wildlife seemed to have made itself sensibly scarce. I imagined the Guatemalans were in a lonely spot like this when they were killed.

After about half an hour we reached a bamboo pole blocking the path. The rebels had decorated it with sprays of palm leaves, reminding me of the fronds on the LRA motif that Moses had stitched with a coin. We had reached the gate of Kony's Jerusalem in the jungle. Into the trunk of a tree somebody had gouged in crude letters:

STOP

LRA

CAME
ONE
CAME
OLL

It was not a bad stab at the slogan "Come one, come all," and it must have taken some time to carve.

Captain Sunday ordered the journalists to stand aside as the Gulu district chairman, the paramount chief, and the archbishop led their delegation of elders toward Kony's camp. For all the misery he had caused, these leaders had never completely disowned him. I was eager to hear what they would tell their prodigal son.

Fighters rifled through our bags, checking our phones were off. A condom was discovered in one of the photographer's wallets. Captain Sunday spoke to one of the cameras, sweat pouring down his forehead from beneath his beret: "We want peace," he said. "We want to go back home."

We arrived at the rebels' "parliament" a little further down the trail. It looked like something the Vikings might have built for their chiefs, a thatched canopy lashed to tree trunks forming a kind of covered courtyard. The letters L-R-A were woven into the wicker walls, and more palm fronds drooped from the windows. Further away, the rebels had set up enclosures to house latrines. A scrap of paper torn from an exercise book with the word MEN scrawled in pen was pinned near one the entrances. "C'est Hilton," commented a French television reporter named Valérie Dupont, by far the most glamorous of the visitors to Kony's realm. Perhaps aware of their reputation, the rebels wanted to appear extra refined.

Elders, journalists, and the rebel delegates from abroad crowded inside the hall. I scanned the shadows for any sign of the Chairman, noticing the gray-haired figure of Vincent Otti and some other rather elderly-looking officers. Distracted by the throng of visitors, I almost missed him.

Joseph Kony watched his guests arrive from the comfort of a plastic garden chair.

Journalists engulfed him, clicking their cameras, bodyguards stepping forward to stop them from overwhelming him completely. I pushed to the front, unable to resist taking out my camera and almost forgetting to look at him without the filter of the lens. It was almost impossible to get a steady shot through the press of bodies.

Kony rested his chin on his palm, seeming to stare straight through the crowd. He wore a smart olive uniform with shoulder flashes bearing crossed swords, his feet planted in a pair of the rebels' ubiquitous Wellington boots. But his face was gentle, and he looked more like a teacher, or a priest, than a general. The arm of a pair of sunglasses poked out of his breast pocket. I was glad he wasn't wearing them. I would never have seen the sadness in his eyes.

Elders queued up to shake Kony's hand, greeting him as if he were a celebrity. He seemed to come to life, rising to his feet and clasping his guests' outstretched hands between his own. A smile transformed his face, revealing stained front teeth. He did not look happy, more relieved. It could have been my imagination, but he seemed grateful.

"God bless you," he said, shaking hand after hand. "God bless you."

Once the Acholi elders were installed in their seats, the rebel officers ordered the journalists out. We sat down on the trail, young guerrillas watching us from among the trees. One boy in a cowboy hat gave a cold stare, while another could not resist a smile. Two more sat on the branch of a tree, laughing softly at some shared joke. I wondered how much they knew about what was going on, and whether they too were thinking of home.

I joined Frank, who was straining to hear the voices that drifted from the "parliament."

"It's him, isn't it?" I said.

Frank nodded. Kony was speaking in Acholi, his voice lilting through the trees. Obonyo translated, though we could only catch snatches.

". . . I'm just like you, a normal person with my good qualities, just like you . . . I am not a wizard . . . it's not me who began the war, I only came to help people . . ."

I caught glimpses of a figure pacing up and down in the wicker hall, occasional bursts of applause filling the pauses in his speech. One of Kony's wives wandered past outside with a baby on her back, seemingly oblivious to her husband's oratory.

". . . Two cocks fighting . . . one may be bigger than the other . . . they reach a stalemate . . . chase each other round and round . . . It's the government forces which have been carrying out these atrocities and blaming it on me . . . government has control of the media so they say a lot of things about me . . . let us join our minds . . . go back home and enjoy life in our country . . ."

The pair of young rebels on the branch began to bounce up and down like kids in a playground, not seeming to hear.

"Many times you have heard that Joseph Kony has no reason to fight, no political agenda . . . but all that is propaganda. Joseph Kony cannot fight without a reason . . . You Acholi who gave me the blessing to fight, why can't you give the blessing to talk peace?" Suddenly, Kony himself broke into English.

"For God, and your what? Your country."

Frank grinned—it was Uganda's national motto.

"I would like to declare today clearly why we are fighting," Kony went on, reverting back to Acholi. "Of course our political agenda has already been explained. We are fighting for God's Ten Commandments; we are fighting to eradicate evil. We are fighting for God's power. If you look at the Ten Commandments, are they bad? . . . We are fighting for God's rule, because God's rule is eternal, so that the evil that is in our land, the killing, the rape, is eradicated. I appeal to you so that we work together and find a lasting solution to this conflict."

He gave a resounding "Thank you" in Acholi, repeating the phrase over and over, his voice thundering through the clearing: "*Apwoyo matek! Apwoyo matek! Apwoyo matek!*" Buoyed by the growing applause, he made one final appeal:

"I came to the bush at the age of 23, since then I've not seen my people—not my classmates, not even my mother. If I look at the machine called global positioning system, I can see that this place is very far from home, yet we are still here. I appeal to you, let us join together to find a way to peace. I thank you very much, may God bless you all."

The clapping grew louder. I could see Major Paul's ebony cross dancing in the air as he waved a blessing. Martin called the journalists. It was almost dark, but we only needed a moment. I flicked through the questions in my notebook, unable to decide what to ask first. There were a hundred possible openers, but all I wanted to know at that moment was what had tipped a young man from healer to fighter all those years back.

One of the rebels placed a chair outside the parliament, while a log was found to balance our tape recorders. Photographers and cameramen elbowed each other out of the way, a couple trading angry words. My pen hovered above my notepad, poised to take down Kony's quotes.

"He is coming," said a rebel officer, "just now."

After a few more minutes Obonyo appeared to announce there had been a slight change in the program. The Chairman would not be speaking to us just yet, but he would give a statement on Kony's behalf. As he read out one of his press releases, couched in its usual lawyerly tones, I felt like throwing down my recorder.

There was one more chance. Vincent Otti was still hanging around with the other senior commanders, one of whom was wearing an Arsenal football shirt with the team's cannon emblem, though it looked like a fake. I asked Otti if we could stay. He considered for a few seconds, then said we were welcome, seeming almost pleased. Most of the journalists began to traipse back to the clearing, but a few of us crept into the parliament. There was a tarpaulin we could sleep on, and hopefully water somewhere too. But after half an hour, Otti changed his mind and we were sent back through the forest. By now it was dark.

We came across a fallen log that barred the path. Valérie swore we had come a different way so we retraced our steps, finding another fork. Flashlight beams flickered in the darkness as we tried to work out which track led back to the clearing, but everywhere looked the same. Valérie sent a message on her Thuraya to one of the Italian mediators at the camp. "We are lost," it said. Fortunately, the text turned out to be premature and we eventually found our way out. Somebody had even saved us a helping of leftovers from the buffet.

The next day we returned to the clearing for the final time. I watched one of the Sudanese soldiers swaggering around with his hand on the Beretta pistol strapped to his hip. Every few minutes he would squirt a gob of spit from between his teeth like a bullet. The soldiers were as frustrated with the waiting as we were.

Captain Sunday appeared first, followed by more than a hundred rebels walking in single file. Kony and Otti strode along in suits that stood out from the jumble of uniforms worn by their men. Kony was striking in white, his smartly creased short-sleeved shirt, matching trousers, and polished black shoes lending him an almost nautical aspect. I wondered who did his ironing.

Kony took his place in the pavilion flanked by Martin and Vincent Otti, who had adopted the same smart-casual look as his boss. Pensive once more, Kony mopped his brow with a blue flannel. When the Sudanese officers began to hustle the journalists out, I realized it was now or never.

I extended my hand for Kony to shake. He looked up at me with startled eyes. My hand remained suspended in mid-air. Kony glanced to the side, as if waiting for someone to tell him what to do. Martin gave a nod, and Kony darted his hand forward. We shook hands for a split second, before he almost recoiled from my grip. But the shake had been firm enough, if a little clammy, perhaps from all that hiking through the forest. I saw a couple of the Londoners on the rebel delegation laughing. Sudanese soldiers bustled me outside and the meeting began.

My Thuraya trilled, its screen signaling a call from the Netherlands. A researcher from the International Criminal Court was on the line from the Hague. I had given him one or two updates on how the talks were going, and he was eager for the latest. I told him I was standing about fifty meters from their number-one suspect, but otherwise there was nothing to report.

The journalists waited under their shelter as Kony made his speech to the Sudanese elders, its ending marked by a round of applause. I wondered what he could have told them that had gone down so well. Later I discovered that he had apologized. As the clapping subsided, Kony came out to meet the press.

The journalists surged forward, forming a tight semicircle around his chair. Obonyo read a statement urging the government to declare a truce. I thought Kony might not even speak, until reporters began to throw questions.

"*Ladit* Joseph Kony," Valérie began, the respectful Acholi term of address sounding silky smooth in her French accent. "People all around the world see you as a devil because of the way you wage war. Today, it's a good opportunity for you to tell us who is the real Joseph Kony. Can you tell us in a few words please, who you are?"

Kony looked up at her, apparently giving the question careful consideration.

"I am a man, I am a human being, I am Joseph Kony," he said. "Those words people say to me, that is propaganda, because they spoil my name like that, so that people will not love me as a human being. But I am also a human being, I am a soldier, I am educated also."

He appeared to have finished, so I asked why he had started fighting.

"What was happened, Museveni come to our place, or to my home, and killed my fathers, killed my sister, destroying all property of my fathers and some other people also, and burned the houses, do many things. That is why most of our people also they went in the bush."

A Dutch television journalist asked: "Mr. Kony, what about the atrocities?"

"Those atrocities which was happened in Uganda, that is not me or that is not my people. Atrocities which was taking place in Uganda was done by Uganda government only that I don't have means or I don't have good communication to the world which can inform the people that those things which was happened was not LRA. But the government they have many machineries to inform the world what was happened. But those things was not LRA. Museveni who is fighting me, so he cannot say good things to me."

A young Sudanese journalist called Irene piped up, asking what would happen to the abducted children. Captain Sunday had invited her back to the rebels' camp on at least one occasion, although she had politely declined.

"I did not abduct anybody which was in the bush," Kony said, "and there's no any children in my position or in my camp, as you know very well the children cannot walk 60 miles as I do. I cannot fight with children, there's no any children in my position, there's no abduction with LRA."

A Sudanese journalist asked why the war had gone on for so long.

"I don't know," Kony replied, starting to look agitated.

A young British woman called Katy Pownall from the Associated Press asked if he would go and face trial at the International Criminal Court. Kony looked confused, almost anguished.

"Me?" he asked.

Frank repeated the question, and he seemed to come to his senses.

"No, no, no, no," he said, "because I did not do anything."

He stood up to leave. The entire question and answer session had lasted five minutes and 32 seconds. I stumbled away to phone in my quotes to Reuters in Nairobi. Screens in newsrooms around the world would give a little "ping" and his words would appear in red. A longer story with more of his quotes would follow, and then they would be forgotten.

When I looked up Kony had vanished back into the bush.

I smoked a cigar that night, huddled around a fire with Frank, Katy, Valérie, and some of the other reporters. I had saved a single Cuban cigar for just this occasion, though in truth I did not feel the buzz I had anticipated after all the months of searching.

Kony may have emerged, but I felt no blinding flash of revelation. My notebook was full of things I never had the chance to ask. I wanted him to explain what had happened at the beginning of the war, to trace his decline in support, to try to justify the massacres and the mutilations, and explain the role of the spirits that had summoned him up to Awere Hill in the driving rain. I almost regretted that I had not followed him down the trail; I had been too wrapped up sending his quotes to the newsroom to chase him. Frank had gone after him and Kony had shaken his hand, saying: "God bless you." I felt I had somehow missed out, as if a few extra seconds in his presence would have revealed something more.

I began to obsess about my own handshake with Kony, trying to recreate it in my mind. In truth, it was over so fast it was as if it had never happened. My abiding memory is the look of alarm on Kony's face. Used to a world he controlled, Kony seemed disoriented by so many strangers. I'm not even sure he really saw me. When I went to play back the press conference on my digital recorder, I found it blank. Even the picture Frank had snapped of our handshake was so dark you could barely make out Kony's face.

For Reuters, what Kony had said was not really the story; it was that Africa's most-wanted man had appeared at all. One of the editors would later remark that he was surprised by how apparently normal Kony looked: "We didn't know what to expect from some guy who had just crawled out from under a stone." A television producer in Nairobi had half expected him to emerge in a dress. Perhaps Kony's first news conference in twenty years had only served one real purpose, summed up by a Canadian researcher who'd joined the trip. As we walked back from the clearing, she had said: "At least we know he doesn't have cloven hooves and horns."

Riek's circus began the journey home the next day. Despite all the effort made to assemble members of the commanders' families, Otti still would not consent to join the peace negotiations in Juba.

Kony's young rebels delivered his wives, children, and the other relatives back to Nabanga, along with their friends from the diaspora with their sleeping bags and suitcases. I began to shoot pictures of some of the young gunmen, who posed once again with stony faces. When Wilson Owiny saw me, he tried to shoo me away from the boy soldiers with the kind of gesture you might use to scare a flock of pigeons.

As the convoy formed up to leave, there seemed to be some kind of argument developing near the front. It was hard to see what was happening from the back of the car carrying the reporters so I tried to get out, but Major Paul snapped at me to stay where I was. Wilson, Obonyo, Martin, Josephine, and their colleagues stood fuming by their luggage, which still hadn't been loaded onto the roof racks. For a second time, Otti had refused Riek's entreaties to come to Juba, and the vice president had decided to ensure Kony's people understood the depths of his displeasure.

A minute later the convoy began to roll. Shocked faces flashed past our car window. Riek had left Kony's followers stranded. They could wait for rescue in Nabanga, or start the long trek back to their boss's camp in the Congolese forest. In spite of myself, I could not suppress a smile.

14. "I AM REFORMED"

Dancing at a meeting for ex-abductees

The pathologist snapped on latex gloves and drew back the blanket. Camp dwellers gathered around the gurney, bare feet squelching in the mud. Some crossed themselves, others covered their eyes. Children peered between the adults for a glimpse of the body. Pink froth bubbled from the dead man's lips, flies feasted on blood crusting his closed eyes. The pathologist probed the gunshot wound in the back of his head, withdrawing fingers stained with red. I did not take a photo.

Kony's guerrillas had shot the man the previous evening on the edge of a camp outside Gulu. It was the most memorable image I had of the war, mainly because the others were too grim to think about for long. There was the farmer with no hands, chewing the white thread of the bandages on his stumps as if biting a phantom nail. The rebels had forced his friend to chop them off with an axe. There was the young woman who had arrived at the hospital with a shredded mess of flesh around her mouth instead of lips, and the man in the camp whose entire body suppurated with sores. The scale of the suffering was too enormous to grasp. All I had were notebooks, recorded conversations, and a not very good snapshot of Kony—minus the dreadlocks.

Heading back to Nairobi from Juba for the final time, I returned to my original question. How could one maniac hold half a country hostage for twenty years? I was beginning to realize that, even before I met Kony, I had begun to find the answer.

He hadn't. At least, not by himself.

As I traveled through Sudan and Uganda, I began to see that my obsession with Kony had blinded me to the deeper causes of the war. I thought back to my visit to his sacred hill at Awere, where the lieutenant had compared the rebels to "groundnuts." Chatting to people in Gulu, it became clear that the conflict had much clearer origins than talk of Satan or spirits would suggest. The roots of Kony's war stretched all the way back to the north–south divide crystallized under colonial rule, then nourished by Uganda's cycles of post-independence bloodshed. But as long as the conflict was portrayed as the result of one man's seemingly inexplicable "evil," there was no need for people to look any deeper. And blaming one "madman" played right into Museveni's hands.

It was hard to think of two more contrasting public personas than the soldier-scholar who was welcomed to the White House and the dreadlocked clairvoyant who spoke to angels, but they shared one thing in common. Both seemed oblivious to the suffering their strategies were causing. Casting Kony as the arch villain of the piece made it easier for Museveni's powerful backers in London and Washington to turn a blind eye, not only to his failure in dealing with the conflict, but to their complicity in tacitly endorsing his strategy.

Museveni's response to the insurgency had been to lock up 90 percent of the population around Gulu in camps where disease killed more people than the rebels, and then to deny that there was a problem. For years, Museveni repeated the platitude that

Kony's "bandits" had been "crushed," despite all evidence to the contrary. Army officers would routinely dismiss massacres conducted by the rebels as "the last kicks of a dying horse." Vacillating between futile jingoism and demanding the surrender of men he had branded "terrorists" or "hyenas" when the time came to talk, Museveni never really seemed to acknowledge the genuine grievances nursed by the Acholi, let alone come up with a convincing plan. But Museveni was a useful ally, so few questions were asked.

As long as Museveni maintained Uganda as an island of relative calm sandwiched between war zones such as eastern Congo, southern Sudan, and at one point Rwanda, the suffering of the people of northern Uganda was of little strategic consequence. Britain and the United States, both of whom provided large amounts of aid to Museveni, were permanent members of the United Nations Security Council, but it was twenty years before the conflict was discussed in any detail. Humanitarian aid salved consciences, but at the same time only supported the encampment policy that caused so much suffering. As long as Kony was seen as an isolated lunatic, constantly on the verge of defeat, there was no compulsion to look at the reasons the conflict persisted or think more carefully about what might be done to end it. The rebellion's longevity was not so much a tribute to Kony's skill as a leader, more the symptom of a deeper malaise.

The war was the shadow cast by Uganda's success. Museveni had taken power promising to rid the country of the tribalism and divisions that had caused so much misery. Uganda's rapid recovery in the early years of his rule seemed like a miracle. Many people regarded Museveni as a savior, the only person who could guarantee peace and prosperity. Given the contrast with Amin and Obote, their enthusiasim was easy to understand. But twenty years on, he had failed to find a formula for creating a genuine sense of national unity. The fate of the Acholi in the north was the most glaring example. Moses summed up the divide perfectly: "If you ask children to draw pictures, northerners will draw guns, armored vehicles, people running. In Kampala, it will be motorcars, skyscrapers, safe families." As long as the Acholi felt excluded from the progress made elsewhere in Uganda, the dangerous ambiguity in attitudes to Kony would persist. A generation imprisoned in camps might hate Kony's methods, but it was not surprising that some sympathized with his aim—to get rid of their president. Museveni's failure was not his inability to kill one man, it was his failure to convince people north of the Nile that he cared.

When foreign ambassadors began to raise questions, Museveni herded them into buses for a tour of the mass graves in Luwero. Flinging open tombs, he told them not to forget what the Acholi soldiers had done when he was fighting Obote. Twenty years after he'd taken power, Museveni's election video still featured images of the "skulls of Luwero," a reminder to southern voters of the "barbarians" he had banished across the Nile. It was no wonder many Acholi concluded that he was content for the war to continue. For all the new shopping malls and hotels opening in the capital, I could not help feeling that Uganda was frozen in time. As long as both Museveni and Kony justified themselves by pointing to atrocities committed twenty years ago, it was hard to see how any genuine reconciliation could come about.

Many Acholi had hoped the elections in 2006 might mark a new start. A change of president would prove for the first time that power in Uganda could be transferred by a means other than at gunpoint, passing the ultimate test of a democracy. But the man who had once criticized African leaders for staying in office too long had broken his promise to step aside. Despite Museveni's undeniable achievements, Uganda's first real chance since independence for a peaceful handover had been postponed until further notice. Uganda's stability was guaranteed by Museveni the man, rather than the institutions he had built from the ruins left by his predecessors. Uganda's population was among the fastest growing in the world; it was hard to see how growing expectations among a new generation would be met. The potential for more conflict seemed clear from the map of the election results— the Nile cut the country in two.

Given the depth of the divide, it was perhaps no wonder that some Acholi leaders began to float radical solutions. The Gulu district chairman, Norbert Mao, told me just before he was elected in 2006 that he would start a debate about northern secession, reviving the idea of a "Nile Republic" to merge with southern Sudan. The concept had at one time been ascribed to Kony, but Mao wanted to bring it into the mainstream. At first it seemed to me that he was using the debate to dramatize the problems of the north, rather than seeing separation as a genuine possibility. Later I began to wonder. Kony would be gone one day, but the Acholi's need to feel they belonged would not. In 2011, southern Sudan was due to vote on independence. Should a permanent peace take hold on both sides of the border, Gulu would benefit from trade and find a market for its potentially huge agricultural output. But if things did not go quite so well, if the north's alienation deepened, the idea of joining an independent south Sudan with its oil wealth and shared cultural heritage might seem more appealing. Unlikely as it seemed, I imagined returning in twenty years and needing a passport to cross the Karuma Falls.

For all the more profound questions about Uganda's future, Kony's infamy had always made the best copy. Amidst the horror, there was something almost comic about the idea of a grown man talking to many-faced spirits. Once I was filing a story to the Reuters desk in London when the phone rang. "Get the bit about the Ten Commandments up high," an editor told me, and I dutifully shuffled the paragraphs to emphasize Kony's apparent insanity. Seduced by the legend, I had set out to find a God-king, a fairy-tale shaman humming with evil, a medium from one of Lloyd's adventures, an African Osama in his cave. The man I met was none of those things.

What was so striking about Kony was the discrepancy between his own view of himself and the image others had of him. Sponsored for years by the Sudanese government, flattered by accomplices in the Diaspora, he saw himself as a genuine freedom fighter. At one time he had even recorded taped messages to his people that were passed around furtively in Gulu. I never managed to get hold of them, but I was told that in one he had compared himself to a villager clinging onto a lion's tail, the only man with the courage to fight the beast that threatened the community. Somehow he had been able to convince himself he was the victim of a "betrayal." The would-be hero turned into a destroyer.

When, after twenty years, he emerged from the forest in a crisp white suit, I assumed he would exude something of the aura that held his army together. But, facing questions from a bunch of bedraggled journalists, he looked almost pathetic. The best defense he could muster for all his crimes was: "I am a human being." The wizard of the Nile was simply a man, and he was afraid.

When I looked back on my days as a correspondent in Nairobi, I saw that I had been an enthusiastic peddler of the myth. There was something irresistible about the idea of Kony as darkness personified in the heart of Africa, enslaving women, summoning spirits in the smoke. Voodoo, harems, barbarism, and magic—he was every primitive cliché rolled into one. The legend pandered to an idea of the continent as the natural home of pointless brutality; Europeans have clung to this image since the days when Lloyd wrote of "heathens" and "savages." I might never know the whole story, but at least I now knew there was more to the war than one man's madness.

A tolling bell summoned worshippers into church for Good Friday. Women wore shimmering dresses in purple, gold, and peach, leading children in outsized hand-me-downs and sailor's caps. Father Carlos entered from a side door wearing his alb, taking up position behind an altar engraved with palm leaves and a crown. Outside the church door, a brown cow browsed in the grass, flicking away flies.

I sat in a pew and listened as Carlos read the Gospel of St. John, the Passion, in Acholi, betraying only a trace of his Spanish accent. A painting behind the altar showed a traditional homestead, the husband sawing at a carpenter's bench, his wife arriving with a pot of water balanced on her head. A child knelt on the ground with a raised hammer. It was the Acholi version of the Holy Family, their ideal home a complete contrast to the huts huddled outside the chapel. Carlos's parishioners formed a queue as he handed out wafers from a goblet, before swallowing the last one himself.

He drove me back toward Gulu in his white pickup, passing a dispensary he had set up with the help of a donation from the council in Madrid, the city where he was born. Moses had painted the sign in neat letters. As the camp trailed away behind us, I asked him what message he had given for Easter.

"In twenty years as a priest I've only spent two or three years in Europe. While I was there I used to stress that we were living in an affluent society, where we have to ask ourselves, 'What is the cross?

And what is suffering?' Here, you don't have to tell them that, you don't have to convince them, this is the kind of life they have."

We drove past a boy playing by the roadside with a model truck made of wire. It could have been a food lorry, or an armored car.

"I said that living in a camp is a big cross for all of us," Carlos said. "But God will not permit this situation to last forever. You always find somebody who has a life harder than yours; let's try to help people carry their own crosses.

"Two years ago people were dying because of a lack of medicine and treatment, so we united and started a dispensary. What you need in a situation like this is to come together to help one another, to think of God, of something which goes beyond what we see, another reality. It can give you hope when you lose any other hope."

I thought back to the boy who told Carlos, "God will help me," as the rebels dragged him out from under a bed. He had eventually escaped and returned to his home near the mission where Carlos's friend di Bari was buried. I met him on my way back from Patongo, finding him studying diagrams of Flemish joints and T-junctions for his brickwork course. Carlos was helping pay his fees.

"Even if they threaten you and shoot at you," Carlos said, "even if it is only making a difference in the life of one person, certainly it is worth the effort."

We returned to his church at dusk. A bonfire blazed outside the entrance. Carlos lit the giant Easter candle and led his catechists inside. Men, women, and children in the congregation gathered round to light their individual candles from his flame. Slowly the church began to glow, the gloom banished by a hundred tiny stars. With a small branch Carlos flicked holy water from a calabash over his flock, and I felt the droplets tingle on my arm. I could recognize enough Acholi now to hear the words *"Tipu Maleng"*—Holy Spirit—during the prayers.

Over the years the Comboni order had offered Carlos postings in the Philippines, Peru, and beyond, but he had always turned them down. As he put it: "I came to Africa, and I forgot the way back." Finally, after two decades, he was wondering whether the time had come for him to return home to Madrid for a year. Perhaps he would spend some more time with his parents in Las Ventas, the old bullfighting quarter where he grew up, and watch Real play a few matches at the Bernabéu stadium. Somehow, I did not quite believe he would leave. It was pouring by the time we were heading once again toward Gulu. He dropped me back at the Franklin and I stood under the veranda for a moment, watching his pickup vanish into the rain.

"I am reformed," Moses told me. "You'd never know I had been a soldier."

He was right. When we shook hands at the girl's tailoring school all those months before, I would never have guessed his past. Perhaps that was what made Moses special. He had been dragged through the gates of Kony's kingdom and come back intact. Few were so lucky. Now he was trying to help others like him. Before I left Gulu, we had one more trip to make together.

Wearing the salmon-pink shirt and tie he had worn when we first met, Moses led me down a muddy side street to a pair of metal doors. He undid the padlock and we stepped into his office. Photographs of meetings in the camps plastered the walls along-side clippings of articles about the war. Gradually a dozen more young people turned up, Christine among them. Some wore white T-shirts with his group's name: IYEP—Information for Youth Empowerment Program. Moses was the chairman.

Former abductees in his group spent their weekends trying to help people understand their plight. Many of Kony's erstwhile followers struggled to cope when they returned to life in the camps, where they had to deal with suspicion as well as the pain they carried. Moses wanted to convince others that accidental rebels deserved another chance.

We piled into a minibus and drove to a camp about half an hour south of Gulu. A group of locals had gathered in anticipation of the visit, drums and calabashes at the ready. Moses stood up to make his speech, wagging his finger and spreading his arms, captivating his audience. Christine translated for me as he explained that Kony's kidnapped fighters had never wanted to cause such suffering. And then he said something quite unexpected, something I had never heard in Gulu until then.

"The conflict is already there in our lives, it's within us, and it's there in the world," Moses said. "We have to face up to it. In China they say conflict is a crisis, and an opportunity."

Men and women formed a circle, smacking whisks against calabashes in time to the frantic beat of drums. Stamping feet kicked up dust, sweat glistened on skin. Somebody blew a whistle and the circle stopped as one, impossibly precise. The dancers swapped high-fives, laughing with exhilaration, lost in the moment. Moses said something to Christine, and then the dance began again.

A man snapped pictures with a camera. I wondered if they would end up in Moses's album. The last photograph showed him on the day he was elected health prefect, his too-long tie dangling past his belt. Ten years later, he was again surrounded by cheering friends.

On the phone near the Sudan–Congo border

A t the time this book went to press in the summer of 2008, a peace of sorts had returned to northern Uganda. For almost two years, the talks begun with Riek Machar's first barnstorming expeditions into the bush had yielded steady progress. Rebels and government signed a ceasefire leading to one of the quietest seasons in the north anyone could remember. Even Joseph Kony's mother eventually made the trek to Nabanga, hoping a dose of maternal love might convince her wayward son to return.

In the Lango area of northern Uganda, hundreds of thousands of people left the camps and returned to their villages. But in Acholiland, the crucible of the conflict, everyone was wary. Many felt safe enough to move to new settlements closer to their fields, but very few ventured back to the mango trees guarding their original homesteads. Some of the camps had acquired such an air of permanence that it seemed the men, women, and children trapped inside might never leave. The war had altered Acholiland forever.

Father Carlos moved to Kampala to edit the *Leadership* magazine run by the Combonis, then returned, for a time at least, to Spain. Moses remained in Gulu, caring for his mother. He sat the O-level exams he had been planning to take a decade earlier, and worked toward his A levels. The last time I saw him he had managed to find sponsors to buy a motorbike for IYEP and a laptop. He wore the computer on a strap around his neck, never letting it go even when he sat down to eat. I could not shake the image of a soldier carrying a gun. When I mentioned this, he just laughed.

Mystery still surrounds the fate of the eight Guatemalan special forces soldiers killed during their attack on Vincent Otti's camp. Rival theories say they were either shot by rebels or may even have been victims of "friendly fire" in the confusion of the jungle.

As the Juba talks wore on, Kony seemed to become more suspicious, perhaps sensing a reckoning was due. In October 2007, he accused Otti of being a government spy. Otti, who had been so anxious to avoid spending his old age in prison in the Hague ended his life in the bush, killed by an executioner's bullet.

Despite the turmoil in the rebel ranks, the negotiations sputtered on, until April 2008, when Kony finally seemed ready to sign a deal. Machar, with his entourage of mediators, journalists, and diplomats, again found himself waiting in a damp clearing near Nabanga. Days passed, but Kony never appeared.

A few weeks later, there was shooting near the village; it seems LRA fighters attacked the southern Sudanese soldiers stationed on the border. Several dozen people were killed, including children caught in the crossfire. The rebels vanished back into the forest. In Juba and Kampala, there was talk of war.

Once more, Kony was adrift in the wilderness, the immense spaces of central Africa stretching away over every horizon. Perhaps, to the Wizard of the Nile, they seem to beckon.

SELECT BIBLIOGRAPHY

Having barely set foot in a library since I started work as a journalist, I was humbled by the excellent work by academics on the conflict in northern Uganda. Researchers including Tim Allen, Ronald Atkinson, Christopher Dolan, and Sverker Finnström have shattered stereotypes and challenged propaganda. I have not provided a complete list of sources or documents consulted, but I hope this gives a flavor, acknowledges at least some of the debts I owe to particular authors, and provides a starting point for anyone who wants to read more.

News reports from Ugandan press including the *New Vision*, *Daily Monitor*, the *Weekly Observer* and others have all found their way into these pages, many of them written by journalists working at considerable personal risk, as have stories filed by Reuters, the Associated Press, Agence France-Presse, BBC, and the United Nations' Integrated Regional Information Networks (IRIN).

For Acholi spirituality, I relied on *Religion of the Central Luo* by Okot p'Bitek, published by the East African Literature Bureau in Nairobi in 1971. I am indebted in particular to Finnström for his account of the legend of Gipir and Labongo, which I borrowed for Chapter Three, along with numerous other nuggets. Much of the material can be found in his excellent book, *Living with Bad Surroundings: War, History and Everyday Moments in Northern Uganda* (Durham: Duke University Press, forthcoming).

Other works I have used on Acholiland include Sir John Milner Gray's three-part series of articles entitled "Acholi History, 1860–1901" in the *Uganda Journal* (starting in 15 (2), 1951), Frank Knowles Girling's *The Acholi of Uganda* (London: Her Majesty's Stationary Office, 1960), a PhD thesis by John Orr Dwyer entitled *The Acholi of Uganda: Adjustment to Imperialism* (New York: Faculty of Political Science, Columbia University, 1972), and the much more recent book by Atkinson, *The Roots of Ethnicity: The Origins of the Acholi of Uganda before 1800* (Philadelphia: University of Pennsylvania Press, 1994), as well as other writings by the same author.

Sir Samuel White Baker's works are referenced by various authors, including Finnström, though they make rip-roaring reads in themselves. They include *The Albert N'yanza: Great Basin of the Nile and Explorations of the Nile Sources* (London: Macmillan, 1866) and *Ismalïa, a Narrative of the Expedition to Central Africa for the Suppression of the Slave Trade, Organized by Ismail, Khedive of Egypt* (London: Macmillan, 1874). Baker also crops up in William Langer's book, *The Diplomacy of Imperialism—1890–1902* (New York: Knopf, 1951). For an overview, see Alan Moorehead's *The White Nile* (London: Reprint Society, 1960). On slavery, I have also drawn on Ray Beachey's *The Slave Trade of Eastern Africa* (London: Collings, 1976). The exploits of the King's African Rifles in Burma are recorded in John Nunnely's *Tales from the King's African Rifles* (Petersham: Askari Books, 1998).

For the sections on Alice Lakwena, I relied on articles by Heike Behrend and in particular her book *Alice Lakwena & the Holy*

Spirits: War in Northern Uganda, 1985–1997, (London: James Currey, 2000). See also Allen's article "Understanding Alice: Uganda's Holy Spirit Movement in Context," published in *Africa* (61 (3), 1991).

For more details on President Yoweri Museveni's guerilla struggle, it's worth taking a look at his autobiography *Sowing the Mustard Seed: The Struggle for Freedom and Democracy in Uganda* (with Elizabeth Kanyogonya and Kevin Shillington, London: Macmillan, 1997). For a firsthand account of life as a child soldier in Museveni's rebel army, read China Keitetsi's autobiography *Child Soldier: Fighting for my Life* (Bellevue [South Africa]: Jacana, 2002).

For an informative account of the aftermath of Museveni's victory in the north, see an article by Adam Branch called "Neither Peace nor Justice: Political Violence and the Peasantry in Northern Uganda, 1986–1998," in *African Studies Quarterly* (8 (2), 2005). See also Dolan's article "What Do You Remember? A Rough Guide to the War in Northern Uganda, 1986–2000" (London: ACORD, 2000). Amnesty International documented abuses by Museveni's soldiers in *Uganda: The Human Rights Record (1986–1989)* (London: Amnesty International, 1989) and *Uganda—Human Rights Violations by the National Resistance Army* (London: Amnesty International, 1991). Dolan has also written an excellent PhD thesis that examines the role of international donors and other actors in the encampment strategy: *Understanding War and Its Continuation: The Case of Northern Uganda* (Development Studies Institute, London School of Economics & Political Science, University of London, 2005). I drew on Dolan's material in Chapter Four. One of the earlier studies to look at the deeper causes of the war was written for the US embassy in Kampala and USAID by Robert Gersony in 1997; *The Anguish of Northern Uganda: Results of a Field-Based Aassessment of the Civil Conflict in Northern Uganda.*

Atrocities by the Lord's Resistance Army have been widely documented. Details I use of the Atiak massacre in Chapter Seven rely on stories in the *New Vision* by Billie O'Kadameri. I have also drawn on work by Human Rights Watch in New York, including *The Scars of Death: Children Abducted by the Lord's Resistance Army in Uganda*, published in 1997. Human Rights Watch detailed abuses by both army and rebels in the 2005 report *Uprooted and Forgotten: Impunity and Human Rights Abuses in Northern Uganda*. For the army's version, see *Progressive Report on Action Taken against Human Rights Violations by UPDF in Northern Uganda, 2003–2005*.

UN investigators documented crimes committed by the Ugandan army in Congo, notably in the *Final Report of the Panel of Experts on the Illegal Exploitation of Natural Resources and Other Forms of Wealth of the Democratic Republic of the Congo*, issued in October 2002. The figures on ghost soldiers are drawn from an internal report produced by a committee set up by the army High Command that started its work on 30 June 2003, obtained by a Ugandan journalist. Various nongovernmental and UN organizations have produced numerous documents on conditions in the camps. I have used resources on the website of the Internal Displacement Monitoring Center, including *Internal Displacements —Global Overview of Trends and Developments in 2006* (IDMC: April 2007). Human Rights Focus in Gulu produced a report a few years ago looking at the forced nature of displacement called *Between Two Fires, the Plight of IDPs in Northern Uganda: The Human Rights Situation in the "Protected Camps" in Gulu District, Northern Uganda*. Dolan has explored the nuances of the suffering caused by the camps in an article called "Collapsing Masculinities and Weak States: A Case Study of Northern Uganda" published in *Masculinities Matter! Men, Gender and Development* (Frances

Cleaver (ed.), London, New York & Cape Town: Zed Books/ David Philip, 2002). Another Dolan article highlighting the complexities of the humanitarian situation in the north is "Which Children Count? The Politics of Children's Rights in Northern Uganda" in Okello Lucima (ed.), *Protracted Conflict, Elusive Peace: Initiatives to End the Violence in Northern Uganda* (London: Conciliation Resources & Kacoke Madit, 2002). A report by Allen and Mareike Schomerus entitled *A Hard Homecoming, Lessons Learned from the Reception Center Process on Effective Interventions for Former "Abductees" in Northern Uganda, An Independent Study*, (2005) challenges misconceptions about former fighters.

Much has been written about Uganda's relations with its donors. I recommend Andrew Mwenda's article "Foreign Aid and the Weakening of Democratic Accountability in Uganda," published online by the Cato Institute in 2006. I have borrowed some references from Wayne Madsen's exploration of Uganda's strategic importance to the United States in *Genocide and Covert Operations in Africa, 1993–1999* (New York: Edwin Mellen Press, 1999).

My account of the 1993 peace talks relies partly on O'Kadameri's article "LRA/Government Negotiations 1993–1994" in *Protracted Conflict, Elusive Peace: Initiatives to End the Violence in Northern Uganda,* cited above. Simon Simonse has also produced a balanced overview in his *Steps Towards Peace and Reconciliation in Northern Uganda, An Analysis of Initiatives to End the Armed Conflict Between the Government of Uganda and the Lord's Resistance Army 1987–1998* (Pax Christi, Netherlands, 1998). For a discussion of the impact of the International Criminal Court, see Allen's *Trial Justice: The International Criminal Court and the Lord's Resistance Army* (London: Zed Books, 2006).

On Sudan, I have made extensive use of *Islamism and its Enemies in the Horn of Africa*, edited by Alex de Waal (London:

Hurst & Company, 2004). For more on Uganda's role in the region, see Gerard Prunier's article "Rebel Movements and Proxy Warfare: Uganda, Sudan and the Congo (1986–99)" in *African Affairs* (103 (412), 2004). The International Crisis Group has produced numerous reports on Sudan and Uganda, including the book-length *God, Oil and Country: Changing the Logic of War in Sudan*, published in 2002. For details on Riek Machar's militia, see *Sudan, Oil and Human Rights* (New York: Human Rights Watch, 2003). For a recent account of the Lord's Resistance Army's activities in Sudan, see a report by Schomerus entitled *The Lord's Resistance Army: A History and Overview* (Geneva: Small Arms Survey, Human Security Baseline Assessment, Working Paper 8, 2007).

The interview with Joseph Kony conducted by Schomerus and television journalist Sam Farmar was aired on BBC's *Newsnight* program on 28 June 2006. An extract was broadcast on BBC World Service radio, part of which is quoted in Chapter Ten. Schomerus discusses the interview in "Chasing the Kony Story," published in *The Lord's Resistance Army: War, Peace and Reconciliation* (T. Allen and K. Vlassenroot (eds.), Oxford: James Currey, 2008).

Details on Kony's family in Chapter Nine are drawn partly from a story by Associated Press reporter Katy Pownall, who scored a lesser-known scoop by interviewing Kony's mother Nora, a feat I deemed too problematic to attempt. Her story appeared on 2 May 2007. Pownall quoted Nora as saying "I wish my son wasn't a rebel."

A NOTE TO THE READER

This book is based on a journey through Uganda and Sudan I made between January and July 2006. Alice Lakwena's funeral took place on 3 February 2007, although I decided for simplicity's sake to describe it at the start of the story.

In some cases I have slightly tweaked the language between quotation marks to make the kind of English phrasing commonly used in the region easier to understand for people unfamiliar with the area, without altering meaning. I have anglicized some Acholi spellings in the same spirit.

I have also taken the liberty of referring to the White Nile throughout, whereas in fact the stretches of the river in Uganda are known as the Victoria Nile then Albert Nile, before the river becomes the White Nile proper in southern Sudan.

ACKNOWLEDGMENTS

I could never count the number of people in Uganda and Sudan who helped me with this book, let alone name them. Everywhere I went, people gave time and knowledge freely, often reliving painful memories for my benefit without any expectation of reward. Thank you. It was a privilege to have had the chance to spend time in such company. The idea for *The Wizard of the Nile* grew out of my experiences reporting for the Reuters Nairobi bureau, whose members past and present have done more to shine a light on east Africa than any number of books. I owe a particular debt to former bureau chief Nicholas Kotch, who gave me my break into Reuters as an intern in 1997, and subsequent bureau chief William Maclean, who was a constant source of wisdom, expertise, and support in the four years I worked for him until 2005. I also owe a big debt to my Reuters editors for granting me a long sabbatical to work on this book. In particular I would like to thank Paul Holmes, Michael Lawrence, and Barry Moody. One veteran Reuters correspondent, Nicholas Moore, who worked in Uganda while Amin was in power, taught me more than he knows. Some of the people who helped me the most during my journey along the White Nile are mentioned in the text. In Kampala, I am also particularly indebted to Paddy Ankunda, Lilliane Barenzi, Paul Busharizi, Tim Cocks, Euan Denholm, Angelo Izama, Elizabeth Kameo, Richard Lough, Tristan McConnell, Frank Nyakairu, Katy Pownall, Sam Rich, Tiggy Ridley, and Will Ross. In Gulu, I would like to thank Bob Leitch, Mike McNulty, Charles Odora Oryem, Esteban Sacco, and many others whom I cannot name. Huub Gales and his wife Jennifer put me up in Juba for weeks, somehow managing to tolerate my Kony obsession. In Khartoum, I was given huge help by Nima Elbagir, Opheera McDoom, Seif el-Din Dirar, Merethe Borge, Ingrid Breidlid, Jonah Fisher, Brechtje Kemp, and Beatrice Mategwa. In Paris, thanks go to Billie O'Kadameri, Joelle Diderich, and Dominique Vidalon. In Nairobi, special thanks goes to Katie Nguyen, for soothing my constant state of crisis, to Andrew England, for his irrepressible enthusiasm, Cornish wit and cottage pie, and Daniel Wallis, always ready for a jerk chicken and White Cap at Sippers. Jonathan Clayton, Rob Crilly, and Jason Stearns kept me laughing. Elizabeth Kennedy arrived at just the right moment. Michael Holman and Michela Wrong, formerly of the *Financial Times*, have been a constant source of inspiration, guidance, and care.

In London, Daniel Simpson had more faith in the idea than I did. Chris Bostock, Matthew James, James Lacey, John Power, Justin Quirk, Jonathan Spence, Matt Steel, and Luke Sweeney know their contribution.

Many people were generous enough to read and comment on part or all of the manuscript, including: Tim Allen, Ronald Atkinson, Charles Okello Ayai, Erin Baines, Paul Busharizi, Andrew Cawthorne, David Clarke, Jeremy Clarke, Tim Cocks, Sverker Finnström, Joyce Laker, David Mozersky, Joyce Neu, Frank Nyakairu, Betty Achan Ogwaro, Charles Odora Oryem,

Michael Otim, Ben Parker, Will Ross, Hugo Slim, Nicholas Tattersall, Alfred Taban, and Alex de Waal. Any errors in the text are entirely mine.

I could never have attempted this project without the faith of my agent, Kevin Conroy Scott of Tibor Jones, who was willing to take a long shot, and my publishers at Portobello Books, Laura Barber and Philip Gwyn Jones, who took an even bigger risk on a plan that turned their competitors pale.

Lastly, I reserve the biggest thank you for my parents, John and Susan, and my sister Katie, for bearing with my wanderings.